CZECHOSLOVAKIA

John Burke

CZECHOSLOVAKIA

B. T. Batsford Ltd, *London*

First published 1976
Copyright John Burke 1976

Published by B. T. Batsford Ltd,
4 Fitzhardinge Street, London W1H 0AH

ISBN 0 7134 3222 5

Text set in 11/13 pt Monotype Baskerville, printed by letterpress,
and bound in Great Britain at The Pitman Press, Bath

Contents

Acknowledgments

The Author and Publishers wish to thank Čedok for the cover illustration and all other photographs reproduced in this book save for plates 4, 5, 6 and 9, which were supplied by the Četeka agency.

List of Plates

EAST

GERMANY

P

Frýdlant
Špindlerův Mlýn
Teplice
SEVEROČESKY
Liberec
Železný Brod
Chomutov
Litoměřice
Terezín
Labe (Elbe)
Ohře
Mělník
Jičín
VYCHODOČESKY

Loket
Karlovy Vary
STŘEDOČESKY
Hradec Králové
Karlova Studánka
Cheb
Křivoklát
Poděbrady
B
Mar. Lázně
Teplá
Karlštejn
Prague
O
Labe (Elbe)
H
M
I
Litomyšl
A
Berounka
E
Slapy
Kutná Hora
Čáslav
Bouzov
SEM
Plzeň
Příbram
Konopiště
Sázava
Olomouc
ZÁPADOČESKÝ
Vltava
Havlíčkův Brod
Žďár
R
Orlík
Jihlava
Pernštejn
A
Domažlice
Tábor
V
Klatovy
Kroměříž
JI
I
Písek
HOČESK
Brno
A
Strakonice
Y
Telč
Slavkov
M
WEST
Vimperk
Husinec
Jindř. Hradec
JIHOMORAVSKY
Uherské Hradiště
O
Prachatice
Třeboň
Kobylí
GERMANY
Vltava
Strážnice
České Budějovice
Hodonín
Český Krumlov
Valtice
Břeclav
Lipno
Rožmberk
Smolenice
ZÁPAD

A U S T R I A
Bratislava

CZECHOSLOVAKIA

To all those unfailing friends who have made each visit and each new exploration more rewarding than the last

Notes on Pronunciation

Although the Czechs and the Slovaks have slightly differing languages, the gap is not so great as to prevent one understanding the other—rather as a Dane, a Norwegian and a Swede chatting together can each use his own language and with little effort grasp what the others are saying. The English visitor or reader will probably have little cause to study the finer distinctions, but a few basic principles of Czech spelling and pronunciation may be helpful.

Unlike English pronunciation, that of Czech letters and syllables is fairly consistent. The main stress always falls on the first syllable of a word, but without the heavy emphasis found in our own speech. Subsequent unstressed syllables are neither swallowed nor given a markedly higher or lower intonation, but kept on a steady level. Pronunciation and speed of utterance of a syllable do not vary according to whether it is stressed or unstressed. The cadences of Janáček's distinctively vocalized music, so strange at first to the unaccustomed ear, demonstrate these balances and rhythms very clearly.

Once one has mastered the apparently alien accents of certain letters in the alphabet, and summoned up the courage to pronounce them, there are few difficulties. Grammar is quite another matter, presenting great complexities; but we are not concerned with that here. Those wishing to study further could make a good start with *Teach Yourself Czech* by W. R. and Z. Lee (English Universities Press, London, 1959). There is also a very useful phrase-book, *Say it in Czech* by Alois Krušina (State Pedagogical Publishing House, Prague, 1963), distributed in England by Collet's, London.

Although standard English pronunciation of letters such as *a*, *b* and *d* varies slightly in Czech, especially at the end of words, our normal usage will pass well enough. But there are others which do have to be watched.

á is 'ah' as in 'half'.

aj is 'aye' as in 'fly'.

au is 'ow' as in 'now'.

c is neither the hard nor soft version we know in English, but always 'ts' as in 'pots'.

č is 'ch' as in 'church'.

ch is the 'ch' in the Scottish pronunciation of 'loch'.

dz is 'ds' as in 'pods'.

é is slightly more pinched than the 'ai' in 'pair'.

ě is 'ye' as in 'yes'.

ej is a cross between the 'ay' in 'day' and the 'ai' in 'dairy'.

h becomes the 'ch' of 'loch' when used at the end of a word.

í is 'ee' as in 'feed'.

j is pronounced as the 'y' of 'yes' of J(Y)ugoslavia.

ň is the 'ni' of 'onion'.

oj is 'oy' as in 'boy'.

ř is the test piece with which Czechs like to torment their foreign friends. An explosively trilled 'r' runs into a sound like the French 'je'.

š is 'sh' as in 'she'.

ú or *ů* both approximate to the 'oo' in 'food'.

ý is 'ee' as in 'feed'.

ž is like the French 'je', or a shortened version of the 'su' in 'measure'.

For those who still do not care to risk entering a restaurant and ordering, say, *vepřový bůček* with a helping of *brambory smažené* (pork chop and fried potatoes), some knowledge of German will help. Many restaurants in larger towns and cities have English menus, and most museums, historic centres and tourist regions have brochures with at least an English summary; but German texts are usually given in full, and the language is spoken nearly everywhere. Nevertheless it is worth attempting a few approaches in Czech itself: such efforts are rarely greeted, as in some countries, with derision, but with admiration and immediate helpfulness.

In this book I have tried to keep spellings of people and places consistent without being too pedantic. In most cases I use the Czech version which visitors are likely to find on maps or in reference books, but I think it would be absurd to present the English reader throughout with 'Praha' rather than 'Prague', 'Václav' for 'Wenceslas', and 'Dunaj' for 'Danube'. Where appropriate I give alternatives on first reference and then adopt whatever I think the more suitable usage in this context.

The Golden City

There is a legend that at some time in the ninth century A.D. a princess of a Slav tribe known as the Czechs, after a chieftain named Čech, stood upon a high rock above a river and uttered the prophecy: 'I see a city whose splendour shall reach the stars.' The princess was Libuše; the rock was Vyšehrad; the river the Vltava; and the city was to become Praha, or Prague.

As a mystic, Libuše was far-seeing and accurate. The city whose birth and maturity she predicted is as radiant as she could have wished. And from that same rocky fortress of Vyšehrad she sent out with equal assurance for a husband. Hearing her tribe derided by a male petitioner in a legal quarrel as 'men ruled by a woman', and being advised by her counsellors that a strong male partner would be desirable, she went into another of her trances and sent her white horse to seek for a consort. In fact she had already been pleasuring herself many a time with a farmer known as Přemysl the Ploughman of Stadic, and the horse, knowing the route well, obligingly fetched this same lusty ploughman back for her. The tribe recognized him as a fitting royal mate, and the couple founded the successful Přemyslide dynasty.

Smetana's opera *Libuše* tells the story in a sumptuous tide of symphonic splendour which, frankly, does not add up to an opera. The composer himself decreed that it should be performed only on ceremonial occasions, and obviously saw it as a dramatic oratorio rather than a conventional stage piece. Not wishing it to be presented in inadequate surroundings, he put it to one side for ten years, awaiting the construction of a suitable National Theatre. In 1874 he embarked on what is probably his

14

most famous work, the set of six tone poems making up *Má Vlast* ('My Country')—music which he was never to hear, since by then he had gone deaf. Although it took five years to complete the cycle, he wrote the first movement in a month. This was *Vyšehrad*, whose opening arpeggios—now the call sign of Prague Radio—are taken from a motif in *Libuše*, representing the prophetess plucking her harp. The theme reappears at the end of the best-loved movement in the sequence, *Vltava*, when the river reaches Prague; and yet again, triumphantly, at the end of the last movement.

A royal castle of those early Slav rulers was set upon this rock. Today the fortifications and gateways enclose public parks and shaded walks, tennis courts tucked under high ramparts, and sudden dizzying views of the river below and a main road passing through tunnels in the rock.

In the nearby cemetery lie many famous men and women: Dvořák, Smetana, Jan Neruda—the great story-teller of Prague's Little Quarter—and Božena Němcová, author of one of the most widely read Czech novels of the nineteenth century, *Grannie*. The grave of Karel Čapek, who put the word 'robot' into every contemporary language, is marked by an open book.

Beside the late nineteenth-century church of SS Peter and Paul, upon the supposed coronation site of early kings, stand three huge mythological statues. One of these represents Šárka, another woman from the time of Libuše whose story finds its echoes in Smetana's *Má Vlast*. Šárka is today the name of a rustic valley on the outskirts of Prague, in which a verse chronicle of the fourteenth century tells of an early Women's Lib organization asserting the supremacy of the far from gentle sex. The leader of these Amazons, betrayed by a fickle lover, swore vengeance on all men, and when a campaign was launched against them by a male army she had herself bound to a tree and lured the invaders on by plaintive laments. The men's leader fell under her spell and freed her; and then, under the influence of a powerful potion, he and his followers were lulled to sleep. Šárka summoned her women out of hiding by a vengeful horn call, and they descended upon the drowsy men in an orgy of indiscriminate slaughter.

To reach the heart of the city which Libuše foretold, one can descend by steep flights of steps and narrow streets to the eastern embankment of the river. Along here is a walk past a succession of bridges, road and rail, with the castle and cathedral height gradually taking on substance and colour above the west bank. Canoes, skiffs and rowing-boats with squeaky rowlocks drift lazily out into midstream, and a plume of dark smoke marks the passage of a pleasure steamer on its journey to the great lake and holiday chalets of Slapy dam. What is now the Slavonic Isle was known in Berlioz's day as the Sophia Island, when its concert hall was used mainly by the city's leading choral society. Berlioz was delighted by them and by the receptive Prague audiences, but less so by the island's pleasure gardens—

> where bad musicians shamelessly make abominable music in the open air and immodest young males and females indulge in brazen dancing, while idlers and wasters, ne'er-do-wells, lounge about smoking foul tobacco and drinking beer which is just as bad, and the women sit and knit and wag their sinful gossips' tongues.

There is now no cacophony in the open air, and no brazen dancing; but I have seen some energetic folk-dancing on the stage of the concert hall. One does find women knitting, and young wives wheeling their babies along the agreeable paths, watched over by a statue of Božena Němcová.

Berlioz, who had come only reluctantly to Prague, was even more reluctant to leave it. *O Praga! quando te aspiciam!* 'When shall I see you again?' It is a question we all wistfully ask ourselves when the time comes to depart.

An adjoining island, Střelecký ostrov, supports piers of the bridge of the First of May, known originally as the Francis bridge. Its opening in 1901 was accompanied by festive illumination of the National Theatre, which stands on the corner of Národní třída (National Street) where trams and cars debouch on to the bridge or turn along the embankment. In the days when Bohemia was part of the Austro-Hungarian Empire this National Street, for a time called Ferdinandstrasse, was the traditional Sunday afternoon stroll for Czechs; the German-speaking citizens who held most of the civic power and mercantile wealth favoured the Graben (now Na příkopě) on the other

1 St Vitus' cathedral, Prague

side of the Rossmarkt or Horse Market—today Wenceslas Square.

Czech national pride, never wholly suppressed by the Habsburgs and showing signs of a great political and cultural revival in the middle of the nineteenth century, demanded the construction of a truly National Theatre. Its cost was met by public subscription, and its opening in August 1881 was marked by the deliberately retarded première of *Libuše*. Soon after this it was destroyed by fire. Nothing daunted, the public raised the money once again, and the theatre reopened in 1883 with another gala performance of *Libuše*.

From this point it is possible to cross the river and climb the castle height by tram. Just as devotees of London know that the No. 9 bus route offers the best over-all selection of metropolitan sights, so the lover of Prague has a special affection for the No. 22 tram, coming down the tree-lined slope of Václavské náměstí (Wenceslas Square) and along the bustling shopping street of Národní (the 'třída' or 'street' is usually dropped from the name in casual conversation), across the river and through the Little Quarter, grinding up a hill and negotiating a tight hairpin bend as spires and towers fall away beneath, and then levelling up behind the northern entrance to the castle.

In the years I have been visiting the city there have been several different methods of paying tram fares. Various machines have been devised to eliminate the need for conductors. One of the most infuriating was a device into which you fed your coin, watching it settle in a slot behind glass, and then pulled a handle to extract a ticket. The motion was exactly like that of a fruit machine handle, but there was never any chance of winning the jackpot. At the time of writing, it is necessary to buy a quantity of tickets in advance from tobacconists and kiosks, and to punch these when boarding the tram. If you find yourself late at night without a ticket and with all the shops and kiosks closed, you are doomed to walk—unless you risk an illegal ride at any point of which an inspector may come aboard.

For myself, I prefer to continue walking a while, in spite of the fact that those proud citizens who boast of Prague, like Rome, having seven hills have obviously lost count, and the

2 The Charles Bridge, Prague, seen from the Little Quarter

innumerable cobbled slopes and flights of steps are hard on the feet and the breath.

Narrow streets twist away from the embankment into the labyrinth of the Old Town. Iron-grey walls, pockmarked with damp and decay, rise three, four and five storeys; massive gateways open into secret courtyards; and then at a corner will be a bright church or a cluster of old houses resplendent with florid graffiti, perhaps a wine tavern newly plastered in shifting pastel shades. Here is nothing four-square, nothing sharp-edged. Spires and domes, fading ochre and scratched grey of walls, heavy metal-studded doors, shutters decorated with carvings or patterns of rusting bolts: all are hazed by a dusty luminescence which softens outlines so that many buildings seem to crumble away down the edges. Many are in fact crumbling. Prague seems at times to be slackening its grip on the present and dissolving back into time. And then, at the last moment, up goes a great tangle of scaffolding, and restoration work begins. Will there ever come a time when Prague needs no more scaffolding, when all the façades are safe and whole and sparkling again? One feels as the seeress Libuše must have felt, peering into the future: 'It'll be lovely when it's finished.'

In the Old Town, as in the Lesser Town or Little Quarter across the river, old signs above doors identify occupants from the days before houses were numbered. A star, a black bear, a white lion, each prefaced in local usage by 'U', meaning 'At the': U zlaté studně—At the Golden Well; U tří lvů—At the Three Lions. Many restaurants, wine cellars and beer houses are similarly identified: U zlaté konvice—At the Golden Jug; U zelené žáby—At the Green Frog; the famous U Fleků beer tavern with its interlocking rooms, its inner 'Beer Academy', its accordion and violin music, its students' songs and exuberant uproar; and the nightly tumult of U kalicha—At the Chalice— with wall paintings and captions recalling its most famous fictional patron, the Good Soldier Švejk.

One vista after another is framed in arches, in the heavy colonnades of the Old Town Square and the Little Square: from a coffee bar in the shadows below the Týn church one glimpses, between thick pillars, part of the Old Town Hall, pigeons strutting across the wide expanse of setts—and then birds fluttering and fleeing as a water sprinkler clatters past, leaving the square gleaming and winking under the sun.

The Old Town Square marks the site of an ancient market-place at the junction of important trade routes. The growing community was dominated by a castle on each bank of the river, at first made of wood and then rebuilt in stone. For some time Vyšehrad remained the more important, but between the ninth and eleventh centuries building on the rival height intensified. There are substantial relics of this Romanesque period throughout Prague. In Hradčany itself, a four-apsed rotunda was built, and although this was superseded by a basilica with twin towers, companion pieces to the original are to be found in smaller rotundas such as that of St Martin in Vyšehrad, St Longin's in the New Town, and the Chapel of the Holy Cross in the Old Town. The most impressive survivor is the basilica of St George; and there is the Black Tower, set up in the middle of the twelfth century as the eastern gate of the royal castle fortifications. Frequenters of wine cellars will also find many an ancient cellar of the period below a palimpsest of later houses.

By the thirteenth century a newer town was growing up beside that centred on the old market-place. At first it had a separate identity as St Gallus Town, but then was drawn in by its neighbour to form what is still called the Old Town.

The church of Our Lady of Týn which dominates the square was originally a small Romanesque structure created for the benefit of foreign merchants who had established their staple here. It gave way to a larger Gothic church, the greater part of the present building deriving from the late fourteenth century. Early in the following century work began on the two spiky, soaring towers, but had to be abandoned during the brutal years of the Hussite wars. For a time the church followed Hussite doctrines, and still preserves the arms of John of Rokycany, the last Utraquist bishop—a star and a horse's hoof. A gilded chalice, symbol of the Utraquists who demanded communion in both kinds, once stood between the towers, but when the reformers were finally defeated by the Catholic alliance its gold was melted down by the Jesuits and used to make a crown, sceptre and halo for the statue of the Virgin and Child now in the gable.

The church organ is a baroque extravagance with angelic trumpeters and two suns which spin like gadgets on a fairground organ when music is played. The pewter font is the oldest in Prague. On a marble slab the name of Tycho Brahe commemorates the Danish astronomer who, driven from his homeland by court intrigue and jealousy, became one of the circle of scientists and alchemists around the Emperor Rudolf II and worked fruitfully with Keppler. His death in 1601 was due to one of Rudolf's caprices: when a banquet was in progress the imperial dictum was that no-one should leave the table, which for a copiously imbibing Brahe led to a burst bladder.

Across the square, the Old Town Hall has a tower whose lofty gallery offers splendid views over this core of the city. Cost of construction was met entirely out of duty on the sale of wine. Its most famous feature is the fifteenth-century astronomical clock, whose upper section shows phases of the sun and moon, and the time of day; below are the days of the week and months of the year. Twelve signs of the zodiac illustrate this lower section, and rural scenes were added by the painter Mánes in the nineteenth century. On the hour a tolling bell draws crowds from all around, two small windows open, and Christ and the apostles process past the openings. On one occasion some years ago the attentive public had an additional treat: a craftsman working on the mechanism within absent-mindedly put his cap on the head of an apostle, who duly slid past the window wearing this anachronistic headgear.

On the outer wall beside the tower is the gilded inscription, *Praga caput regni*. Within, the wedding hall does a brisk trade. After the compulsory secular ceremony those who wish for a religious ceremony may make their own arrangements, and many couples like to stroll across the square into the Týn church. I was present on one such occasion when, in the middle of a scorching day, a mighty thunderstorm began. The words of the officiating priest were drowned. So was part of the church: a fierce wind blew open the doors, lifted cloths from side altars, tore down some of the scaffolding outside, smashed in a window, and released a deluge of rain water through the window and from the roof itself. By the time I emerged, traffic signs had been twisted out of the pavements, masonry had splintered down from above, and all the trams in the city had been put out of action for some hours. I have always hoped that the bride and groom did not take this celestial outburst as a bad omen.

Under the pavements, the square, the shops and houses and restaurants, run a number of deep cellars and passages. Many of these were originally the ground-floor rooms and corridors of long-lost residences. When the level of the river was raised to supply power to essential watermills, there was sporadic flooding and earth had to be tipped and built up to make a new, higher ground level. Cellars and passages which had been kept clear, running between various houses and even below the Town Hall, came in useful during the Second World War. Resistance workers operated from here during the final outbreak of fighting around the Old Town Square. The Nazis managed to destroy part of the Town Hall, including thousands of volumes from the city archives. Fire melted the fourteenth-century bell, the oldest in the land; but the old council chamber, hung with insignia of the city guilds, was fortunately saved. In the entrance hall a mosaic shows Libuše prophesying the glory of Prague.

The Gothic style characterizing many a Prague scene owes its richness largely to the creative zeal of Charles IV, King of Bohemia from 1342 to 1378 and Holy Roman Emperor from 1355 onwards. He conceived a great range of building projects, redesigned the royal palace on Hradčany, laid out an entire New Town as a settlement for foreign workers and merchants— soon to become an integral part of the city and to house a larger population than that of the older areas—and provided employment during a period of economic depression by constructing a 'Hunger Wall' below his castle. A number of establishments were ordained for religious orders, among them the Carmelite church of Our Lady of the Snows, the tallest church in the city and the one with the largest altar.

Above all, Charles found in 1348 the first university in central Europe, named after him: the Charles University, or Carolinum. Originally Gothic, it retains some inner sections in this

style, restored in this century with a discreet use of specially
made bricks to complement and yet be distinguishable from the
basic structure. Externally there remains only the Gothic oriel
window of the chapel of SS Cosmas and Damian, patron saints
of the medical faculty.

Another gem of the period is the Old-New synagogue, actually
the oldest surviving synagogue in Europe. It adjoins the seventeenth-century Jewish Town Hall in the heart of a compact
Jewish settlement which existed for centuries in streets behind
the Old Town Square. All the buildings of this quarter have
now been amalgamated into a State Jewish Museum.

Records of significant Jewish settlement here go back to the
tenth century. For some three hundred years the Jews traded
here in reasonable freedom, but then were banned and confined
to the ghetto. In 1357 Charles IV granted Prague Jews the
privilege of flying a standard, and a frayed remnant of this,
many times repaired, is still displayed in the Old-New synagogue. In spite of his tolerance, Jews were not allowed to join
Christian guilds, were forbidden to work in gold or silver, and
suffered from sporadic pogroms, the worst of which in 1389
resulted in the massacre of some three thousand members of
their community. By the end of the sixteenth century, however,
they seem cautiously to have expanded into precious metal dealing. In due course Ferdinand III declared they should be free
to carry on any craft in which they had obtained the necessary
qualifications; but the goldsmiths in particular ignored this, and
entry to skilled trades and the guilds was still well-nigh impossible. It was not until 1797 that Jewish rights were recognized,
and even then their professional examinations had to be held
before masters of the Christian guilds. It took until 1848 for the
last restrictions to be abolished.

Today there are several grim collections of mementoes in
rooms of the different Prague synagogues. Hitler, set on exter-
minating the Jews from all territories under his heel, conceived
the idea of a museum in which the relics of his victims should
be displayed as a mockery of all they had stood for. As thousands
died in Bohemia and Moravia, mainly in the concentration
camp of Terezín, their personal effects and religious objects

were collected here: so many that only about a tenth of the headpieces, crowns, pointers, kiddush cups, alms boxes and so on can be put on show in the space available.

Some historic material of the community is no longer here. Between 1664 and 1736 the largest collection of Jewish prints and documents then known in Bohemia was made by David Oppenheim, later to become part of the Bodleian Library in Oxford. But there is plenty left—textiles, scientific and philosophical manuscripts, guild banners and clothes. The personal banner and robe of Solomon Molko, Portuguese exponent of the Kabbalah, who was burned at the stake in 1532, were acquired by the Pinkas synagogue. The walls of this building carry the most terrible of all memorials: the inscribed names of almost eighty thousand Bohemian and Moravian martyrs to Nazi fanaticism, among them about fifteen thousand children.

Embracing the Pinkas and Klaus synagogues is the old Jewish cemetery. Its earliest identifiable grave dates from 1439, but there were many earlier burials. Beneath the present surface are thought to be some twelve superimposed layers, their mounds and subsidences accounting for the tilting and jostling of the existing stones, which numbered twelve thousand before burials ceased in 1787. A new Jewish cemetery in the suburb of Žižkov accommodates the ancestors of Rainer Maria Rilke and Franz Werfel and of the Kafka family, including their most famous and prophetic son, Franz Kafka. In the old graveyard lie the scholar and bibliophile David Oppenheim and Mordechai Maisel, who gave his name to another synagogue and to the street which still runs beside it. The most frequently visited tomb is that of Rabbi Löw, a sixteenth-century primate of the Prague rabbinical school, best remembered for his creation—long before the days of Mary Shelley's Baron Frankenstein—of an artificial being moulded in clay. This ready-made servant, the Golem, untiringly obeyed his master's commands but, not surprisingly, was later converted by opportunist authors of novels, plays and films into a melodramatic monster.

A short stroll takes us from the rear wall of the old graveyard back to the river embankment and the loveliest way across that river—the Charles Bridge.

In the Square of the Knights of the Cross at the Old Town end of the bridge is a conglomeration of churches, monuments, dome and tower and spire and rooftops, all best viewed from halfway across the bridge and frequently photographed from there. The dome balancing the whole pattern is that of the baroque church of St Francis, designed by a French architect in the seventeenth century. On the other side of the narrow street, where pedestrians are continually menaced by trams and cars erupting murderously from a narrow arch through the Colloredo-Mansfeld palace, is the church of St Saviour. Interred within this is one of the most unsparing priests and preachers of the Counter-Reformation who, after orthodox Catholicism had been reimposed upon the Czech lands after the battle of the White Mountain, went throughout the city and across the whole land denouncing and burning whatsoever he deemed to be heretical. How many invaluable manuscripts and books were forever lost in this campaign it is impossible to estimate.

The statues in the square are those of St Wenceslas, supported on a column garnished with vine tendrils and grapes, and of Charles IV. The Emperor's monument was commissioned by the Charles University in 1848, the five-hundredth anniversary of its foundation, and the figures below him symbolize the four faculties of the university. In his right hand Charles holds the foundation charter, whose original is no longer to be seen: it was removed by the Nazis during the occupation and never recovered.

To one side, in a complex including the Colloredo-Mansfeld palace and the Smetana museum, is the clock tower of the Old Town mills. Taking pride of place in Plate 3 of this book, it is of comparatively recent date but, frivolous and out of keeping as it may be, somehow contrives to blend most happily into the scene.

Behind the congested square, Karlova ulice—Charles Street —meanders its narrow way below one side of the Clementinum, once a huge college testifying to the Jesuits' determination to extirpate every heresy which they believed had taken root in the footsteps of John Huss. It incorporates the churches of St Clement and St Salvador, and a chapel of the Assumption.

Although the extensive buildings have now been incorporated in the university and the National Library, they retain many features of the past: a statue of St John of Nepomuk, chosen as the symbol of the return of the true faith, ceiling paintings of St Ignatius of Loyola and St Francis Xavier, a wonderful collection of breviaries, early music and illuminated manuscripts including the eleventh-century Vyšehrad Codex, and a baroque astronomical tower housing many of Tycho Brahe's instruments.

Like Karlova and like the large square in his New Town— indeed, like so many large and small features of grateful Prague —the Charles Bridge is named after the Emperor who conceived it and whose tower at the Old Town end carries decorative reliefs representing the countries under his rule, together with some motifs associated with his son, Wenceslas IV. There is also a plaque recalling an attack on Prague by the Swedes in 1648, during the closing stages of the Thirty Years' War, when the townsfolk turned out to block the bridge and, in the fighting, all the ornamentation on the bridge side of the tower was ruined.

For centuries the only crossing of the river other than by ferry had been at this point. An earlier Queen Judith bridge had provided an essential part of the coronation route along which kings of Bohemia went from their court near the present Powder Tower through the Old Town Square and the adjacent Little Square or Little Ring, along Karlova, and over the river on their way to the cathedral.

The thirty statues lining the bridge were not part of the original concept of Peter Parler, builder of the bridge and master of the workshop responsible for so much in Prague castle and cathedral, the Týn church, and elsewhere. These figures date mainly from the eighteenth and nineteenth centuries, some having been restored and replaced—such as that of St Francis Xavier, who came down in the floods of 1890. Someone else who is reported to have gone into the water, this time in real life, was St John of Nepomuk, whose seventeenth-century statue, the oldest on the bridge, stands close to the spot where he was hurled over by royal decree. There are two versions of the story. One, propagated by the Jesuits when they urged his canonization and set him up in rivalry to the revered memory of John

Huss, was that he had refused to divulge the queen's confessional secrets to her husband, Wenceslas IV. The other claims that John, as Vicar-General, confirmed the appointment of a new abbot of Kladruby monastery against the king's express wishes. Either way, Wenceslas is said to have authorized his being tied in a sack and tossed into the Vltava.

Recent scientific investigation into a possible historical basis for the legends has produced some interesting results. The body in the vast silver tomb in St Vitus' cathedral cannot be positively identified; but it has been confirmed that it is the corpse of a man who, after being severely assaulted, was drowned. One much venerated relic, the saint's tongue, was on display for many years, looking—as I recall it—like a fragment of dried-up leather. On examination it was found to be not a tongue at all, but a sliver of brain tissue. Inexplicably, when moistened with a sponge it refused to dry up again and, according to one account, has remained moist ever since.

But in the centre of the Charles Bridge, in recent years a pedestrian thoroughfare mercifully free from other traffic, we would do better to occupy ourselves with present beauties rather than past mysteries. 'Earth has not anything to show more fair,' said Wordsworth on the prospect of the Thames from Westminster Bridge. He could hardly be so ecstatic at the modern prospect. But, apart from a few television masts and a hint of new housing blocks along the horizon, the view from this vantage point above the river Vltava has suffered little over the centuries. Mozart, who knew the river as the Moldau, might be bewildered by the proliferation of bridges and some other intrusive features since he was last here; but would still recognize most of what lies spread out before him.

Looking back we see the Old Town bridge tower, the square we have so recently left, and a fine panorama of the eastern waterfront. Allowing the eye to be coaxed round a full hundred and eighty degrees, over the curve of the river and along the grassy, wooded slopes of Letná, we are suddenly confronted by two opposing bridge towers and, beyond, a dazzling uprush of multi-coloured houses, palaces, domes, copper spires and gilded pinnacles. Some houses appear to have been stacked one on top of another; and closer inspection reveals this to be true. Little penthouse sheds lean against chimneystacks; vertiginous cat-walks lead from one dormer window to the next; and right at the top, seemingly supported by the closely packed shoulders of russet-tiled roofs and gables, the cathedral and castle shine against the sky.

Below us, Kampa island is divided from the west bank by the arc of the Devil's Brook, slowly turning the old waterwheel. Canoes sweep in and out of a slalom marked by dangling poles strung between the tall houses—a Venice in miniature. Women gossip at the foot of the steps or, avoiding the cameras which seem to be forever making children's television films here, settle themselves on seats facing the weir and vie with the chatter of birds an octave or two higher in the trees above.

From the gable of a house rising from the island to the level of passers-by on the bridge juts a tiny balcony with a window-box and a holy picture, before which a little light has burned day and night ever since I can remember.

The archway leading on to the Charles Bridge from the Old Town end cuts right through the bridge tower itself. Here, at this far end, the arch is a later addition linking two separate towers: the tower to the left was part of the original Queen Judith Bridge; its higher partner dates from the middle of the fifteenth century. A gallery around the top of this latter gives incomparable views over the bridge, the Old Town, and the Little Quarter. It can also provide unexpected sights at times. I recall a hot summer's day on which a young man wearing only black socks and skimpy red swimming trunks was somnolently practising the guitar in a top room with the windows wide open, oblivious to the sightseers along the parapet.

The Little Quarter or Lesser Town—the Kleinseite to the many Germanic residents of its earlier days, today Malá Strana —came into being in 1257 and expanded rapidly. In its un-spoilt, picturesque streets are even more of the ornamental house signs we met in the Old Town—At the Red Lion, At the Golden Stag, and the house of several generations of distinguished violin makers, At the Three Fiddles, now an agreeable little wine res-taurant. In 1541 a disastrous fire destroyed whole rows and squares of houses, and spread to the growing township of Hradčany on top of the hill. The wide spaces thus devastated offered wealthy nobles the chance to lay out the great palaces bearing their names—Kolovrat, Ledeburg, Lobkovic, Liechtenstein—which have now been adapted as foreign embassies or government departments. Two giant stone Moors support the balcony of the richly ornamented Morzini palace, today the Rumanian embassy. The Thun palace, where Mozart stayed on his first visit to Prague, has become the British embassy and possesses the trimmest lawn in the city: the Czechs themselves quite genuinely, and not from laziness, prefer their greensward a bit wild and romantic.

The most lordly of these homes is the Valdštejn palace with its spacious gardens, pool and fountain and folly and colonnade, all conceived by the arrogant Valdštejn or Wallenstein to compete with the royal palace itself. In spring and summer, like many of its partners, it is the setting for chamber music and orchestral concerts, silently watched over by bronze casts of classical and hunting statues by Adriaen de Vries. The originals of these figures were looted by the Swedes during the Thirty Years' War.

Of other great mansions echoing with history, the Vrtba palace beside the Little Town Square, refashioned in the Renaissance period, houses the offices of the Czechoslovak Foreign Institute. Across the square the palace once occupied by Charles of Liechtenstein, remembered for his savage execution of anti-Habsburg leaders in 1621, was for a while during the eighteenth century Prague's main post office.

Much less grand but perhaps better appreciated by the townsfolk, a demure little café in the centre of the Little Town Square is always quietly busy. At any time of day you will see, through its side window by the tram stop, women sipping coffee and eating cream cakes, and men browsing through the papers. This rendezvous once bore the name of Marshal Radetzky, whose statue stood close by until pulled down in 1919, after the establishment of an independent Czechoslovakia.

Behind it soar the tower and great cupola of the church of St Nicholas. Preliminary designs of this baroque masterpiece were prepared and carried through by the gifted Dientzen-hofers, father and son, whose influence was to appear in many a project throughout all Bohemia. There are some fifteen hundred square yards of frescoes in honour of St Nicholas, painstakingly treated and fixed in this century to avoid dissolution. A large statue of the saint dominates the high altar, and within a glass case to one side is a statue of Our Lady of Faenza, brought from Belgium by Jesuits in the middle of the Thirty Years' War.

From the south side of the Little Town Square we can make a leisurely way towards the Maltese Square, passing a plaque of Beethoven on a house where he once lodged, and the originally Romanesque church of Our Lady Below the Chain, which underwent a typical Prague transmutation through fourteenth-century Gothic to seventeenth-century baroque. In the Maltese Square one is soon conscious, especially when windows are open, of the existence of a music school. And there is a further diplomatic concentration hereabouts: the embassies of Japan and the Netherlands and, a few steps away, those of France and Yugoslavia.

Always the cathedral and castle and the spires of the Strahov monastery beckon the stroller to the summit. It gets less of a stroll and more of an endurance test as the inclines sharpen. But there really is no better way to approach the castle height if one is to get the full spread and savour of Prague.

The pattern of Hradčany was evolved from 1320 onwards within fortifications aimed at protecting the castle. More extensive defences were developed by Charles IV, and he incorporated the area still known as Nový Svět, the New World, whose cobbled lanes and little cottages are just about as old-world as one could imagine. One of these lanes leads up to a square overlooked by the Černín palace, now the Ministry of Foreign Affairs, refashioned along with the surrounding walls and buildings between the First and Second World Wars. Below the palace, on the other side of a sloping street inlaid with interwoven fans of stone setts, is the Loretto.

This takes its name from the Italian town to which in the thirteenth century the Santa Casa, or Holy House of Nazareth, was miraculously transported from the Holy Land to save it from the infidel. There have been many imitations of this building in which Mary is thought to have received the Annunciation from Gabriel, all of them aspiring to become places of pilgrimage. The shrine and church on this spot were donated by Benigna Catherine of the rich Lobkovic family in 1626, six years after the final defeat of the Protestant cause in Bohemia and Moravia. The donor did not have to pay much for the land, abandoned by fleeing Protestants.

In the Holy House itself, key to the whole architectural complex, murals illustrate the life of the Virgin. Her statue—strikingly, that of a black-faced woman—is of cedar set in a silver frame, the whole thing donated by the lady of another devout Catholic family, the Kolovrats. Beneath the shrine is the family vault of its original sponsors, the Lobkovics.

Cloistered chapels grew up around the first buildings, and ultimately a baroque façade by the brilliant younger Dientzenhofer was added to hold together the accumulation of styles. The carillon in the belfry rang for the first time in 1695, and continues to drop its limpid notes over the roofs and statues, and the terrace of the neighbouring restaurant.

Some of the courtyard chapels were neglected for decades, and restoration work now proceeds slowly. Among the occupants of these glassed-in recesses, some lying in undignified piles with limbs, a torso, or distorted fragments each carefully wrapped in plastic sheeting, is the strange St Vilgefortis. This Spanish martyr defied her father's command that she should marry a pagan, and prayed to God to rescue her from such a union. In answer to her plea, an unsightly beard grew on her face overnight. Her enraged father ordered her to be crucified.

The most visited and most awe-inspiring room in the Loretto is its treasury. This was part of Benigna Catherine's primary intention, and as the years went by it acquired a succession of priceless gifts from the faithful. Wealthy families competed with one another to provide new and more elaborate goblets, reliquaries and monstrances. Members of religious orders which had profited from the renewed supremacy of the church added their trophies. There are small and large pearl monstrances, a beautiful ivory crucifix, and the Valdštejn mitre of silk set with precious stones. But the glowing centre-piece of the whole collection is the incomparable 'Sun of Prague', the great diamond monstrance. While on a visit to Spain one of the Lobkovic family heard of the Kolovrat legacy to the Holy House and, fired with competitive zeal, at once ordered the creation of a monstrance by the court goldsmith at Vienna. When completed, it incorporated 6,222 diamonds shimmering within the gilded rays of a great sunburst. A dragon, reptiles, clouds and an exquisitely wrought Virgin all lead the eye towards the centre in which the host would be set. When Marie Lobkovic was charged with its transport from Vienna to Prague she was provided with an escort of five trusted men from the royal guard. Today this blazing golden miracle is protected behind plate glass and a barrier of electronic alarms, often difficult to see properly through the shifting reflections of other visitors; best contemplated in solitude when, by some lucky chance, ten or fifteen minutes elapse between coach tours and school parties.

Another religious foundation in the vicinity is that of the Strahov monastery. In a courtyard surrounded by monastic buildings, including a brewery, stands a statue of St Norbert, originator of the Premonstratensian order. The first structure here in 1140 was wooden, but this was soon amplified into a Romanesque stone building. The abbey church in its surviving form is mainly baroque, with many individual chapels and altars, and murals illustrating St Norbert's life. Strahov became famous for its collection of manuscripts and incunabula, and distinguished patrons added to this store, forming an appropriate basis for the monastery's present use as a Memorial of National Literature. Some of the most beautifully proportioned and decorated rooms in the city are to be found here. Religious books are kept in the Theological Hall, with a ceiling painted by one of the monks. A corridor lined with material on law and natural sciences leads to the Philosophical Hall, a high, gleaming room with polished galleries of finely bound editions and a resplendent ceiling, the work of the eighteenth-century Viennese rococo painter, Maulpertsch. Original letters of John Huss, disputatious pamphlets, and the recurrent attempts to reinstate the

Czech language in defiance of German-speaking overlords: all are here.

Below Strahov, paths through the old monastic and aristocratic gardens disclose the cathedral spires to one side and the whole of Prague laid out in the valley below, hazed in the morning when the sun is in the east, at its loveliest on certain late afternoons when light from the west picks out every gleaming detail. In spring the blossom, starting slowly like specks of hoar frost incongruous in bright sunshine, thickens until the whole hillside of gardens above the Little Quarter is a white tumult of overlapping waves. The scent drifts down upon the city to blend with that of Eastern European petrol and a chemical used for cleaning the streets, producing a distinctive and utterly unforgettable incense. Set down blindfold after years of absence I am sure I should be able to tell exactly where I was.

Rather than descend with it we should turn across the hill towards the cathedral, up a steep flight of steps and then inevitably down another slope until we reach the wide square before the main entrance to the castle. To one side is the archbishop's palace. Facing it, the palace of the Schwarzenbergs has become the Swiss embassy, and beside it the Lobkovic palace with its black and white geometrical graffiti is now a museum of military history, in whose courtyard displays of duelling are often given.

So to the castle itself.

Even before religious buildings and fortifications appeared on this summit in the ninth century there is known to have been an ancient Slavonic burial ground in the heart of the present castle area. The earlier Přemyslide rulers did not live here but six miles or so north at Levý Hradec. Then, as the trading post on the Vltava became more important to the emergent nation, adequate defences had to be provided, and by the twelfth century a royal palace had been set within the battlements. This was burnt down in 1303, after which we can begin to trace the influences of two men on both castle and cathedral. First came Matthias of Arras and then Peter Parler, a young man from Gmünd whose talents in his early twenties were recognized by

3 The banks of the Vltava in Prague

the discerning Charles IV, and who was to work on the cathedral for almost half a century until his death.

Following the ill-starred rule of Charles' son, Wenceslas IV, there was a period of stagnation during which the rulers of Bohemia were crowned here but chose to live in the Old Town. It was not until late in the fifteenth century that the palace was reoccupied and significant building work was resumed under Vladislav Jagellon, after whom the great Vladislav Hall is named.

This was conceived as a throne room to accommodate the coronation and other ceremonials on the accession of a new king. Tournaments were held here, and a wide, shallow-stepped staircase had to be installed so that horses could be brought up to the hall. Hall and staircase have Gothic ceilings patterned with interlaced stone ribs: hardly the intricate fan vaulting we are accustomed to in certain English masterpieces of the kind, but fascinating in their interwoven cat's-cradles of arcs and coils. To one end of the hall is the Old Diet, where the Czech Estates met for election of their king and all other major administrative sessions until 1847. It is still the venue for swearing in the President of the Republic.

The fire of 1541 was a serious setback, destroying large tracts of the castle, its chancelleries and offices, and many valuable records. The Vladislav Hall was badly damaged, but happily its ceiling survived. Reconstruction was entrusted to Boniface Wohlmuth, who created new formal rooms and houses within the walls, and completed the Italianate summer house, the Belvedere, which after a confused career as a royal retreat, an observatory for Tycho Brahe, a market, a dance hall and a timber store, now shelters frequent art exhibitions in a setting of trim paths and flowerbeds, with a reverberant 'singing fountain' forever thrumming a song.

When Rudolf II settled permanently in Prague in 1580 the castle became a centre of the arts and sciences. He installed collections of works of art and curios, surrounded himself with artists, miniaturists, philosophers and scientists, and provided accommodation for alchemists and astrologers. A new palace which he ordained along one side of the second courtyard included a Spanish Hall and a gallery for his treasures.

4 Karlštejn castle, Charles IV's treasure house

The glittering Spanish Hall, damaged in 1757 by Frederick the Great's troops, owes its present appearance to lavish refurbishing undertaken between 1865 and 1868 in anticipation of the Emperor Franz Josef's coronation here as king of Bohemia —a calculated political gesture which in the end was not carried through.

Many of Rudolf II's treasures were carried off by Swedish looters in 1648, and during subsequent years of Habsburg rule the castle was only intermittently occupied. The present main gateway, with its guardian giants, bears the initials MTI— Maria Theresa Imperatrix—but the fabric as a whole sported more scars than ornaments as a consequence of the Empress's complicated wars, suffering especially from Frederick the Great's attack. After that humiliation, gradual repairs and further additions gave it the general proportions we know today.

During Frederick's siege many valuable paintings were hastily removed from their walls and hidden in a number of odd, improvised caches. The imperial court in Vienna had already acquired many choice items from the Prague collections, and now others were bundled off to join them. Even worse, some canvasses were sold off without any reasonable supervision: works of Titian and Dürer fetched a few shillings. Condescendingly Vienna filled in the gaps by transferring a number of undistinguished works by lesser painters to Prague. After the First World War the newly independent Czechoslovak Republic asked for numerous works of art filched by Vienna to be returned, but with little success. Later investigation showed that in fact a fair number of interesting works, if not those of the mightier geniuses, had been left behind. In the company of paintings by Titian, Veronese, Tintoretto and Rubens these are now on show in two halls which were once stables, together with some smaller linking rooms.

Works of more specialized national significance are to be found in the Šternberk palace across Hradčany Square, where the National Gallery displays old monastic paintings, fine carved Madonnas in the old Bohemian tradition, and some Gothic panels by Master Theodoricus.

Yet another exhibition of past glories is housed in the chapel of the Holy Rood, in the second courtyard of the castle. Here are treasures acquired over the centuries by St Vitus' cathedral: jewel-encrusted crucifixes, reliquaries, monstrances, chalices, episcopal robes, and the sword of St Stephen; Venetian glass and onyx, and tenth-century hunting horns. Some are gifts from Charles IV, a pursuer of holy relics so assiduous that no saint's tooth or toenail was safe from his possessive adoration.

The cathedral itself is an amalgam of several styles and several centuries. The original tenth-century rotunda gave way to a Romanesque basilica at just about the time William of Normandy set his sights on England. When Prague became an archbishopric, Charles IV celebrated this by lavish endowments and the engagement of the academic Matthias of Arras and the more imaginative Peter Parler and his sons. Political, dynastic and economic conflicts halted or diverted work between one generation and another, and the cathedral was not effectively completed until 1929. Sculpted portraits in the triforium, some installed by the Parler workshop and others in more modern times, commemorate the men who contributed distinctive touches to the ultimate achievement.

At St Vitus' altar took place the coronation ceremonies of the Bohemian kings, and before that altar is the mausoleum containing the remains of many of them, including Charles IV and his four wives.

It was Charles who put his personal weight behind the cult of St Wenceslas, originally buried in the early rotunda but rehoused by Peter Parler in a richer tomb complete with his helmet and armour, in a chapel whose walls are studded with semi-precious stones. At the same time Charles made the St Wenceslas crown a sacred object in itself by inserting into its sapphire cross a holy relic, supposedly a thorn from Christ's crown of thorns. From then on no other crown could be chosen by a putative ruler, and no Bohemian coronation could be considered valid without the use of this crown. It was said that anyone so much as setting it upon his head without due authority would meet a violent end. The last man known to have risked this was Heydrich, Hitler's sadistic 'Protector' of Bohemia and Moravia, who presumed to take even the crown jewels under his personal protection and decked himself in the regalia for the amusement of his family. It was only a matter of weeks before he was assassinated. After many vicissitudes and many occasions on which they have had to be hidden away from barbarians and usurpers, the crown jewels are now lodged in a chamber reached by staircase from the Wenceslas chapel, protected by seven locks whose keys are held by seven separate officials and institutions. They are rarely displayed, on average about once in ten years. I was lucky enough to see them in 1975 when, under heavy guard, a patient queue filed past them in St George's basilica. Presumably we must now wait until 1985 for another glimpse.

There is some striking modern stained glass in windows above the side chapels and altars, glowing with flame when the sun strikes from the right angle. Tombs of Přemyslide kings are to be found in the chapels of the Virgin, of John the Baptist, and of the Holy Relics, and those of the great builders themselves, Matthias of Arras and Peter Parler, were rediscovered in 1928 in the Valdštejn chapel.

From beside the Wenceslas chapel the Golden Portal leads out into the third courtyard of the castle. Above it is a fourteenth-century mosaic of the Last Judgment, several times restored and showing signs of serious deterioration by the middle of our own century. It was restored again in 1959 and looked splendid for some years, but is already showing signs of fading once more.

On most days these courtyards are filled with strollers, but on Sunday mornings during the milder months they tend to empty out on to the castle ramparts. There an orchestra plays to an audience divided between those who are content to sit in the chairs provided and those who prefer a saunter through the Paradise garden and along the paths, looking down on to jumbled rooftops, hints of café umbrellas, the terraces of long-vanished noble families, and even a compact little vineyard on the steeper slopes. And when all this palls, if it ever does, there is the solace of the Vikárka restaurant on 'Vicar's street', under the far side of St Vitus' great bulk.

This little warren of rooms and corridors, one stretch running along the edge of the old moat, was once a tavern of some rowdiness and disrepute. Perhaps it has now gone too smartly to the other extreme as a tourist attraction; but it still has its club-room for those in the know, and still relies largely on the support of its regulars during the quieter winter months.

Janáček's opera, *The Excursions of Mr Brouček*, little known in this country because of its localized appeal, offers a character-istically sardonic slant on the goings-on in this establishment. The composer had always regarded music as a tragic rather than a comic medium, but when he found the bourgeois Brouček in the pages of Svatopluk Čech's satirical novel he was so taken by him that between 1908 and 1917, battling with difficulties imposed by a succession of librettists, he produced the two sections of this unorthodox opera.

The name Brouček means a beetle. Many Czech surnames have explicit meanings of this kind, not always welcomed by those who inherit them. Among my own acquaintances are a Mr Sadness, a most amiable and generous man, and a Dr Peasant, a man of great discrimination and culture. However, Mr Brouček is, it must be admitted, a bit of a beetle. Owner of an apartment house, he is forever lamenting the dilatoriness of his tenants in paying the rent, the greed of tax collectors, and the depressing news in the papers every day. Grumbling and drinking away his sorrows at Vikárka, he comes out one evening in maudlin mood and, longing to be on the trouble-free Moon instead of this exasperating Earth, collapses and dreams of being whisked through space to his heart's desire. On the Moon he finds himself in an airy-fairy world of pretentious writers, painters and critics, and cannot even fortify himself with a good piece of Czech sausage taken from his pocket because this is regarded as a bestial, degrading appetite. In the music we hear parodies of the Czech national anthem, some shameless paro-dies of Richard Strauss whenever sentiments get too high-flown, and the laments of the Moon-folk that even up here you can't get away from that troublesome tribe, the Czechs.

Fleeing from the amorous advances of a Moon woman, Brouček is glad to find himself back in Prague, even if in a somewhat undignified position—in the long, coffin-like basket on two wheels used to trundle 'beer corpses' home after a heavy night.

Still Brouček goes on dreaming. In the second part of the opera he again takes too much beer—a difficult thing to resist, considering the quality of the beer in Vikárka!—and blusters his way into an argument with his cronies about Prague's secret tunnels and their place in the city's defence against the Holy Roman Emperor, Sigismund. In no time at all Brouček finds himself, in contrast to his trip to a futuristic Moon, back in history. He also finds that he is not the stuff of which heroes are made. After a cowardly plea to the enemy he is crammed into a barrel by his enraged comrades, who have the faces of the innkeeper and his twentieth-century friends in new guise, and thrown on the fire . . . waking to find himself with a hangover in a dirty, empty barrel at Vikárka.

This seems as appropriate a point as any at which to take a steadier look at the history of the Czechs and Slovaks. First visits to a city or a country produce visual impressions rather than an interest in names and dates. But after a while, passing references which have been brushed aside on preliminary sight-seeing tours begin to return and to nag. The Přemyslides, the Jagellons, the invading Germans and Magyars and Turks and Swedes, kings such as Wenceslas and Vladislav and reformers such as John Huss: in what order did they come, why are they still revered or excoriated, what mark have they left on stone or earth? It is impossible to pack every significant detail of every development and every conflict in this contentious region of Europe into one coherent chapter, and I am all too well aware that a brief summary will omit too much and probably throw false emphasis on some things which have been included. The relation of potentates and politics to places on a visitor's itinerary makes for a complex jigsaw; and I apologize to any reader who discovers, at the end, that some key pieces are still missing.

Frontiers

The state of Czechoslovakia, created in 1918, has an area of some 50,000 square miles and a population of fourteen and a half million. In size, then, it is much the same as England, but with a population less than a third of ours. Rich equally in mineral resources, agricultural land, and timber—forests still cover almost a third of its territory—the country lies perilously across the map of central Europe, enclosed by West Germany, East Germany, Poland, the U.S.S.R., Hungary, and Austria: a ring of neighbours whose varying ambitions have allowed Czechs and Slovaks few periods of tranquillity over the centuries. The mountain ranges of the borders are impressive, but have never presented a solid enough obstacle to really determined intruders.

We know from the Romans that a Celtic tribe, the Boii, settled and gave their name to Bohemia late in the sixth century B.C. Other Celts established themselves on the fringes of Slovakia and in Moravia, the central region of the present republic. All were driven out by Germanic invaders about 100 B.C. For many centuries there was no single dominating group until, in the sixth century A.D., the Slavs appeared on the scene and, after a period of subjugation by nomadic Avars, began to dig themselves in.

One of these tribes was that of the Czechs, their name deriving from a chieftain called Čech who led them into Bohemia. The daughter of one of his successors was the princess Libuše. However mythical the story of her choice of Přemysl as husband may be, there is no doubt of the existence of a Přemyslide dynasty or of its importance in the growth of the country.

While the Czechs were consolidating their position, the tribes which had settled Moravia expanded over neighbouring territories until they could justifiably boast of having created a Great Moravian Empire. In the ninth century Christianity began to reach these pagan lands, though by devious routes and with some clashes of opinion. Prince Rostislav of Moravia, whose conquests extended as far as Saxony, was displeased by missionaries from Rome who taught in a tongue incomprehensible to most of his people, and sought for preachers in the vernacular. Historians have two conflicting versions of his purpose and procedure. One school holds that, having asked Rome to send Christian missionaries who would speak the language of the people and been ignored, he turned defiantly to the Emperor Michael of Byzantium. The other sees cunning rather than impatience in this move: fearing that subservience to the church of Rome would probably mean subservience also to the ambitions of German princes who supported that church, Rostislav preferred to seek a spiritual alliance with Constantinople, at a time when spiritual and temporal alliances went hand in hand.

Whatever impulses or calculations there may have been, the Byzantine Emperor answered the Moravian plea. Two priests with a knowledge of Slavonic tongues, Constantine (later and better known as Cyrill) and Methodius were sent to spread the gospel. Among many stories told about them is one of a revelation vouchsafed by God just as they were about to set off. Cyrill had a vision of an alphabet capable of interpreting the sounds of Slav speech and so of recording essential liturgical texts. This Glagolitic script, derived from Greek, was adapted in later centuries as the basis of, among others, Russian orthography, and called the Cyrillic alphabet. Cyrill eventually went to Rome and continued to specialize as a Slavonic interpreter. Methodius became Bishop of the Czechs and then Archbishop of Pannonia, the ancient name of the plain covering a wide region of Slovakia and Hungary, most of it controlled by the Great Moravian Empire. Unfortunately his patron Rostislav was overthrown by a usurping nephew, who blinded the prince and imprisoned him in a monastery, thereafter playing off Rome against Byzantium, harassing Methodius and, after the Archbishop's death, driving his followers out of the country.

It is true that under this despot, Svatopluk, the Great Moravian Empire grew greater. But when he died, a Magyar invasion robbed it of Slovakia. Czechs and Moravians banded defensively together. The Slovaks did not rejoin them until after the First World War: a divorce of a thousand years.

In 921 A.D. Bohemia came under the rule of a Přemyslide duke, or prince, or (according to one's favoured terminology) king whose name will be preserved in, if nowhere else, an English Christmas carol. Good King Wenceslas did his Christian best to come to a reasonable accommodation with German rulers and other greedy neighbours. His piety was rather out of tune with the spirit of the age. His own mother had murdered her mother-in-law, later to be canonized as St Ludmila; and his brother Boleslav, greedy for power, gathered dissidents about him to challenge and finally assassinate Wenceslas in 935 at mass in the royal township of Staré (Old) Boleslav. A Romanesque basilica built as a shrine on the spot of the martyrdom was rebuilt in baroque style in the eighteenth century, but the original crypt has been preserved.

Both Wenceslas and his grandmother have lived on as protective saints. Ludmila has given her name to the excellent wines of Mělník. He, like our own King Arthur, is said to be not dead but sleeping until the hour of his country's greatest need. When this time comes, Wenceslas will arouse the Bohemian knights who slumber under Blaník hill (depicted in the final section of Smetana's *Má Vlast*) and lead them towards Prague. As they cross the Charles Bridge, Wenceslas' horse will stumble above the spot where the knight Bruncvík, whose statue stands beside the bridge, hid a magic sword brought back from foreign parts. Wielding this, Wenceslas will destroy the enemies of his people. During an economic crisis in the late nineteen-fifties a widely circulated joke told of President Novotný's alarm when the statue of Wenceslas in Václavské náměstí (Wenceslas Square) came to life and rode purposefully off towards Blaník. Summoning his Minister of Finance, the President managed to intercept Wenceslas and the knights on their way into Prague. Novotný

ordered that the Minister of Finance should, in order to calm
the warriors, read out reassuring details of the country's new
Five Year Plan. When he had heard it, Wenceslas turned to his
followers and said: 'This, gentlemen, is not the hour of our
country's greatest need. Back to Blaník: they will be in much
greater need of us five years from now.' With very little adaptation the story could surely be used in a contemporary English
context!

Bohemia was now growing in strength. Prague had become
one of the richest and most important trading centres in Europe.
The Přemyslide monarchs played the usual medieval game of
alliances and treacheries with as much skill as any, but made
one move which was to provoke discord far into the future: they
not merely allowed but invited German settlers into Bohemia
to colonize field and forest, and to develop the country's
resources.

In 1198 Přemysl Otakar I succeeded in having himself acknowledged as a king, his predecessors having been technically
no more than dukes or self-styled princes. Before his death he
had his son also crowned so that there should be no quibbling
over the succession. This son became the first true King Wenceslas. During his reign the Tatars invaded central Europe, and
local conflicts were suspended so that a concerted defence could
be mounted. After some successes in Hungary and Poland,
the intruders withdrew.

Wenceslas I's heir, Otakar II, by two shrewdly planned
marriages acquired Austrian lands and extended his country's
boundaries to the Adriatic sea. Unfortunately he became too
bold, set his sights on winning the German crown, and after a
succession of blunders managed to lose all his new acquisitions,
most of them claimed by the Holy Roman Emperor Rudolf I.
With his own nobles turning against him, Otakar attempted one
last attack on Rudolf, but in 1278 was killed at the battle of the
Marchfeld. Rudolf took personal charge of Moravia, and in
Bohemia appointed Otto of Brandenburg as regent to Wenceslas, the dead Otakar's seven-year-old son.

This was a dark time for Bohemia. The Brandenburgers
behaved as exploiters rather than protectors of the realm.

Otakar's widow was virtually imprisoned in the castle of Bezděz, far to the north-east of Prague, with her son; and when at the age of twelve Wenceslas was entitled to ascend the throne, the regency demanded a ransom from the Czechs before releasing him. There was widespread famine which was not, however, allowed to distress the German part of the populace, who were everywhere shown favour. A romantic, patriotic treatment of this period of history is found in Smetana's first opera, *The Brandenburgers in Bohemia.*

Young Wenceslas II was not long in finding his feet. With the Brandenburgers out of the way and the feud with Rudolf patched up by marriage to his daughter, Wenceslas turned on the Vítkovci family who had conspired against and ultimately abandoned his father. By now his mother had married one of them, who hoped to use the young king for his own ambitions. Instead, Wenceslas had him executed and then proceeded to massacre the rest of the family. After rebuilding the prosperity of his country and attempting one or two more or less obligatory campaigns of expansion and conquest, Wenceslas was succeeded by his son Wenceslas III, assassinated in Olomouc at the age of seventeen with no heir to carry on the Přemyslide dynasty.

To maintain this level of prosperity and continue on peaceable terms with the Emperor Rudolf, the Czech nobles thought it politic to nominate Rudolf's son as king of Bohemia. In return the young man had the good sense to marry Wenceslas' widow; but within a year was dead. After a number of false attempts and potentially dangerous squabbles, an invitation was extended in 1310 to John of Luxembourg, son of the German Emperor. He accepted the throne and proved a more determined ruler than his proud sponsors had quite anticipated. But by 1318 they had combined to extract from him an agreement weakening German influence in the administration and putting more power in the hands of the great Czech families. John was a courageous and much respected monarch and when, in spite of having been blinded in battle against the Lithuanians, he decided to offer his personal services to France against an English invasion, his knights were eager to follow. At Crécy they were mown down by Welsh archers. The blind king, charging on when the French had already turned to flee, was killed; and his son Wenceslas was lucky to escape with his life.

Bohemia, too, had reason to be thankful for this escape. This son, who changed his name and chose to be crowned not as Wenceslas but as Karel, was to prove the most enlightened and creative of kings and emperors as Charles IV.

We have seen his imprint upon Prague. Less apparent but of equal significance to the country were his legal and economic reforms, and his policy of winning and safeguarding territory by diplomacy rather than war. His four successive marriages all won land and allies. He curbed the arrogance of the nobles, personally led a punitive expedition against one of the more defiant and hanged him within his own castle, and gave royal authority to independent courts in place of subservient manorial ones.

Charles' daughter Anne became the first wife of Richard II of England as part of a scheme conceived by the Roman Pope to contain the troublesome French, who were backing his rival. This marriage took many young courtiers to England in Anne's entourage, and there was an increase in the number of Bohemian students at Oxford. Some had already come under the reformist influence of John Wycliffe, in serious trouble towards the end of his life because of his outspoken criticism of clerical abuses and ecclesiastical greed for earthly possessions, and his heretical views on transubstantiation and the interpretation of the Scriptures. Queen Anne herself, whose marriage was a direct result of the turbulent papal schism, was interested in many of these views and encouraged their dissemination through her homeland. Wycliffe died in 1348, and in England much of the vitality of his doctrines died with him; but in Bohemia they continued to provide food for argument, helped by the transcription of two of his books taken to Prague by Master Jerome. By the turn of the century they had made a fateful impression on another reformer, Jan Hus, or John Huss.

The teachings of Huss and the strife to which they led so soon after his death and long, long afterwards are of far greater import in Czech history than any conceivable parallel in English history. Czechs today still argue the rights and wrongs where we could rarely be found arguing with any great heat about, for example, Oliver Cromwell or William III (except, of course, in Ireland). To some, Huss was an unyielding fanatic and unquestionably a heretic; to others, a man of good will who nevertheless unleashed brutish wars from which the nation never entirely recovered; to others, the most heroic national symbol of them all. The attentive foreigner sometimes gets the impression that all Czech history before 1415 was merely leading up to that death at the stake in Constance, and all Czech history since has led away from it. Without an understanding of the Hussite explosion there can be no understanding of Czech aspirations and sufferings over the last five hundred years.

One of the troubles Charles IV had laid up for his successors was in the wording of his university's foundation charter. This, devised from the most enlightened motives to allow equal administrative rights to the four main communities in the realm —Saxon, Bavarian, Polish and Czech—in effect produced an almost unvarying coalition of three to one against the native Czechs. Nationalist resentment built up, and at the same time religious doctrines began to be questioned. Quite apart from reformist murmurings in many parts of Europe, the Czechs had their own grounds for associating orthodox religion with oppression: church and priesthood were dominated by those Germanic elements which ceaselessly, in spite of all checks and reversals, sought to control the key posts and most profitable concerns in the land.

John Huss, born in Husinec in 1371, was the son of poor cottagers. In Prague he was first a student and then a professor at the university. After studying, copying, annotating and translating some of Wycliffe's pamphlets he began to spread controversial ideas of his own. In 1402 he was appointed preacher at the Bethlehem Chapel in the Old Town, a great austere barn of a place from whose pulpit he addressed audiences of up to three thousand. A persuasive evangelist, he called for a return to the humbler, ascetic concept of Christianity, and denounced church wealth and temporal power. Though not subscribing to all Wycliffe's doctrinal deviations, he supported the common man's right to judge from the actual words of the Bible what was right and wrong rather than submit to the self-perpetuating glosses of the clergy. In pursuance of this belief in the need to make Holy Writ available to all, Huss reformed Czech orthography, established the Czech alphabet and accents still in use, and encouraged his disciples to disseminate this knowledge.

Local priests were not slow to complain to the king or to report the dangers to Rome. The establishment of the Bethlehem Chapel in 1391 by radicals among the Czech gentry had never met with papal approval, and observance of the mass had never been allowed in it. In due course, long after the Hussite cause had been defeated, its demolition was ordered; but between the First and Second World Wars the main entrance, the bases of some columns, and outlines of the original windows were rediscovered, and after the Second World War the chapel was faithfully reconstructed from old plans and measurements.

Charles IV's son, Wenceslas IV, was a complete contrast to his father: a feeble vacillator with little grasp of his country's needs. He allowed himself to be imposed on by German courtiers and then, badgered by the indignant Czech nobility, would go to the opposite extreme in the hope of appeasing his latest malcontents. On one occasion he was imprisoned by his nobles, with the connivance of his own brother Sigismund, and released only after making humiliating concessions.

In 1409 Wenceslas bowed before a storm of complaint about German domination of the Charles University and reversed the administrative balance, giving three Czech votes to one foreign vote. Many non-Czech professors and students left at once; and the German rector, compelled to resign, gave way to the jubilantly elected John Huss.

This was a further irritant to the Pope and his local representatives. The Archbishop of Prague made a public bonfire of Wycliffe's writings so that there should be no doubt of the official view on such perversities. For a time Wenceslas remained on the side of Huss, approving the logical implications of the Wycliffe–Huss view that temporal power was no concern of the church and should rest with secular authorities; and the Czech nobles had every reason to feel the same. Even when Archbishop Zbyněk laid a temporary interdict upon the city, rendering impossible the solemnization of births, weddings or funerals, the king allowed Hussite preachers to celebrate mass in their own parishes and in churches under his jurisdiction.

In 1412 the Pope authorized the sale of plenary indulgences, an international money-making scheme whereby sinners could lessen their sentence in Purgatory according to the amount they were prepared to pay to the retailer. Huss stepped up his diatribes from the Bethlehem Chapel pulpit. Three young admirers fired by his denunciations attacked an indulgence seller and were swiftly condemned to public execution. Students turned out in force to carry their corpses solemnly to the chapel for burial. At last the Pope excommunicated Huss. To save not only himself but his king and his loyal followers from direct confrontation with the spiritual overlord they still in principle acknowledged, Huss was prevailed on to retire for a couple of years to the mellow countryside of Southern Bohemia. There he was well looked after by the local gentry, and continued to preach in the open air to enthusiastic congregations.

Still unappeased, the Pope threatened a crusade against rebellious Bohemia. Wenceslas was finally persuaded that Huss should attend a general council which had assembled in Constance to discuss schismatic problems, and there explain and justify his views. Wenceslas' brother, King Sigismund of Hungary, Holy Roman Emperor since 1410, gave a solemn undertaking that the preacher should have safe conduct there and back. In spite of warnings that such promises from the notoriously treacherous Sigismund could not be relied on, Huss went in the company of Jerome of Prague and several attendant nobles to Constance in the hope of obtaining a fair hearing.

With scant ceremony he was arrested and thrown into prison. Jerome and the other members of the party demanded his release and Sigismund's honouring of the promise of safe conduct. The most they were granted was a public hearing before the council—which in the event could hardly be called a hearing. Whatever point Huss tried to make was shouted down. The verdict had been reached in advance, and on 6 July 1415 he was burnt at the stake. The executioner's assistant was ordered to sweep the ashes into the river so that no trace of Master Huss should remain to contaminate his misguided countrymen. A year later his companion and fellow reformer, Master Jerome, was also burnt.

But 'the truth', Huss had roundly declared, 'shall prevail'. The Czechs were appalled by the wicked charade at Constance. Few even of the orthodox faithful found it easy now to respect the authority of their pastors. Large numbers asserted their independence by taking up the cry of communion in both kinds—ironically, not one of Huss's own essential doctrines, though in his last hours at Constance he had expressed approval of it. Now the Utraquists (*sub utraque specie*, under each kind) or Calixtines (so named after their symbol of the chalice) defied all commands to bow to the authority of Rome. The new Archbishop of Prague, a German, refused to ordain priests declaring their allegiance to Huss; whereupon the pro-Hussite queen used her prerogative to dismiss any priest on the royal estates who did *not* declare such allegiance. Ordered by the new Pope Martin V to restore such priests to their incumbencies, the king surrendered. The returning priests, most of them German, at once abolished the service of communion in both kinds which the Hussites had instituted. This left them with derisory congregations: the majority of worshippers went out into the fields to attend mass and take communion from their exiled preachers.

In July 1419 there was a riot in Prague. A Hussite procession, marching with the host elevated in a monstrance, was observed by newly appointed anti-Hussite councillors from a window in the New Town Hall. One of them is said to have thrown a stone at the priest or at the monstrance, though after all this time the evidence can hardly be regarded as water-tight. Whatever the provocation, the marchers stormed the Town Hall and threw several councillors out of the window to friends below, who promptly lynched them. King Wenceslas, terrified and incapable of coping with the situation, died of a heart attack the following month.

His brother Sigismund was next in line for the Bohemian throne. But the memory of his betrayal of Huss rankled. The Czech Estates could see no way of accepting him without certain stringent conditions, including his toleration of Utraquist beliefs and practice; while the peasantry and provincial townsfolk preferred to do without him altogether and concentrate on means of sharing out the great church estates and establishing a fairer society.

The Pope certainly had no intention of countenancing any compromise with heresy. Early in 1420 he ordered a crusade against dissidents which Sigismund himself must lead. Indulgences were guaranteed to all who eradicated sin by killing Czechs. Catholics, largely of German extraction, set about the task with a will. Mercenaries and genuine anti-heretics of all nations assembled to invade Bohemia under the banner of the Holy Roman Emperor.

But by now a champion had arisen to rally the forces of reform and become as great a national hero as Huss himself: another Jan, or John.

Squire of a small and none too prosperous country estate in Southern Bohemia, John Žižka of Trocnov had encountered some troubles early in his career with powerful neighbours, the Rožmberks. At a time when he was supposedly in royal service there were rumours of his belonging to a band of brigands which harassed the Rožmberk lands; but there is not necessarily an inconsistency here, since the king often gave sly support to free-booters who would keep his over-powerful lords busy. For a while, probably with royal connivance, Žižka left the country to serve the Polish king against the Teutonic Knights. The loss of his left eye has been attributed to an encounter in battle; but other chroniclers say young John lost it in a boyish escapade when he was eight. On his return to Bohemia he became a favourite at court and is known to have accompanied the queen more than once to listen to Huss in the Bethlehem Chapel.

Setting himself at the head of religious idealists inflamed by Huss's death, of peasants weary of clerical avarice, and Czech nobles and burghers eager to settle once and for all their feud with the German patricians, Žižka improvised an army equipped with flails, hideously spiked balls on the end of lengths of chain, home-made spears and daggers, and heavy waggons linked by chains into pre-fabricated forts, against which many a cavalry charge was to smash itself to pieces. The tactics of his peasant rabble have been denounced by many who, with reason, deplore the sacking of monasteries, the destruction of holy statues and works of art, and the savage maiming and murder of opponents. But neither side in the seventeen or eighteen years of the Hussite wars can claim to have been especially merciful. Germans in the mining town of Kutná Horá, with the full assurance of papal clemency, tossed hundreds—some claimed thousands—of Hussites down disused mine shafts.

The Czech Diet, endeavouring to rule the country without an acknowledged monarch, found itself not surprisingly faced by an anarchy of local lords taking matters into their own hands, splinter groups forming, and groups of peasants leaving the land to shelter in larger town communities able to withstand attack.

The most influential and well disciplined of these sectarian groups was that of the Taborites, so called after a Biblical mountain. Long before Luther they were, in essence, zealously reformist Protestants. They believed in the literal interpretation of the Bible as the only path to truth, in abandonment of ritual, in the imminent Second Coming of Christ, and in social egalitarianism. Seeking a secure base in that part of Southern Bohemia where Huss had written and preached during his period of exile from Prague, they took over a nearly derelict fortress on a granite hill above the river Lužnice, set about refortifying it, and named it Tábor. It became a commune of equal 'brothers and sisters' in which property was shared, no distinction was admitted between peasant, gentleman and burgher, and intensive daily reading of the Bible took precedence over all else.

But military as well as spiritual strength was needed. Hard pressed in Plzeň and forced to negotiate a withdrawal, Žižka set out with his few hundred men and a few waggons towards Tábor. The Catholic lords who had negotiated the truce and promised his safe withdrawal did not hesitate to break the promise once he was on the move, and sent a force of two thousand men, including a large body of armoured cavalry, to intercept him. By using his waggons in a defensive arc, similar to those which later cinema-going generations have seen a hundred

times in Wild West films, Žižka protected his flanks and concentrated his forces to their best advantage. The vastly superior
forces were beaten off, and proved reluctant to renew the attack
in darkness. Žižka was met by a welcoming committee and
escorted in triumph into Tábor.

The Hussite forces were still small and ill coordinated, and
Sigismund, concluding he could rely on the support of the
Czech nobles once he had made a real show of strength, decided
to set out for Prague. His intention of suppressing Hussitism
once he was firmly installed was so blatant that Prague councillors and priests held hurried meetings and began to prepare
defences against their would-be king. At the same time a manifesto was prepared embodying the Four Articles of Prague,
varying slightly in order and emphasis through later drafts but
unequivocally demanding:

1. That the body and blood of Christ be given everywhere to the
   common people.
2. That the Word of God be proclaimed and freely preached
   everywhere.
3. That the church exercise no worldly power and possess no
   worldly property.
4. That sins, including those of clergy as well as of laymen, shall
   be denounced and punished by the appropriate authority.

In May 1420 Sigismund entered the country he considered
to be his and marched towards the capital. Vyšehrad was in the
hands of loyal supporters, and at the news of his approach
waverers within Hradčany decided to yield this fortress also.
When news of this defection circulated through the city there
was an outburst of protest and fighting which devastated large
parts of the Little Quarter below the castle. Sigismund hurried
on through Kutná Horá, where he was rapturously received by
the German community and refugee clerics. More than ever
determined to resist, in spite of royalist forces in both Prague
castles, the city councillors appealed for help from Hussite
communities in neighbouring regions.

They did not have long to wait. Žižka at once set out from
Tábor on a brisk forced march with his army, blockaded sup-
plies to Hradčany, and moved so purposefully to the east that
Sigismund hastily backed away to Kutná Horá. Then, fearing

the loss of the royal castles, he tried to subdue other towns which were supplying troops and provisions to his enemies in the capital, and in one bold stroke managed to get food through to Hradčany, though he did not risk a head-on battle at this stage. The puritanical Taborites expelled from Prague all families who would not acknowledge the fundamental Hussite principles, concentrating especially on Germans who might be expected to aid Sigismund should he breach the city defences. Then Žižka set up individual command posts at strategic points, and prepared for both a siege and a possible all-out assault.

With two main approaches blocked by the loyalists on the castle heights, he had to do something about the unprotected, vulnerable supply road entering the city from the north-east. Above this stood a hill named after St Vitus—Vítkov. Žižka erected earthworks and some makeshift towers here, together with a palisade in which he did not hesitate to use wooden pews torn from a church. His foresight was soon confirmed. On 14 July 1420 Sigismund's crusaders attacked the hill. With his usual cunning Žižka had shaped his defences so that only a small number of cavalry could charge abreast at any one time, providing easy targets for the Hussites. But attackers outnumbered defenders four or five to one, and before long succeeded in getting over the wall. At this crucial stage Žižka led a contingent of his most trusted warriors through the vineyards of the district known today as Vinohrady (literally 'vineyards') and, followed by a large body of Taborites singing a thunderous chorale, took Sigismund's troops on the flank. These chorales were almost as terrifying a weapon as any axe or flail in the Hussite armoury: the most celebrated of them, 'Ye Warriors of God', still echoes through *Tábor* and *Blaník*, the last two movements of Smetana's *Má Vlast*. The nerve of the crusaders on Vítkov failed, and they fell back.

A new name was given to Vítkov. Henceforth it was known as Žižkov, as is the residential and industrial area which has now grown up around it. On its summit today stands a massive equestrian statue of the one-eyed leader, backed by the somewhat heavy block of the National Memorial containing the grave of the Unknown Soldier, those of twentieth-century working-class revolutionaries, and a hall commemorating the achievements of the Soviet Army.

Sigismund did not immediately renew his attack. Pressure was brought to bear by moderate Czech lords and, hoping that with their aid he might avoid bloody and protracted campaigning, Sigismund stayed his hand and, a mere two weeks after his defeat, was crowned in St Vitus' cathedral. He appeared to give grudging assent to the over-all terms of the Four Articles in order to be allowed to accede to the throne, but in fact avoided committing himself irrevocably. The Czech lords soon realized they were not going to get much from Sigismund, and he in his turn realized that the throne was not going to offer him much comfort. The Prague authorities made it clear that they proposed to ignore his coronation and seek elsewhere for a royal candidate. A Polish regent was accepted for a short time, but then ejected by the more radical Hussites. In the meantime Sigismund made another attempt to bring Prague to its knees, but failed. During the years which followed, increasingly unenthusiastic crusades from outside were beaten off by the Hussite fraternities now skilled in war. They even, as if to keep in practice, began to make swift raids out into surrounding countries and spread their own interpretations of the gospels.

Things went wrong only when there was no immediate threat to their existence. Then theological differences between and within the communes led to internal strife, and even to the more puritanical Taborites denouncing their more moderate brethren as heretics and in some cases putting them to death. Žižka himself became involved in wrangles with the Taborites and finally left them to take over military command of the Orebites in Eastern Bohemia. In 1424 he was hammering royal towns in Moravia when he was stricken by the plague and died. The desolate Orebites referred to themselves thereafter as 'The Orphans'.

Resistance to the mere idea of Sigismund continued for several years, but moderate Hussites longed for a settlement which could restore peace to the land without robbing them of their hard-won freedoms. In 1433 John of Rokycany, Hussite claimant to the archbishopric of Prague though not recognized as such by the Pope, led a delegation to a council assembled in Basle to discuss schismatic problems. At this the Four Articles of Prague were watered down, and the essential demand for communion in both kinds was conceded only as a special privilege for convinced adult Utraquists who specifically asked for it. The extremist fraternities did not think this was good enough, and intensified their activities against non-Hussite communities in town and country. Weary of this perpetual feuding, the moderates allied themselves with Catholic forces and, in May 1434, defeated combined Taborite and Orebite armies at the battle of Lipany.

Sigismund was at last invited to Prague, which he had so long sought to enter as conqueror. True to form, after agreeing to accept the terms drawn up at Basle and to share out certain ecclesiastical properties among nobles who had assisted his return, he at once repudiated most of his promises, hunted down survivors of the extreme Hussite factions, hanged the leader of the Taborites, and drove Archbishop John of Rokycany from his post. Trouble in his other kingdom, Hungary, diverted him in 1437; and on his way there he died unexpectedly in Znojmo, leaving no heir.

The Duke of Austria claimed the throne but was not recognized by the nobles. When he conveniently died they decided to elect his posthumous son Ladislas: a protracted regency would suit them very well. Ladislas was six before being formally proclaimed king, by which time the most influential figure in the ruling council was that of Jiří (George) of Poděbrady. This Hussite nobleman succeeded in counteracting attempts by Catholic associates to continue Sigismund's persecution of the Utraquists, restored many Hussite priests to their pulpits, and managed by a remarkable blend of persuasiveness and firmness to bring rival factions into something approaching harmony. When young Ladislas died of the plague in November 1457 there was no question, in spite of claims from the Habsburgs and others, but that the next ruler should be King George. In all he held the country together for more than twenty years, and dreamed of an even greater unity: his ideas for a confederation of European states to resist the Turks on one hand and the

Roman theocracy on the other, and to settle all mutual disputes within an international council of kings and their delegates, presaged the League of Nations or United Nations Organization.

A persistent challenger throughout his reign was King Matthias of Hungary, who also fancied himself as King of Bohemia. Several times Matthias invaded, was defeated, swore not to do it again, and then came back for more. On one occasion he actually won the backing of some Catholic nobles in a spurious coronation ceremony. When George of Poděbrady died, Matthias again sought the crown, but the Czech Diet offered it to Vladislav Jagellon of Poland. Vladislav found that he, too, had to spend part of his reign battling with Matthias; but the situation was abruptly turned right round when Matthias died and Vladislav was elected to the Hungarian throne also, after which he was rarely seen in Bohemia. The next Jagellon king, his son Ludvík, was also by choice an absentee monarch, so that administration of the Czech lands was yet again left in the hands of a clique of contentious noblemen. Some attained the status of petty princelings on their own vast estates. Widespread revolts by hungry peasants and townsfolk, and by industrial workers such as the Kutná Horá miners, provoked few concessions and many vicious reprisals; but made evident the need for a stronger and less fragmented central authority.

Ludvík Jagellon died in Hungary in 1526 while fighting the Turks, and the Estates made a decision whose long-term repercussions they could hardly have foreseen. In the belief that Habsburg family ties would strengthen Bohemia itself and its resistance to the Turks, they accepted the claim of Ferdinand, son-in-law of Vladislav and brother to the German Emperor, and elected him king. In due course Ferdinand succeeded in having himself formally acknowledged as hereditary ruler. So far as he was concerned, that put an end to the impertinence of royal elections: Bohemia belonged as of right to the Habsburgs.

The effects were not at first too alarming. The country had for long needed a firm hand, and now got it. A large element of the populace approved of the subduing of the arrogant aristocracy and of the new stability. But the spread of Jesuit activity and growing harassment of Hussite and newer Protestant sects led to growing unease. Many fled the country, and in 1547 Ferdinand had to quell a near rebellion and imprison many Prague councillors and notables for their resistance to his dictates. Property was confiscated and civil rights revoked.

Rudolf II proved for a while more amenable, and his decision to settle in Prague with his distinguished artistic and scientific entourage endeared him to the people. But the scales tipped again. Forced by outside pressure to step up persecution of unorthodox religion, Rudolf floundered from one confrontation to another, driving his exasperated nobles to contemplate alliance with growing Protestant forces outside Bohemia. They forced a 'Letter of Majesty' from Rudolf, reasserting the principles of religious freedom, and when he subsequently attempted to bring them to heel once more they forced his abdication. His brother Matthias who succeeded him had no greater success in reconciling the opposing Catholic and Protestant influences.

On a fateful day in May 1618 Protestant nobles, followed by rowdy supporters, marched to Hradčany to denounce royal policies and the conduct of Catholic officials. Three dignitaries were thrown out of a window of the castle in what was to resound through history as the Defenestration of Prague and, like a spark dropped on a waiting fuse, ignite the Thirty Years' War.

Looking at the sheer walls of Prague castle today, one may shudder at the thought of being flung from such a height. In fact the window through which the offenders were ejected was that of the chancellery in the Vladislav Hall block, so close to the ground that they picked themselves up and set off hot-foot to Vienna to report on this latest insult to Habsburg authority. Without waiting for the royal reaction the Czech Diet nominated a national council to preserve the country on Protestant lines and thwart any attempt by Matthias to reimpose himself. Early in 1619 Matthias died. His successor was, according to the Habsburg view, automatically Ferdinand II. But with the Moravians and Silesians rallying to their cause, the Czechs denied this and offered the crown to the Elector of the Rhenish segment of Germany known as the Palatinate.

The Elector Frederick was a Lutheran. His sixteen-year-old

wife Elizabeth was daughter of King James I of England, and the Bohemians perhaps hoped for English support against Austrian domination. If so, they were disappointed. James, 'the wisest fool in Christendom', shied away and left his daughter and son-in-law to their fate, in spite of a public outcry in England. Hard pressed by the Habsburgs and the Catholic League, the unhappy Frederick reigned for such a short season that he was dubbed 'The Winter King'. On 8 November 1620 the battle of the White Mountain, just outside Prague, smashed the pride and independence of Bohemia and Moravia, not to be restored for three hundred years.

Ferdinand II offered no leniency to his opponents. The leaders were publicly executed on the Old Town Square in Prague, the Habsburg claim to the Bohemian crown in perpetuity was reaffirmed, the Catholic religion was declared the only true faith, the German language was not merely encouraged but forced to supersede that of the Czechs, and those of the broken nobility who wished to survive found it necessary to transfer their allegiance and their theatre of operations to the Viennese court. Prague declined to the status of a provincial resort for the wealthy—but such a beautiful and favoured one that, over the years, it grew in stature as a cultural centre.

Things did not settle into this mould in a matter of months or even of years. In these pages there is no space for even an attempted summary of the Thirty Years' War. Briefly and brutally it can be said that each tide of battle in this protracted struggle between the forces of the Reformation and Counter-Reformation broke most shatteringly on the hapless Czech lands. If one name can be singled out of the tumult of contestants it must surely be that of the Czech who became the greatest of the royalist generals: Valdštejn, or—in Schiller's play and most history books—Wallenstein. His father had been a Protestant but Albrecht turned Catholic, supported the Habsburgs at a very early stage, threw out German and Danish forces coming belatedly to the succour of Protestant Bohemia, killed King Gustavus Adolphus in battle and ultimately compelled his whole Swedish invading army to surrender. The military skill and riches he offered his king were considerable; but his ambition was greater. In 1634 he had become such a threat to the régime, with sycophants urging him to seize the crown for himself, that it was found expedient to assassinate him.

The Swedes continued to attack the kingdom. For some time they were virtual masters of Moravia, infiltrated into Bohemia, and by 1648 felt strong enough to attempt the capture of Prague. Some Protestants hoped they would succeed. But most of the townsfolk were moved by civic pride rather than a hope of dubious liberation, and poured into the streets to resist the attack. The Swedes were beaten off, though they did not completely withdraw from the country until 1650.

By the end of the war, Bohemia was exhausted. Hundreds of towns, villages and castles had been ruined. Some estimates say that a quarter of the population was destroyed; others, taking into account refugees who never returned, calculate that a reasonably prosperous population of three million had been reduced to a poverty-stricken million.

Confirmed in office, the Habsburgs made of Bohemia and Moravia no more than outer suburbs of their growing empire, into which Slovakia had long ago been swallowed. Mercenaries who had helped the Catholic cause were richly paid off. Czech estates were apportioned among foreign nobles. The cult of St John of Nepomuk was forced into every spiritual niche once occupied by the shade of John Huss. The Czech language was scorned as that of peasants and servants. Until well into the nineteenth century the Austrians relied on the repressive methods of a police state, and all attempts at revivifying Czech music and literature were derided or, if thought to be seditious, stamped upon.

Yet cracks duly appeared in the surface. Conditions of the industrial revolution encouraged workers' rebelliousness here as elsewhere, and rekindled the embers of old comradeship between Czech and Slovak. In the heady year of 1848 a Slav Congress was held in Prague at which far-reaching nationalist ambitions were over-optimistically discussed. The accompanying demonstrations by students and workers gave Prince Windischgrätz an excuse to bombard the city and quash what he saw as incipient revolt. Still the reformers edged their way forward, playing on the Austrian need for a united community, especially after the disgraceful defeat in the war with Prussia. The 'Compromise' of 1867 granted the Hungarians nominal equality within the empire. The Czechs sought similar concessions, and were incensed when they did not get them. But step by step the Austrians were persuaded to allow the reintroduction of the Czech language into general use, into the law courts, and into schools. Czechs were accepted in important official positions. By the time the First World War broke out the reinvigorated Slav nationalists were in a position of some strength.

Yet few of even the most ardent really believed that complete independence was feasible. More autonomy within the existing framework was all they dared hope for. Not until they were conscripted into the service of the largely Germanic war alliance, with all the unhappy echoes this was bound to arouse, did many of them see the chances which might be grasped. Reluctant to fight Serbs or Russians, thousands deserted to join the Allies; wholesale arrests of Czech radicals did nothing to persuade those still at home that an imperial future boded anything but ill; and in 1915 Professor Thomas Masaryk, who had fled abroad shortly after the outbreak of hostilities, appealed to all his countrymen to work against the Central Powers in the assurance that the Allied Powers would support the creation of an independent Czech and Slovak country. 'I kept the inclusion of Slovakia constantly in view', wrote Masaryk in his memoirs, 'for I am by descent a Slovak, born in Moravia.'

This country came into being on 28 October 1918 with the proclamation of the new Republic of Czechoslovakia.

The Austro-Hungarian administration had gone. The new nation had to start from scratch, and was eager to face the challenge.

All noble titles were abolished, settling a historic score with the foreign opportunist families who had acquired the estates of dead or expatriate Czechs after the battle of the White Mountain. Land reform carved up these estates and allocated them to individual farmers or cooperatives. The previous owners were allowed a measure of such tracts as they were willing to work, and were compensated for the balance.

Creation of a sound currency was essential. One day all frontier posts were closed and the depreciated paper money of defeated Austria overstamped with new values, prior to the introduction of a completely national currency. This prompt action saved the young republic from much of the inflation soon to plague its neighbours; though that inflation created inevitable trading restrictions which could have crippled a less resolute youth.

An early problem was that of integrating the Slovaks in the new society and of raising their living standards. The harshness of alien rule had been mitigated in the advanced Czech lands as time went on, but for a thousand years the Slovaks had been kept so ruthlessly down by Hungary that it was a wonder they retained any enduring sense of national identity. From the moment the Magyars took over the country they dispossessed all Slovak leaders and landowners, allowing the conquered people only the most frugal existence in the barest farmlands and mountain regions. As in Bohemia and Moravia, German immigration was encouraged to exploit natural resources and supply specialized skills; and, in Slovakia, to build up a population capable of resisting the Mongols and the Turks. Only a few defiant barons in isolated rocky fortresses displayed a lingering Slovak defiance, and the history of these castles usually introduces a Magyar conqueror before long.

As if the Magyar domination had not proved demoralizing enough, the Slovaks were hemmed in even more tightly after Ludvík Jagellon died and the victorious Turks occupied wide areas. When the Habsburgs claimed what was left of stricken Hungary, the Slovaks continued to be treated as they had always been treated: useful beasts of burden, and no more. Having been themselves mistreated by Habsburg Austria, the Hungarians might have been expected after their achievement of near-equality in the 1867 'Compromise' to show sympathy to Slovak aspirations. Instead, given a freer hand in the empire, the Magyars intensified their earlier policies of barring Slovaks from the few educational opportunities which the Austrians had grudgingly allowed: all Slovak secondary schools and four out of five elementary schools were abolished.

Doggedly the Slovaks, who through all the centuries of sub-jugation had responded sympathetically to religious convulsions and Slav protest from across their borders, pursued the belief that if only they and the Czechs could be reunited they might forge a lasting partnership. Their handicap in the councils of this reunited family after 1918 was that, despite the endeavours of their indomitable scholars and idealists, they had been for so long second-class citizens of a land in whose development they had been allowed no say, debarred from learning or profiting from industrial expansion—and now had suddenly to compete with more advanced, thrusting nations, and to some extent with their own brothers in this new venture. They had a lot of ground to make up.

Matters were not helped by the presence of a resentful Mag-yar minority incorporated willy-nilly into the new state. Having always regarded themselves as a higher race than the servile Slovaks, they now, like the once superior Germans of Bohemia, faced some unpleasant truths.

The Bohemian Germans constituted an even tougher prob-lem. Of the three million settlers and descendants of settlers in the Sudetic mountains and other border areas, a vociferous pro-portion tried, in spite of the collapse of the Central Powers, to claim union with Germany or Austria. The idea of chopping off an essential part of the old Czech lands at this formative stage of the reborn state was untenable, especially as it would have meant handing over some forty per cent of the country's indus-try to folk who had not been noted in the past for their 'good neighbour' policy. Some Germans were happy enough under their new régime, with fair representation in Parliament and many special concessions to soothe their doubts. Others re-mained surly and, when the opportunity offered, grew bellige-rent. Even early in the century it had been common to find notices in German-owned shops, grimly prophetic of the decades to come: 'Jews, Czechs and dogs not admitted.' Now the more aggressive pioneered a German Socialist Workers' Party before Adolf Hitler had even thought of the name.

By 1936, with Hitler tightening his grip on Germany and promising a Reich which would embrace all the Germanic peoples, the leader of the Sudetenland malcontents, Konrad Henlein, who had at first denied being a Nazi, was now proudly admitting to the fact. Eduard Beneš, President of Czechoslovakia, agreed that the German minority might have some grounds for complaint but repudiated any idea of their setting up an autonomous state within the republic. In 1938 Hitler seized Austria and then demanded new frontiers which would incorporate the Sudetenland in the Reich. Neville Chamberlain flew from London to meet him in an attempt to avoid war over 'a quarrel in a faraway country between people of whom we know nothing'. After shameful negotiations in which Britain and France brought pressure to bear on the appalled Czechoslovak government, an agreement was signed at Munich whereby this vital industrial region of the Czech lands was handed over to Germany. Hitler pledged himself as having no designs on the rest of Czechoslovakia, but in March 1939 the Nazis invaded and annexed all that remained.

Bohemia and Moravia were declared a German protectorate, and Hitler tried to win at least the tacit goodwill of the Slovaks by confirming their secession from the republic, for which some had been working on the grounds that the Czech-dominated government had been treating them as poor relations rather than equal partners.

When the Second World War broke out in September 1939, demonstrations by the Czechs led to a declaration of martial law. Czechs abroad joined the Allies, contributing especially effective units to the army and R.A.F. in England. In spite of the familiar pattern of Nazi brutality, resistance groups functioned throughout the occupation; and the refugee President Beneš travelled widely in Britain, Canada and the U.S.A. and in 1943 was in Moscow for the signing of a treaty of mutual co-operation, making it clear that in the eyes of the world there still existed an independent Czechoslovakia. Nor did the Slovaks prove as amenable as Hitler had hoped. Partisan activity intensified until, on 29 August 1944, there was a Slovak National Uprising in Banská Bystrica. Two days later a newly formed Slovak National Council issued a manifesto which included a firm commitment to the Czech and Slovak alliance. By early

October, Russian and Czechoslovak troops had crossed the border into the country from the Carpathians. Russians from the east and Americans from the west squeezed the Germans into surrender; though in fact Prague was the last European capital to be liberated, and the townsfolk were still fighting the last intransigent Nazis in the streets while D-day was being celebrated in London.

After Czechoslovak independence was again acknowledged, the Sudetenland and other Germans were thrown out *in toto* and dumped in the American and Soviet occupation zones. This time there was to be no lingering menace of the post-1918 fifth column. Land from which German and other collaborators had profited was confiscated and shared out among native small-holders. A large part of the country's industry was nationalized. In 1946 a coalition government was set up after elections in which the Communists won almost forty per cent of the votes.

President Beneš had been reinstalled as head of state, but effective power was in the hands of the Premier and Communist party leader, Klement Gottwald. There were many causes for conflict between the older elements and this strongly entrenched new one. Some wished, in spite of the unforgotten betrayal of Munich, to restore traditional ties with the west; others regarded Marshall Aid and all such offers from the United States or her associates as suspect, and turned towards the Soviet Union. A number of ministers mistrusted plans for further nationalization. On the other hand there was resentment from the left against attempts through the courts to rehabilitate some bankers and businessmen convicted of dubious relationships with the Nazis during the occupation, and of their attempts to reclaim their assets or substantial indemnities. By the time the next elections fell due in 1948 many key posts had been allocated to Com-munists, and the replacement of senior police officers by Communist security officers was taken as a direct challenge by ministers of other parties. In an attempt to force the President's hand, a number resigned and hoped that Gottwald would con-stitutionally be obliged to follow suit. Instead, he organized a mass rally in Prague, blamed the resigning ministers for the country's ills, announced the formation of action committees to purge industries and offices of anti-progressive elements, and forced Beneš to accept a substitute government. In May 1948 elections were held on a single list of candidates and, not unexpectedly, ninety per cent of the votes were for the new National Front. President Beneš resigned in June and died in September. Gottwald took over the presidency.

Gradually Czechoslovakia was incorporated into all the economic and military strategies of the Eastern European bloc. Critics within and without the Communist party were silenced, some after public trials, some not. The structure of the Catholic church within the country was demolished, and many of the clergy were imprisoned or driven out; but the early mood of almost vindictive iconoclasm has softened over the years, and although the rich monastic communities have long since ceased to exist there is, today, little really purposeful opposition to freedom of worship.

Stalin and Gottwald both died in 1953, and in the revulsion against the worst excesses of the Stalinist era a markedly less stringent administration was shaped. The new secretary of the party, Antonín Novotný, also had himself declared President in due course, and warily rehabilitated victims of earlier political purges; but at the same time harried other so-called deviationists. By 1967 he was beginning to find that he had not got the balance quite right. The intellectuals didn't like him; the economists didn't like him; the still critical Slovaks didn't like him; and his own friends ceased to trust him. In January a reformist group who had for some time urged the separation of Novotný's party and state functions and the bringing of government into closer touch with the people managed to unseat him and, after some remarkably free speech in the country and in the press, force his retirement. The new party secretary was a Slovak, Alexander Dubček. The new President was a much-decorated hero of two world wars, General Svoboda.

The rest of the story is known in a thousand details to anyone who watched television and read the newspapers in the summer and autumn of 1968, though it is doubtful whether the Soviet-baiting glee of the western media allowed for as objective a presentation of those details as one could have wished. Certainly

5 Husinec, birthplace of John Huss
6 Tábor, stronghold of the Hussite 'brothers and sisters'

it did the cause of Dubček and his colleagues no good. Alarmed by social and economic reforms carried through with such speed and enthusiasm, and by the lifting of censorship and restrictions on international travel, Russia uttered grave warnings and summoned the new leaders to a number of conferences. Warsaw Pact manoeuvres brought Soviet and other troops into the country, but Dubček refused to believe that they meant any harm. Czechoslovakia had no intention of seceding from the Communist bloc or succumbing to the temptations of the west: all that was sought was 'socialism with a human face'.

But on 21 August 1968 Soviet and allied forces marched in and, as they saw it, restored order.

British holidaymakers and other travellers may wonder how attitudes and restrictions in such a country will affect their visit. I can only refer to my own experiences. As a non-communist, with that dangerous word 'author' clearly recorded in my passport, travelling not as a neatly packaged tourist but as an individual making individual arrangements in all parts of the country, I have made repeated visits of varying duration since the 1950s without ever encountering any mistrust or lack of hospitality.

Even after so many visits I would regard it as indiscreet, often presumptuous, to pontificate about the post-war failings or achievements of that 'faraway country' of whose people we still know far too little. Neither official pronouncements nor the sincere opinions of rebels and disillusioned refugees tell even half the story. One cannot help observing, though, that the most implacable denigrators tend to be found among well-paid columnists and commentators who, preferring never to visit the regions from which they derive such profitable wordage, avoid having their income reduced or their outlook confused by anything so irrelevant as first-hand experience.

Whatever conflicts and setbacks there may have been, and whatever may be yet to come, I cannot write about Czechoslovakia with anything but affection. Should this blur the picture which this book attempts to present, there will undoubtedly be found many a dissident expert to redress the balance.

7 Český Krumlov

Hussite Bohemia

South of Prague are many routes to tempt the traveller. Steamers plough upstream to Slapy dam and its twenty-five-mile lake, fringed by houseboats, speedboat and dinghy moorings, and holiday chalets. Only a few miles from the city the banks of the Vltava steepen. We glide beneath the film studios and restaurant of Barrandov, named after the French geologist Barrande who made important discoveries of trilobites here, and soon there are crops of summerhouses perched high on the rock face, reached by precarious paths. Locks are so deep that it seems we shall never sink to the bottom; and then, as the water plops and surges away, huge grey gates open on to a golden sky and rolling hills. Approaching Slapy, the river weaves so much that the sun is first on one bank and then on the other, striking a glow from the varnish of a wooden house far above and colouring the oil drums which support some improvised landing-stage.

Parallel with the river for some way, then crossing it, the railway disappears from time to time into little tunnels. Echoes skim across the water as an unseen train strikes a resonance from a rocky overhang. The country's rail network is still impressive, compared with our own severely truncated lines, though so much of it involves single-track working that even expresses are somewhat staid and cautious. Out in the country a station may be no more than a slightly elevated island like a tram stop, with grass and wild flowers forever encroaching. Paths lead across undulating fields to a gleam of lake, distant summerhouses, and perhaps a secluded, invisible hamlet. A yellow church spire beckons, coloured with the same wash as farm buildings below so that it seems an integral part of the group, all of it fading into the brighter background of toasted golden grain. Outside trim little station houses an inspector comes to attention with his baton under his arm, ready to salute the more important trains. Somewhere, surely, a Czech poet must have written verses as evocative as those of Edward Thomas, hearing the name of Adlestrop and its birdsong forever. If not, we must be content with the poetry of that unforgettable film, *Closely Observed Trains*, and the vision it has left us of Loděnice station.

A stranger choosing the highways rather than river or rail will be surprised by the size of some roadside supermarkets. These cater largely for the weekend stream of city dwellers on their way out to summerhouses along the Vltava and its tributaries, the idyllic Sázava and Berounka. The wire baskets are familiar, the layout of the shelves would make any visitor from Luton or Yarmouth feel at home. But there are certain formalities: the number of baskets is regulated to ensure that the flow of customers does not become unmanageable, and without a basket nobody is admitted. Nor are dogs admitted. Living as I do in a delightful east coast town in England, which is being made progressively less delightful by the uncontrolled fouling of pavements and greens, I cannot but feel respect for authorities who levy a licence fee of up to £50 a year on a dog, according to its size. Such measures might decontaminate the streets and parks of England, both by reducing the numbers of animals and providing a subsidy for the cleaning operations entailed.

Once you have collected your weekend food and drink, you are all set for the cottage or chalet. Accommodation in towns and cities, especially the capital, is strictly allocated and hard to come by, but inexpensive. A hard-working family can save enough to lease a plot of land outside the city on which to build a holiday home. Some of these are little more than allotment huts in which to spend weekends developing an orchard, growing vegetables, or lying in the sun. Others have been built with the aid of neighbours or a local commune, to which everyone contributes in the digging of drains and the laying of main services. There is an amiable barter system: you can have my cottage for a fortnight if you'll deliver some slabs for the path, or keep the outhouse well supplied with home-made cider; I've got some linoleum to spare . . . I could do with some nails. Twenty minutes from Prague, and within the same range of most towns of any size, there are little colonies of these rural and riverside retreats: timber huts, stone cottages, orchards and rock gardens and pools. From Zbraslav to Slapy it is difficult to be more than a mile or so from such a group, though they are rarely obtrusive, tucked away in woods or shaded little dells.

Zbraslav is a small town set at a junction where the main A4 road leaves the Vltava and heads for Příbram, and a side road sets off beside the river Berounka towards Karlštejn. It grew up around a royal hunting lodge and a richly endowed Cistercian monastery founded towards the end of the thirteenth century. Many of the Czech kings were laid to rest here, and King Wenceslas IV had made it clear that when he died he wished to join them. This presented his loyal courtiers with some problems. After his death from a heart attack during the Hussite demonstrations of 1419, turbulence in the city was such that it was unsafe to move him openly through the streets, and his nobles had to wait until nightfall to get the corpse from the Old Town into Prague castle. There it lay for some time before it could safely be shifted—again at night—to Zbraslav and its monastic burial place.

Sigismund encamped here before his abortive attack on Prague. In 1420 fanatical Taborites who had already demolished monastic properties in Prague turned their attention to the idolatrous decorations and unseemly riches of Zbraslav, and marched from the city to deal with them. Unfortunately the temporal wealth of the place included well-stocked cellars, and the less ascetic soldiers got so drunk that they forced open Wenceslas' tomb, tipped his remains on to an altar, poured wine over him, and set fire to the building. What remained was finally destroyed during the Thirty Years' War.

At the beginning of the eighteenth century a baroque château was built on the site. Today it houses the National Gallery's collection of Czech sculpture from the end of the last century to the present, some of it imaginatively displayed out of doors in the gardens and among the trees. The Madonna of Zbraslav in

St James' church is one of the few treasures surviving from the original monastery.

The Berounka meanders along an almost indecently seductive valley towards the town of Beroun, which retains little of its past apart from two towers and a few fragments of other fortifications. A little way to the south are Golden Horse hill and the caves of Koněprusy. Celtic remains have been found in the neighbourhood, and after the Second World War the karst caves were discovered in a disused quarry. Relics of prehistoric animal and human occupation were identified, and there were signs of more recent occupation: a quantity of counterfeit silver coins of the Hussite period scattered about a forge.

But the real treasure of the valley is itself a treasure chest, the castle of Karlštejn.

Charles IV built this fortress in the heart of one of his game forests as a safe repository for the crown jewels both of Bohemia and of the Holy Roman Empire, and for his extensive collection of holy relics. One wall painting in the castle shows him receiving a thorn from Christ's crown of thorns; its companion piece has him setting it in a reliquary. When at his protracted devotions, he could be given even the most urgent message only through a slit in the wall of his private chapel. It is also said that he liked the periods he spent at Karlštejn in hunting and holy meditation to be uninterrupted by women, so that even his wife was not allowed to enter the castle. One of his four wives, however, grew so suspicious that she determined to enter the forbidden gates disguised as a page, to see what went on. A light-hearted comedy by Jaroslav Vrchlicky based on this story is often performed on summer evenings in the courtyard; and a year or two ago was transformed into a witty musical film, with a blend of modern pop songs and classical pastiche which could have been a whimsical disaster but proved to be a delight. For film purposes the wife, usually thought to have been Blanche of Valois, was featured as Charles' fourth wife, Elizabeth of Pomerania, reputed to be so strong that she diverted herself by bending iron bars and snapping swords in two. Perhaps Charles' insistence on complete seclusion at Karlštejn was not entirely due to religion or blood sports.

The most important feature in his original building was the great keep in which the jewels and relics were lodged, and so it remains today in spite of Renaissance alterations to the exterior and some attempts to restore the whole complex in Gothic fashion at the end of the nineteenth century. Within, few features remain quite untouched, but an attempt has been made to preserve the essential qualities of Charles' concept. As well as the depictions of himself, a precious fourteenth-century fresco from the Apocalypse has been carefully restored, and in the emperor's own chapel of St Catherine are similarly tended murals of Czech saints. Everything leads up to the culminating Chapel of the Holy Rood, high in the tower, where the crown jewels were deposited in a shrine. The vaulted ceiling gleams with gold, more than two thousand semi-precious stones are embedded in the walls, and there are a hundred and twenty-eight panel paintings by Master Theodoricus.

During the Hussite wars the imperial jewels were removed, but the Bohemian regalia stayed here in safe keeping. The fortress represented a constant challenge, and in 1422 the Hussites made a determined attempt to take it. In spite of prolonged bombardment by siege guns from the surrounding slopes, the castle held out. The besiegers settled glumly in, making an occasional futile attack and hoping that if all else failed they would eventually starve the defenders into submission. Later in the same year one of the crusading forces launched into Bohemia tried to relieve the Karlštejn garrison. The besiegers, making a desperate attempt to get into the castle first, were thrown back yet again. Needing to release troops for their other campaigns, the Hussite leaders at last offered an armistice to the garrison. Karlštejn's record remained unblemished until 1620 when, at the time of the terrible battle of the White Mountain, an Anglo-Scottish infantry detachment—one among many volunteer groups which did not share King James' apathy towards his daughter's adopted land—tried but failed to hold the castle against Habsburg forces.

One of the most popular regular coach tours organized from Prague by Čedok, the state tourist agency, takes in Karlštejn, Slapy and its spacious lakeside restaurant, and another castle which shelters quite different collections and relics from those of Charles IV.

Above rich parkland Konopiště château raises one red-capped, tall cylindrical tower whose unbroken column suggests an illustration to *Rapunzel*. When built for the Šternberk family in the fourteenth century it had seven towers in all, but later reconstruction lowered the level and squeezed some of them out. What remains is a bit of a hotch-potch, made worse by the extravagances of the Archduke Franz Ferdinand around 1890. The interior is, to me, horrific. Heir to the imperial throne, Franz Ferdinand was a keen and sensitive landscape gardener, whose 'organizational mastery and fine colour sense' were much admired by the Kaiser Wilhelm II after a visit to Konopiště. But he was also an obsessive huntsman, loving nothing better than to roam this and other estates slaying any animal incautious enough to raise its head. Of the three hundred thousand beasts he is said to have shot during his lifetime, a fair representation of those heads can be seen stuffed and mounted on wall after wall of Konopiště, labelled with time and place of execution and the name of the executioner.

There is also a fine bag of statues, figurines and other representations of St George, a saint as revered in Bohemia as in England. Visiting the Prince of Wales, later to become King George V, Franz Ferdinand was so impressed by his collection of such effigies that he immediately wanted to start, as it were, a rival shoot, and sent his beaters to flush out every possible trophy in Europe.

The Weapons Hall contains a display of arms from the sixteenth and seventeenth centuries. It seems too grimly appropriate that this collector of murder weapons and murdered animals should in the end have fallen prey to a young hunter's bullet at Sarajevo, thereby provoking even greater killing, this time of humans by humans.

Slapy dam created one of forty-seven similar lakes in the country. On the Vltava alone, the Slapy waters have hardly been pinched back to river width before we reach the dam at Orlík and another lake which at its southern end is fed by both the Vltava and the Otava. The royal castle of Orlík has suffered many transformations since its birth in the thirteenth century, and has sheltered many a controversial owner or guest: Wenceslas IV was fond of hunting here; Žižka is thought to have served as one of his local huntsmen; Napoleon's son and heir, '*L'Aiglon*', spent some time here when the Austrian authorities were keeping an attentive eye on him, and the castle derives its present name from him. Boats make a leisurely journey from Orlík to the lake's complementary guardian, Zvíkov, which once perched on a commanding cliff but is now lapped by waters which have robbed it of its lower baileys. It first took shape in the time of Wenceslas I, and its main tower with embossed masonry survives from that era. The main building and courtyard arcades were added soon after; and there is a detached watch-tower with fifteenth-century frescoes. Closely packed trees seem at times to threaten suffocation of the remaining stretches of battlements.

High up near the source of the Vltava, in the far south of the country, is Lipno, another magnet for skiffs and powered craft and holiday houses, its dam holding back or judiciously releasing waters over the great boulders and promontories of the Devil's Pulpit and the Devil's Wall (about which Smetana wrote an opera). Its neighbouring woods and jostling shoulders of hills blend into those of the region known as the Šumava.

This mountain range forms a barrier between Germany and a stretch of Southern Bohemia from near Lipno to the fringe of the Chodsko area south of Domažlice. Its highest peaks reach about four thousand feet, but their granite harshness is mellowed by dense coniferous forests from which through many centuries timber has been floated downstream or used in local paper, glass and match factories. In the fifteenth century there were many charcoal-burning glass manufactories in this region, before the main concentration of the industry was drawn away to Northern Bohemia. The Devil's Wall presented a fearsome obstacle to the rafting of logs down a key section of the Vltava, and because the terrain did not encourage profitable farming settlement there was always a shortage of labour in the region. But in the years leading up to the Second World War the timber trade received nation-wide encouragement to meet large orders

from Germany, mainly for military use—supplies all too soon
to be turned against the suppliers—and during the Nazi occupation forests were exploited greedily with no thought for the
future.

Still those forests are luxuriantly healthy, and shelter many
other growths: mushrooms are as varied and plentiful as the
mushroom growth of camping sites under the trees. Trails lead
in all directions to hazy summits, infrequent little villages, and
glacial lakes far up in the mountains such as the Black Lake and
the darkly gleaming Devil's Lake. Below the high peak of
Boubín is an unspoilt primeval forest.

Field and forest trails are a feature of most holiday regions.
Discreet wooden signs in village squares or at major junctions
of the woodland paths direct one to local beauty spots, towns
and hamlets, specifying distances so that one can choose a three-
kilometre stroll or a fifteen-kilometre hike according to mood
and stamina. Different routes are identified by differently
coloured blazes on tree trunks, always clear but never garish.
There are few restrictions on walkers who wish to explore un-
marked paths for themselves; but the newcomer is advised to
follow the better trodden trail, on which he will rarely, even at
the height of summer, be interrupted by the occasional sight of
a fellow human being.

One of the more substantial gateways to this national park
region is Klatovy, a Přemyslide royal town founded by Otakar
II. Crowning the gentle hill is the sixteenth-century Black
Tower, matched by the White Tower of the Gothic church's
detached campanile. In the crypt of the Jesuit church are
mummified bodies of monks.

Some little distance south-east of Klatovy the great keep,
overgrown grey stone walls and bastions of the most extensive
castle ruins in Bohemia rise from a hilltop commanding the
river Otava, overawing Rabí village like some Welsh border
fortress. The earliest parts of the castle and a fragment of its
original church date from the fourteenth century, when it was
set up to guard the extraction of gold along the Otava. The
fifteenth-century church of the Holy Trinity by the main gateway was at one time joined to the castle as its chapel. Žižka took

the castle early in the Taborite campaigns but left no garrison to protect it. The enemy took possession again, so in due course Žižka himself came to reclaim it. It was here that he lost the sight of his remaining eye, pierced by an arrow from one of the defending archers. For many weeks he was out of action, and when he finally insisted on soldiering on the world knew that he was now totally blind.

Another fortress set up to protect gold mining in the region was that of Kašperk. Only a few spikes of masonry thrust up from the undergrowth to commemorate an industry which flourished from the early Middle Ages until the nineteenth century. Bohemia's reserves of gold and silver brought many traders into the country; and many would-be robbers; and, in this field as in others, German immigrants with mining and refining skills. At Rejštejn, gold was panned from the river. The very name of Písek derives from its gold-bearing sand.

There are other richnesses in Písek. Its seven-arched bridge is even older than the Charles Bridge in Prague, with similar statuary, all belonging to the late eighteenth century. There were once two bridge towers, but one was brought down in a flood just before the statues were erected, and the other destroyed in 1825. Although it was a royal town from the mid-thirteenth century onwards, the royalty it favoured was always indigenous Bohemian, and right from the start of the civil wars it declared itself for Žižka and the Hussites. Taken only once by the enemy early in the campaigns, it was soon liberated and thereafter remained faithful to the cause. All that survives of its original castle after a great fire in 1532 is the hall beside its courtyard, now serving as a local museum. The church of the Birth of the Virgin Mary suffered in the same blaze, but traces of its frescoes have survived two major rebuildings and various bits of piece-meal restoration. The core of the old town is still traceable around the main square, and fragmentary old fortifications link the architecture of successive centuries.

Some of the most productive silver mines in the country were at Příbram, as well as lead mines in the neighbouring hills, many dating back to the thirteenth century. The town has a mining academy and a museum devoted to the history and practice of mining. On nearby Holy Mountain stands a huge baroque monastery. My wife and I have a memory of mixed pleasure and exasperation in fitting together the cardboard segments of a model of the Příbram Nativity, with a manger scene surmounted by a pert Bohemian township and a flying angel.

To the west run the cloaking forests of the Brdy hills, relieved by a pattern of streams and attractive lakes. To the south, we are drawn back into the Šumava. Strakonice merits a courteous nod in passing. It has a flourishing motor-cycle factory, but is better known—and joked about by its neighbours—for its brisk trade in, of all things, oriental fezzes. The Jelenka tower of its castle dominates the bridge across the river. The castle, guarding the junction of the Otava and the Volyňka, began life as a farmhouse, but this was presented to the order of St John of Jerusalem so that they might build a hospital and church. In due course the tower and substantial fortifications were added.

The hills beckon us upward. Vimperk is well worth the journey. Set in the most beautiful wooded surroundings and capped by a castle, with steep streets, tilting squares and pleasant little gardens, it offers the Boubín primeval forest on the one hand and favourite ski resorts on the other. As if to compete with Strakonice in eastern matters, it specializes in the printing of miniature editions of the Koran, in type so small that one requires the eye of faith or a first-rate magnifying glass to read it. There is also a long tradition of glass making and cutting here.

I recall one somnolent morning in a cobbled square with nobody moving but with the sounds of sociable chatter drifting out of a tavern. On the pavement outside were stacked musical instruments. After a while the musicians emerged, looking well satisfied with their refreshment; and we waited for what promised to be a brass band concert. Instead, we witnessed a funeral procession. Traffic in the narrow streets was brought to a standstill as a long file of people, headed by their priest, marched slowly to a graveyard somewhere on the outskirts of the town. The band, very sober in mien now, played a succession of dirges in a minor key. Apart from the dress, it had all the elements of a New Orleans funeral. We did not stay to find out whether the mourners returned to the brisk beat of a rousing march, but made our way up to the castle.

As in so many cases, the general appearance of the building is the result of nineteenth-century restoration. All that remains of the original stone castle, begun in the middle of the thirteenth century by the burgrave of Zvíkov royal castle, is the square tower. Later owners, a powerful local family, extended it and added a whole new township just below its outer walls. In modern times the enclosed courtyard, with its bright window-boxes, looks less like that of a castle than some slightly faded, exclusive apartment block.

Below the foothills, with the dark heads of Boubín and Bobík to the south, a pleasant road leads to Husinec. A room in the house where it is thought John Huss was born forms part of a small museum, standing on one slope of the village street which dips and then climbs again to the church. In a square facing the church is a statue of Master John. As a boy he walked three miles to school in Prachatice, and it is tempting to think he may have trodden that same path which now follows a tinkling stream for a while, climbs through patches of woodland, and then starts a gentle descent beside an undulating line of white wayside shrines. The main tower of the Gothic church of St James thrusts up from the trim little town like a marker on a route which in fact existed long before church or the present town were built: the 'Golden Trail' linking Bohemia with the salt mines of Passau in Bavaria. The trail was already in use in the ninth century, and Prachatice dates its prosperity from the time of Wenceslas IV's decree that all the country's salt should follow this route. The remains of fourteenth-century fortifications are impressive, though the inner gateway is overshadowed by the massive Písek Gate of 1527. Within the older part of the town one still has a feeling of being securely locked in at night, as though gates had thudded into place and guards been set along the walls. The main square, enclosed like the courtyard of Vimperk or some other similar château, sometimes has a bustling, colourful market, and serves also as a car park; but at twilight this has all gone. There is a glow from the window of a wine tavern, perhaps a snatch of music from the hotel in one corner. Only every now and then is there a sudden burst of noise from the gipsies who sit on the pavement or in little alcoves, talking and squabbling in unpredictable fits and starts.

The school which Huss attended, and where Žižka is also thought to have spent some time, still exists, though Prachatice did not show itself as loyal to his memory as other towns in the region. Under the sway of the Rožmberks, it was captured by Žižka and agreed to accept the Hussite tenets; but once his forces had moved on it repudiated this promise, and burnt some of those who clung to the symbol of the Chalice. Žižka returned and launched a savage attack on the sturdy defences. Once he had forced his way in he was merciless: all the anti-Hussites who had not been killed defending their town were shut into a building and burnt to death.

For the greatest concentration of Hussite memories, however, we must go to Tábor.

In this century the town has expanded to take in a fair amount of light industry, sprawling out to mask the original proportions of its granite redoubt, but one can still get some impression of the old conformation from certain angles along the river Lužnice, a section of which was diverted by the Taborites to form a moat.

Žižka Square is the focus of the Old Town, and retains some of the stone tables at which communion was celebrated in both kinds. The Taborite church of the Transfiguration has been preserved, and the Town Hall is just one of the buildings serving as a museum—the whole historic section of the town being, in effect, a museum. There is an exhibition of the brutal weapons used by the peasant armies, and an example of Žižka's fortress-waggons. From maps and battle plans one can trace the course of various campaigns and disjointed crusades. Double walls and stepped ramparts of the old fortifications hold the survivors steady on their pinnacle, with the original Bechyně Gate of 1420 still in place. Later incorporations include a street like a film set, Praské ulice (Prague Street), lined on both sides by picturesque houses from the fifteenth and sixteenth centuries. And there is one pre-Hussite feature—the Kotnov tower of the earlier castle.

A few miles from Tábor are the ruins of Kozí Hrádek, where Huss stayed and worked during his exile from Prague.

Signs on the main road and on many a secondary road direct the motorist repeatedly to České Budějovice; but before being drawn into the administrative centre of Southern Bohemia it is worth making a detour through Jindřichův Hradec, placed to the best pictorial advantage on the river Nežárka and the Malý Vajgar mere. An ancient water castle between these two stretches was converted early in the thirteenth century by Jindřich of the Vitkovci family into Nova Domus, the new castle, which in Czech soon became Jindřichův Hradec, Henry's Castle. The graceful arcades and the Renaissance rooms within were the work of Italian architects three hundred years later. They house a collection of period furniture, paintings and porcelain, and the lovely panel painting of the Madonna of Jindřichův Hradec. The potential visitor to the collections should, however, be warned. All too often one sets out for such places only to find, on driving or walking up the dusty approaches, a pile of rubble, some fractured limbs of masonry stacked against a wall, a cement mixer, and one of those familiar pyramids of sand which indicate that somewhere not far away will be a notice incorporating the word with which one also becomes increasingly familiar: *Adaptace*. Adaptation or reconstruction—so many castles, mansions, museums and other buildings have to be closed for long periods as the overworked restoration teams reach them. The magnitude of the task throughout the country is daunting; yet slowly, selectively, one historic place after another is reopened.

In the museum of the Nežárka gateway, on our way out of the town, is a fascinating nineteenth-century fantasy in wood —a crèche scene with a hundred moving figures.

Around Jindřichův Hradec and Třeboň are some of Bohemia's most extensive lakes. Quite apart from its mountain lakes, Czechoslovakia has over twenty thousand meres, nearly all of them artificial. With no access to the sea and, before the days of the deep-freeze, with no easy way of importing more than small quantities of salt water fish from great distances, the country's kings, lords and monks set about installing their own fish ponds. Many date from the time of Charles IV, but the main expanses in Southern Bohemia were the work of the Rožmberks after the Hussite wars. Largest of all is the Rožmberk lake north of Třeboň. They used as a basis the scattered pools left by the post-glacial fresh-water lake and threaded them together with a linking canal system. Thousands of other individual meres were dug, fed by rain or river water, specifically as fish farms. The favourite Czech dish is carp, which takes the place of our turkey in the Christmas menu. These are bred in tanks and put into selected meres, then fished out and moved to other 'reservations' at the end of the first and second years. Every three years the adults are fished out, and the up-and-coming generation moved into their place. Of them all, Třeboň carp are said by connoisseurs to be the most succulent.

Designed for strictly practical purposes, these linked waterways are also ideal for canoeists, and for sailing.

Třeboň itself is a state reservation town, one of several protected for their architectural and historic interest. Its medieval town square has a fine skyline of assorted gables, which continue down some of the side streets. Three gates remain in the old fortifications, one of them adjoining the fourteenth-century monastery. Many of the community's religious treasures have been distributed among various state museums, but in the Gothic church of St Giles remain substantial parts of frescoes restored after a fire in 1781, and an especially fine Bohemian Gothic Madonna. Large peat deposits in the neighbourhood were found in the nineteenth century to have valuable curative properties, and a spa grew up, specializing in rheumatic and muscular treatment. It continues to offer an enviable regimen which leads the convalescent patient from pleasant spa gardens to more strenuous activity rowing on the lakes, fishing, or hunting.

The pattern of meres and streams continues almost to the outskirts of České Budějovice, and here we are joined again by the Vltava. At the crossroads of ancient trade routes, Budějovice (called České, Czech, to distinguish it from a smaller Moravian place of the same name) has for centuries been the key town and effective centre of Southern Bohemia. It was founded in 1265 by Otakar II, and as a royal town owed allegiance to no one but the king himself. In recent centuries it has prospered as a market centre for the timber trade; and one aspect of this, allied with the extraction of graphite near Český Krumlov, led to the foundation of the famous Hardtmuth pencil factory, later Koh-i-Noor. Perhaps even better known is the local beer, Budvar, or Budweis—a name used by breweries of other lands without any concern for an *appellation contrôlée*.

The medieval town square is one of the most spacious in northern Europe and is truly squared up, with straight roads striking out from each corner and straight lines of arcades along its sides. No two of the pastel-coloured façades are alike, yet all blend in the most appealing harmony and contrast effectively with the more substantial town hall, bishop's palace, and the Black Tower, from whose gallery there are extensive views over the square, roofs, and gentle countryside. In the centre of the square, the fountain with figures of Samson and a lion once provided the city's only water supply.

During the Thirty Years' War the Bohemian crown jewels were moved here for safe keeping in the chapel of the smiths' guild in St Nicholas' cathedral church.

At least the name of Žižka Square seems destined for immortality. In some towns and villages of Czechoslovakia many once-revered identifications have vanished. Strolling along an Avenue of the Red Army or Street of the Yugoslav Partisans, or into Gottwald Square, one wonders how they used to be labelled, how many of an older generation still think instinctively of the older names, and how long it will be before these fade utterly away: Maria Theresa Square, Francis Joseph Street, and so on.

By Žižka's time the predominating influence in Budějovice or Budweis was that of German burghers and merchants, and over the surrounding rural areas that of the Rožmberks or Rosenbergs. At the time of his anti-Rožmberk guerilla activities, Žižka seems to have had clashes with the city authorities and later had to seek clemency from Wenceslas IV. As commander of the Hussite legions, he found his old feuds with the Rožmberks not ended. Budějovice remained true to its royal faith; and after playing a leading part in early Hussite councils, the Rožmberks fell out with Tábor and with Žižka, made approaches to

8 Zvíkov castle
9 The Šumava reserve seen from Kašperk castle

Sigismund, and so incited Žižka to attack and reduce several of their castles.

There are not just hundreds of baronial castles and mansions in the Czech and Slovak lands but thousands. In Slovakia the Magyar lordlings needed watchtowers to keep an eye on a peasantry which, in spite of centuries of subjugation, regarded them as aliens. In Bohemia, shifts of power involved so many tricky liaisons between barons and their neighbours, and barons and their elected kings, that each local lord needed his own stronghold to meet the worst that might come from any direction. The more estates a nobleman had, the more castles he needed. Of all the landed nobility, the Rožmberks were for a long time the most powerful, and regarded Southern Bohemia almost as their private kingdom.

They sprang from the Vitkovci family as a result of five sons in the late twelfth century sharing out their inheritance. To distinguish each scion and each estate from the others, their insignia incorporated roses of different hue. Rožmberk approval was well-nigh essential in the election of any king. Grateful monarchs behaved accordingly, and the Rožmberk wealth accumulated. In return, these 'Lords of the Rose' tended in any dispute to espouse the royalist cause, though if dissatisfied with any current tenant of the throne they were quite capable of sounding out other claimants and assessing the odds. Wenceslas IV's surreptitious approval of Žižka's skirmishing with these local despots may not have been altogether unconnected with the fact that he suspected them of planning to depose him— and, in fact, at one stage they imprisoned him (doubtless excusing it as 'protective custody') in the Rožmberk castle at Krumlov, or Krumau.

The entire region still echoes with them. Třeboň, the inheritance of the fourth son, owes its Augustinian monastery to them. At Bechyně, the château beside the stream has a Rožmberk hall and an entrance tower built for Peter Vok, last of the line. The Rožmberk house in Soběslav has become a museum of local crafts, costume and folklore. The Landštejn castle near the Austrian border was theirs. On a rocky headland above the Vltava they built a castle called simply Rožmberk, and then

10 The ski resort of Špindlerův Mlýn

started a new one lower down the slope in the fourteenth century. In 1522 the upper castle was gutted by fire and abandoned. Thirty years later the lower castle was extended, and then transformed in the nineteenth century into a fashionable piece of neo-Gothic. A park was laid out on the upper slopes, now leaking its glowing greenery in between sections of the castle, threatening to overtop roofs and choke the old round tower. There is a so-called Crusaders' Gallery featuring representations of supposed knights from the Crusades; and in the Rožmberk room are documents and exhibits relating to the history of the building itself and to its Bohemian and French owners. The French came into it after the death of the last Rožmberk, when the property became that of the Comte de Bucquoy, the imperialist general whose tactics were to prove decisive at the battle of the White Mountain, and whose descendants lived here until 1945.

At Vyšší Brod a Cistercian monastery was founded by the Rožmberks in 1256. Its cruciform church took two centuries to complete. The library has a collection of early scientific books and papers, including some Tycho Brahe and Copernicus manuscripts. In the art gallery are paintings by Raphael, Rembrandt, and the outstanding Czech artist Karel Škréta; but the monastery's greatest possession, the set of nine fourteenth-century paintings by the Master of Vyšší Brod, has been removed to the National Gallery in Prague, leaving a finely executed copy in the church.

When the body of the last of the line, Peter Vok, was brought here for burial in 1611, the insignia of the rose was symbolically broken over his coffin.

Of all the Rožmberk possessions the most splendid is the great castle of Český Krumlov. It commands a double bend on the Vltava, crossed by bridges binding town and castle together, embanked in trees and balanced by red roofs climbing to castle walls, tower and spire of St Vitus' church, and the galleried tower of the stronghold itself over all. On the main gateway is set the emblem of the rose.

This was originally the domain of the second Vitkovci son, who started with a small fort on the rock. In the early fourteenth century Peter of Rožmberk began afresh with a more extensive château including a small palace, two towers, and a chapel of St George. On this imposing framework the Rožmberks and their successors rarely ceased building, until the existing complex can boast three hundred rooms. Vilém of Rožmberk adapted his home to the Renaissance taste, and it was during this period that the incomparable little theatre, the oldest of its kind in Europe, was built. Performances are still given here from time to time, mainly during the holiday months. Adjoining it is the Masquerade Hall, which also leans to the theatrical: original stage sets and costumes are displayed here, and the walls are painted with *trompe-l'œil* scenes of unruly audiences leaning out and in some cases appearing to climb out of boxes.

The town itself, with streets twisting towards the twisting river and with its sudden glimpses from unexpected angles of the great tower, is an ideal place in which to stay and to stroll. Arcades, narrow cobbled lanes, a sudden pride of Renaissance burghers' houses, an archway and an abrupt turn on to a bridge . . . the eye and feet are led forever on. Some nasty errors of previous years have been remedied. When my wife and I stayed in the hotel overlooking the town square a long time ago, we were appalled by the damage done to one beautiful façade by the chopping out of a channel to carry electricity cables, all in connection with the loudspeakers which in those days blared out patriotic songs and injunctions. The number and volume of such intrusions were toned down as time went on. One may also pray for some alleviation of the town's worst problem: alluring as the river looks on its mazy way through this vale, it brings with it an appalling stench from papermills upstream, a quite inappropriate accompaniment to such towers, cupolas and streets.

In the sixteenth century there was some concern 'up at the castle' for the future of the Rožmberk line. The head of the family was seriously ill, and had only one infant son to succeed him. Special care was taken of this child. A rota of nursemaids watched over him day and night. The story is told of a ghostly visitor, a woman in white, who was known to appear whenever a family crisis threatened, and who now began a nightly vigil beside the baby's cot. When the baby cried, she soothed him. Then one night a nursemaid awoke to find the spectral visitor with the child in her arms, and seized him from her. The ghost declared herself to be the boy's ancestress; but after this incident she would not return. Fortunately the boy survived and in later years, having been told the story and shown the spot through which his visitor was supposed to have vanished into the wall, opened up the wall and found a fortune in gold coins.

But, as we have seen, the Rožmberks did die out early in the following century. After this the castle continued to expand under new owners, the Eggenbergs and Schwarzenbergs, both Catholic families which reaped a rich harvest in Bohemia after their efforts in the imperial cause.

North of Krumlov rises the peak of the Kleť, three thousand feet above sea level. It can be circuitously attained by car, but the happiest ride is that on the cable cars which carry one gently, almost silently up from a station near Holubov railway halt to the summit. As the chairs go up and down on an endless belt, one needs to be fairly sharp hopping on or off at either end. From the top one surveys the far rolling, hummocked carpet of Southern Bohemia, with an occasional village spire glittering between a frame of dark conifers, swathes of dark and light green, hills reasserting themselves and then sliding away again, forests surging on across the Šumava region. Once again there is a cluster of signs indicating trails of different length. Whichever route you choose, there is a consoling thought: it will be downhill nearly all the way.

Perhaps the most rewarding path is that which returns to Krumlov by way of Zlatá Koruna, the Golden Crown. This monastery was founded by Otakar II in thanksgiving for his defeat of the Hungarians at the battle of Kressenbrunn. Žižka's men sacked it during the Hussite wars, and by the nineteenth century it seemed doomed to end its days as a factory. This, however, was shut down; and the buildings have now been carefully restored, using as far as possible the surviving stones of the original edifice. Monastery and church stand as the finest examples of Bohemian Gothic one is likely to find, and it is fitting that Otakar, the founder, should be buried here.

Turning back towards Prague, or heading north-west past Budějovice, I see no reason to spare other travellers the ordeal which confronted us some years ago. Escorted by friends driving us to Krumlov, we were told that we absolutely must stop and see the castle of Hluboká, which once belonged to—well, to whom else?—the Rožmberks. We had a drink in the village and then were led up a path which, in spite of a later investigation which proves my impression false, I still visualize as coiling at least four times round the hill on its upward journey. At last we came out through what was becoming more and more like an English park to find . . . a small-scale, oddly squared-off caricature of Windsor Castle. This pseudo-Gothic oddity was, we were told by our friends and some lamentable phrases in a number of guidebooks, the pearl of Southern Bohemia. Its exterior is in fact a perfect jacket illustration for a Victorian romantic novel.

The original Rožmberk castle, built on the site of a royal fort, passed to the Schwarzenbergs during the smash-and-grab of the seventeenth century. Just over a hundred years ago Count Jan Adolf of Schwarzenberg had it rebuilt and refurbished in pseudo-medieval English style, with the grounds also landscaped in the fashionable English manner. Many of its magnificent furnishings from other Schwarzenberg homes, including some Dutch tapestries, are still in place—paintings, furniture, weapons and porcelain. The former riding school has been converted into a gallery of demure Bohemian madonnas and other statuary and paintings, named after Nicholas Aleš, painter of patriotic subjects such as the murals in Prague's Old Town Hall and many works in the Kinský Palace galleries.

From here there are several options for the thirster after knowledge or other potions: to the east, the vineyards of Moravia; to the north, a leisurely return to Prague; and to the northwest, the beer of Plzeň or the mineral waters of what used to be sparkling Carlsbad and Marienbad and now are sparkling Karlovy Vary and Mariánské Lázně.

Let us go west.

Spas, Forests and Rock Cities

Late in 1941 a number of Czech parachutists trained in Britain were dropped into their homeland on a special mission. The Czech government in exile had decided that some gesture must be made to show that no oppressor was safe, and to encourage the resistance movement. The men went into hiding for a few months, and then on 27 May 1942 appeared at a roadside in Prague to confront a car carrying Reinhard Heydrich, Hitler's bestial Protector of Bohemia and Moravia.

Things went wrong. The first parachutist's gun jammed. The second one's grenade found its target, but did not immediately kill the Protector. Heydrich was able to climb out of the wrecked car and get to safety. When he died a week later, it was from infection rather than from the wounds themselves.

His killers had gone into hiding. Rewards were offered for their capture, and at the same time a campaign of terror was launched. Hundreds were questioned, arrested, tortured, murdered. At last one of the original group of parachutists gave himself up and revealed where the two assassins and five others were hiding. All this time they had been sheltering in the church crypt of SS Cyrill and Methodius in Resslova, a street leading from the eastern embankment of the Vltava to the Charles Square in Prague New Town. The Nazis surrounded the church, and one contingent tried to storm the building. Three men on guard in the chancel met them with a burst of fire and threw them back. Further attacks and the use of tear gas were of no avail. The end came only when a hosepipe was thrust through a window from Resslova to flood the crypt. The defenders had gone on fighting until each had only one bullet left. None was captured alive. The scars of the attack remain as a memorial around the church window on the street.

The parachutists did not fall into Nazi hands; but hundreds of others did. One night, while the assassins were still alive and in hiding, S.S. and Gestapo units went to the village of Lidice, some miles north-west of Prague. On the pretext that para-chutists had been sheltered here and that an example must be made, they took women and children away and then penned all the men of the village into a farmyard and slaughtered them. Any Lidice workers who had been on night shift in Kladno, the nearby mining and steel town, were met on their return home and taken off to be executed. The village was systematically burnt and bulldozed into extinction, and the Nazis decreed that all references to it in official records or on maps should be expunged. A few children were handed over to German parents to be brought up as good Nazis; and there were some sad stories after the war of a few surviving mothers trying to trace these children. Survivors were in fact few: most went to concentration camps and died there, sometimes in the gas chambers.

The German desire to wipe Lidice off the map failed. Word of the atrocity spread all over the world, and after the war many countries followed up the suggestion of British miners to estab-lish a worthy garden of remembrance. Rose bushes from all over the world began the rose garden which now flourishes on a slope near a monument and a tragic little museum. A modern village has sprung up, but even the older one has not, in spite of Nazi savagery and supposed thoroughness, been entirely obliterated: the outline of several foundations can still be traced.

One of the more infamous concentration camps lies almost due north of Lidice. Terezín, or Theresienstadt, was an eighteenth-century Austrian water fortress which never had its fortifications put to the test but was employed almost from the start as a prison. It held Italian and other rebels and then, in the First World War, about 20,000 prisoners of war; and it was in captivity here that the young man whose action sparked off that war, Gavrilo Princip, assassin of the Archduke Franz Ferdi-nand, died. There was really accommodation for only 7,000, approximately half military and half civilian. In 1941 the Nazis

converted it into a concentration camp for Jews from Czechoslovakia and other parts of Europe, and crammed nearly 60,000
within its walls.

Trying to maintain some veneer of civilization in order not to
despair utterly, the inmates wrote, painted, composed music,
and formed a choir. Karel Ančerl, one of the most distinguished
conductors of the Czech Philharmonic Orchestra, assembled
enough musicians to form an orchestra which concentrated,
naturally, on the works of Dvořák and other national composers.
It was even found possible to produce a number of operas. A
revue called 'The Last Cyclist' was built around the sour joke
that everything wrong in this world can be attributed to Jews
and cyclists. At one stage there was a hurried 'beautification' of
the camp for the benefit of a visiting Red Cross team, and such
activities were briefly encouraged.

Everyone played what part he or she could in giving lessons
to the children, although these were officially forbidden. 'The
war will be over before long', was the axiom, 'and then what
will you be? You must be like the children outside.'

Of 15,000 children, only a hundred survived to see the outside.

On any westward route from Prague we are for some time on
the central Bohemian plain, unless we steer a more winding
course along the Berounka valley. On the levels, the roads go
straight on, on and on, without hedges but with many an
accompanying rank of apple trees. A profusion of wild flowers
colours the ditches and the borders of fields. Tyres squeal on the
rubbed, uneven setts of a village street. There are pleasant little
gardens behind wire mesh fences; few lawns. Perky church
spires, bright colour washes—and usually, in a patch of grass or
at the top of some little side street, an eroded statue of some
saint looking puzzled rather than anguished. Stacks of palings
by the roadside, here and over other parts of the country, look
at first like the material for makeshift sheep pens or for the protection of newly seeded patches. In fact they are waiting for the
winter snows. With no hedges, stone walls or permanent fencing
of any kind, the roads can quickly become blocked during heavy
snowfalls; and these wooden sections are quickly set up to break
the force of the snow and hold it back.

Smoke and tall chimneys seen from far away mark the situation of Plzeň, administrative and industrial centre of Western Bohemia. Clamorous factories and a busy commercial life have not altogether suffocated the original heart of the city, however. Standing on the trade route from Prague to Bavaria via the Bohemian and Bavarian forests, it grew up rapidly around the main square and the fourteenth-century church of St Bartholomew, with its slender steeple soaring to more than three hundred feet. The prosperity of merchants of all past ages can be seen in the Renaissance, baroque and neo-Gothic styles of the houses on the square. The church's most cherished possession is its carved limestone Madonna; but in spite of its heavy nineteenth-century restoration it has many other details worth studying, especially in the choir.

Still there is no denying that when we think of Plzeň it is not as a city of historic survivals but as the home of beer and armaments. Beer was brewed in the region for centuries in circumstances common to other countries—local farmers and innkeepers making their own, then small local breweries setting up to meet increasing demand, and finally the larger combine. In 1842 the main breweries around Plzeň merged to form the municipal brewery which now produces the strong, delectable beer known here as Praždroj and marketed in other parts of the world as Pilsner Urquell. Visits can be arranged to the brewery, with its five miles of chill underground passages where the beer is matured; and there is a brewery museum which merits a longer stay than most visitors, with a mounting thirst, are prepared to allow it.

Quite recently the Czechs, incensed by a successful French action to stop them using the word 'Burgundy' in connection with a red wine which they had so described for centuries, brought a similar action of their own to ban the use by other countries of the words 'Pilsner' and 'Budweis'. Such descriptions, they reasonably claimed, should be the prerogative of Plzeň and Budějovice. The case was not upheld.

Some years after the brewery was established, in 1859 an armaments factory known at first as the Valdštejn works was opened. In due course it changed its name to Škoda, by which its motor cars and other machinery are still known in spite of a further, more recent, change: it has now become the V. I. Lenin works, sprawling over an entire quarter of the city.

Plzeň's industrial growth was facilitated by the existence, in the basin scoured out by four rivers, of extensive measures of lignite—brown coal—and the rich mineral deposits of the Krušné Hory, or Ore Mountains. Iron, lead, tin, copper and silver have all at one time and another been mined here, though the veins are now pretty well exhausted, and it was from the uranium deposits of Jáchymov that the Curies first extracted radium.

These minerals and the cracks in the surface caused by ancient volcanic action have given Western Bohemia another of its great assets, the string of spas and curative springs stretching through hills and woods to the north.

The most celebrated of these resorts is said to have been founded by Charles IV. While hunting in the forests which still lap the edge of the present town, he came to a little place called Vary, where one of his dogs was scalded by a sudden jet of hot water shooting up some forty feet from the ground. The king ordered the water from this thermal cleft to be analysed, and it was soon found that not only this hot spring but several others in the vicinity were rich in medicinal properties, especially useful in treating liver, kidney and various gastric troubles. So Charles gave his name to Karlovy Vary or, during the Germanic phase of its existence, Karlsbad or Carlsbad.

Visitors came here to take the waters from Charles' time on, but it was not until the eighteenth century that Jakob Berzelius concluded a really thorough analysis of the waters. The ingredients of the twelve main springs do not show many marked variations, but the differences in temperature between 45 and 72 degrees centigrade produce different effects on the patient and have to be taken into account when evolving a regimen. The first to be discovered, the Vřidlo, still throws its jet high in the air above a warm reservoir. Waters can be tasted freely whether you are under doctor's orders or not. Strolling along the pedestrian precinct on one side of the Teplá stream (Teplá meaning, simply, warm) you will be reproached at either end of the classical Mill Colonnade—now the Czechoslovak–Soviet Friendship Colonnade—by weighing machines; and good resolutions will be undermined by the sight, across the stream, of a string of restaurants. A wooden colonnade built in 1831 was replaced towards the end of the century, when Carlsbad was at its most fashionable, by a new colonnade of glass and iron. Below, hundreds of golden carp fight their way up an extended staircase of shallow weirs.

The taste of some of the waters can be disconcerting, and you may in any case prefer your mineral water cold rather than warm, or even scorching. It is probably the pungent aftertaste which leads so many sippers to undo all the good work they have done on their insides by fleeing to buy the wide, thin, richly creamed biscuits known as *oplatký* which are on sale everywhere. For myself, I favour the local aperitif, Becherovka, made from herbs and local mineral water and known to the natives as 'the thirteenth spring'.

Carlsbad reached its peak in the two or three decades before the First World War. The Grand Hotel Pupp, the Hotel Bristol, the Restaurant Leibold, all the self-satisfied luxuries of the Kaiserstrasse for the half-heartedly recuperative . . . from Smetana to the odd Tsar and Crown Prince or two, all came here for a pretence of taking the waters and the reality of enjoying 'the season'. Names have changed, habits have changed, society has changed. Lenin Square and the Moscow Hotel aren't quite the same. The mud baths and expensive hydro-residences are no longer the resort of aristocrats and financiers filling in their leisure time. Yet they are all still there. The main therapeutic establishments come under the aegis of the Trades Unions, and since the health service in Czechoslovakia is free there are now, in those luxury beds and baths, workers who need treatment. Also, at regular intervals, employees who merit an extra fortnight's holiday or so are given a free spell here, or in one of the other spas—a sort of subsidized romp round a health farm, with plenty of insistence on fresh air and long walks, and not too much on the sulphurous waters. The forest walks, labelled and blazed with directions and distances in the usual way, are also graded by medical advisers to ensure that patients do not collapse from exhaustion on the slopes. Foreign visitors no longer come as part of their annual routine; but with an authentic recommendation from their doctors can, not too expensively, take a course of treatment.

And there is still a 'season': an international film festival, golf tournaments, orchestral concerts and opera, dancing in many hotels—and always the leisurely strolls beside the water, up the embracing hills, through the gardens. The last time I was in Karlovy Vary a startling new hotel was rising to compete with the not-so-faded splendours of imperial Carlsbad. Its sparkling springs show no sign of losing their impetus.

The traveller who blithely asks in Karlovy Vary how he may best get to Mariánské Lázně will be greeted with the sort of raised eyebrow which tenants of a tied public house display when asked about the premises of a rival brewer. Though the two spas are reasonably close, there is only one bus a day, and the train service is built around hours awkward enough to discourage any but the most earnest seeker after comparative truth. If you have a car, and are prepared to risk meeting that one murderous bus coming round hilly corners on the wrong side of the road, as is its wont, there can be little doubt about the best route: instead of following the main road all the way, pleasant as its wooded surroundings undeniably are, you must take in Loket *en route* and then stick to the winding side roads all the rest of the way. The hills are furred with pine and spruce, indented with little clearings and minor forests of wild lupins. An occasional village straggles along the verge of the road, with a couple of shops and, under every awning, heaps of logs and kindling waiting, like the roadside hurdles, for the hard winter.

Clinging to a tree-girt rock in a twisted cleft of the river Ohře is Loket, its name both in Czech and German—Elbogen— meaning 'elbow', from the jut of its promontory into the tight curve of the river. This red and brown castle, built with walls so thick they were once considered impregnable, was a key defence on the western border of the Czech lands. Founded in 870, it came as a dowry to Frederick Barbarossa when he married the daughter of the margrave. John of Luxembourg was very fond of it, and stayed here for some time with his wife and baby son, the later Charles IV. In 1352 Charles presented the little town with a charter relieving it of all taxes provided that on every occasion when he or any of his heirs paid it a visit the burgomaster should be waiting to present them with a wooden beaker holding five pounds of silver farthings. It was during one of his hunting expeditions from the castle that Charles discovered the Karlovy Vary spring.

When the Elector Palatine and his English wife were on their way to become rulers, for such a short time, of Bohemia they stayed in Loket overnight and were treated to an outdoor banquet. We are told that they were also treated to a two-hour sermon by the burgrave's chaplain on their royal responsibilities.

One burgrave was so much hated by the folk he oppressed that they laid a joint curse on him, and soon afterwards he was struck by lightning and turned into a lump of stone. This, at any rate, is the story behind 'the petrified burgrave', a meteorite weighing almost a ton which was found in 1775 during the cleaning out of the castle moat.

In St Wenceslas' church there is a fine altar-piece by Peter Brandl depicting the murder of the saint by his brother. The castle collection, whose opening times need to be checked (since the galleries can be unpredictably under adaptation or reconstruction, or just plain closed), includes some fine displays of local porcelain and glass, and some reminiscences of Goethe. The open air theatre, built since the Second World War, is close enough to Karlovy Vary to be included in the programme of summer attractions issued by the spa.

So to last year, or past years, or this year in Marienbad.

The mineral springs of Mariánské Lázně were known in the seventeenth century, but it was not until 1760 that Antonius Strinci did a thorough analysis of their properties. The spa, about two thousand feet above sea level, did not really find its feet until the beginning of the nineteenth century, trailing after prosperous Karlovy Vary. It owed its swift development then to the commercial good sense of the abbot of Teplá monastery, to whom the entire area belonged. With the aid of a landscape gardener and a doctor who was to become the spa's first fulltime medical officer, the abbot began a programme of drying out the marshes, creating parks and gardens, and exploiting the springs.

The town's name came from the dedication of an early discovery of mineral springs here to the Virgin Mary. In the newly fashionable spa the chief springs were called the Cross, the Rudolf, and the Ferdinand. The Cross stands above a broad walk with the inevitable colonnade, this one of glass and iron adorned with motifs of shells and lions' heads, topped by a frieze of open-mouthed men's heads—gaping secular gargoyles. There is a bandstand, but most of the music nowadays comes, disembodied, through amplifiers; though it must be admitted that the mood is still that of the past, with light classical music and some wistful waltzes. From one end of the colonnade we look across a wide path and flowerbeds to the classical white colonnade and dome of the Rudolf spring against dark coniferous slopes.

Unlike those of Karlovy Vary, each of the waters here has quite different properties, so that a variety of complaints may be treated in the clinics, bathhouses and rest homes set in the town itself and raising their turrets and curlicues from the encircling trees. The Cross spring tastes sulphurous; the Ambrose of iron. Peat deposits rich in iron provide the most efficacious mud baths. In gardens beside the Ferdinand spring, a glass cover shows the water foaming to the surface like an oil gusher.

The octagonal church, with its blue domed ceiling, could almost be taken from outside as one of the more sumptuously conceived bathhouses. But then, everything—colonnades, little temples housing the springs, theatre and casino and arboretum —was planned as a homogeneous whole, and though much smaller than Karlovy Vary seems more spacious.

Most signs on the various establishments include an English translation, but little English is spoken. German may still be spoken, but it is not the prevailing language, as it was for so long. There are not even the descendants of the familes of old Marienbad here: when the Germans were expelled *en masse* after the Second World War, this was one of the towns which had to be virtually repopulated from scratch. Even more noticeably than

Karlovy Vary it has become a Trades Union holiday and recuperative centre, and one main street is actually called the
Avenue of Trade Unionists. They certainly have a good time
here. There is dancing every evening in nearly all the restaurants and wine cellars; and this dancing, and the music played
for it, have a nostalgic, 1930-ish character. Set high above the
town and meriting its name of Hotel Panorama, one establishment has obviously known greater days, with a huge banquet-
ing hall, a café reminiscent of the Holland Park orangery, and
an evening wine bar. Down in the town itself, one of the older
restaurants is an Edwardian dream of thickly carpeted floors
and steps, chocolate-brown marble columns, intimate alcoves,
gilded rams' heads, crystal chandeliers and long lace curtains.
It does not take much imagination to conjure up a picture of
Edward VII pacing through here on his annual visits to the spa.

Although the purpose of this regular pilgrimage was supposedly to counteract the excesses of the remainder of his year,
it is unlikely that Edward adhered to any strict diet or course
of treatment. He is known to have entertained some of his passing *amours* here; and there are testimonies to his other appetites.
He frequently visited the abbot of Teplá, or Teppel, and Hal-
dane tells of his gossiping freely and agreeably with the monks.
The monastery had grown rich on the taxes from its Marienbad
properties and on selling bottles of the various mineral waters.
When Edward was invited in September 1906 to go shooting
over the abbot's lands, he slyly warned his entourage that they
must not expect more than a frugal lunch before setting out.
In fact one sumptuous course followed another, each accompanied by an excellent wine. The royal guest was not expected
to be content with mineral water. They were so late setting out
on the shoot and so erratic in their aim that the bag was no
great success. The king treated the abbot with equal lavishness
the following year during a visit to Windsor, and made him a
K.C.V.O.

From the tenth century Teplá had been a key town in the
defence and development of the sparsely populated western
fringe of the Czech lands. Late in the twelfth century its royal
burgrave, Hroznata, donated land to the Premonstratensians

and, on his return from an unsuccessful crusade, gave up the military life and joined the order himself. Both Wenceslas I and Otakar II granted royal privileges and allowed the monastery to farm and exploit wide domains, coaxing peasants and craftsmen from inner Bohemia to come and settle in the region. After Otakar's death the monastery was several times burnt down and rebuilt; then attacked by plague; and, because of its espousal of the Hussite George of Poděbrady's cause, burnt down yet again. But gradually it regained its old powers, and extensive rebuilding included a new church, a library, a brewery, a hospital, and a slaughterhouse. After further devastation during the Thirty Years' War it set to work again, and established a ring of chapels about the town of Teplá, and a chain of wayside shrines to remind possibly rebellious peasants where their allegiance lay. Growing richer than ever on the proceeds of the Marienbad venture, the monastery remained a religious house until 1950, when it was closed on account of 'anti-socialist activities' and converted into a state library.

The main part of the library is a vast hall with display cases, and two balconies railed in black and gilt ornamental iron. The extensive collection of illuminated manuscripts, hymnals, and philosophical and scientific works is available for the use of all *bona fide* students, and there is ample accommodation for national and international conferences. One interesting item among the documents is a letter of 1528 from Ferdinand I asking the abbot if the local springs would yield salt, which was expensive in Bohemia.

The original Romanesque basilica of the church has gone through various transformations before acquiring its present three naves, the most impressive influence being that of Dientzenhofer, the master of Prague baroque. The Blessed Hroznata's sarcophagus is in a chapel in the north aisle. A reliquary remained here until 1950, when it was moved to the town church. The little single manual organ in the gallery above the choir proved inadequate, so in 1766 Gartner of Tachov built a larger instrument at the west end of the nave. Both were repaired in 1960, and regular organ and chamber music recitals are given in the church.

On the other side of Mariánské Lázně, on the way to Cheb, lies the coolly formal château of Kynžvart in its English park. The estate, known then as Königswart, had been a trophy of one of Metternich's ancestors after the battle of the White Mountain. Originally baroque, it was rebuilt in Empire style to become the famous chancellor's summer residence. His father was buried here, and he used it increasingly as the years went on, especially when working out such knotty problems as the anti-revolutionary measures to be incorporated in the Carlsbad Decrees. In 1856 we find him complaining about the invasion of his privacy by tourists from Marienbad. Kynžvart is now primarily a children's spa, but the tourists still come, in this day and age, to inspect Metternich's relics—his state carriage, the conference table from the Congress of Vienna, and the collections of books, furniture, and Napoleonic weapons and uniforms.

Approaching Cheb by rail or by road we come upon a scattering of smart holiday chalets around the lake and intersecting rivers near the town. The modern railway station buildings are reminiscent of airport architecture, but a few minutes' walk downhill brings us into the medieval heart of the old town.

Once known as Eger, this old Slavonic settlement was favoured by many historic figures. Frederick Barbarossa took the town as his personal property. George of Poděbrady was very fond of it, stayed here frequently, and had his children married here. The arrival of the ill-fated Winter King in Bohemia was jubilantly celebrated in the town. Schiller stayed here in 1791 while studying background material for his *Wallenstein* trilogy.

It is the death of Wallenstein, or Valdštejn, with which Cheb will forever be associated. Born into a Protestant family in 1583, Valdštejn was orphaned when very young. After travelling in Italy he became a Catholic convert, and at the imperial court was quick to ingratiate himself with Ferdinand III. He married a wealthy Moravian widow who conveniently died, leaving him a rich man. When he remarried, it was to the daughter of one of the emperor's closest advisers. He lent Ferdinand money—on one occasion, the pay of Moravian troops he found deserting to the enemy. A brilliant tactician in battle, he was erratic and overbearing in his dealings with allies and with his own king and emperor. Fearful of his ambitions, the lords and generals of the imperial cause could nevertheless not do without him through much of the Thirty Years' War. He pulled off one victory after another. His men were, if not encouraged, at least not officially debarred from torturing and murdering civilians in the territories they overran; and upon this terror Valdštejn built more and more power. His appetites grew. It was he, rather than his supposed master, who decided what wars should be fought and where. By 1633, quarrelling with his superiors and with his own officers, misjudging his tactics and hated by the peasants whose land he devastated, he began to fancy himself in the rôle of King of Bohemia, and it seemed likely that he was preparing to defect to the enemy together with his entire army if he could be given a promise of support to his claim. The emperor decided the time had come to remove Valdštejn once and for all. In February 1634 a decree of dismissal was published.

Hearing rumours that this would not be the end of it, and that his death was intended, Valdštejn fled from his Plzeň headquarters to Cheb. The evening after his arrival, the trusted officers who had accompanied him were attacked and overpowered by a contingent of dragoons under the orders of a group of English, Scottish and Irish mercenary officers in the imperial service. Valdštejn was found alone in his room and killed by a Captain Devereux, who then wrapped the corpse in the carpet on which it had fallen, and bumped it down the stairs into a coach for removal to the castle.

The castle and palace buildings are of different eras, with walls of every kind of stone that could be packed in: chips and slices of shale and slate fill up gaps, later mortared over during renovation. The Black Tower, one of the oldest surviving features, was built of lava blocks from an extinct volcano in the neighbourhood.

An enclosed wooden bridge leads over a now dry moat to a sports stadium called the Red Star. This may testify to a modern political allegiance; but the sign of the Red Star has existed in Cheb in a quite different context since the thirteenth century. In 1271 an exclusively Czech order of the Knights of the Cross was introduced, prophetically taking the red star as its emblem. In 1414 its church was that of St Bartholomew, now a well devised, uncluttered Gothic museum. Another museum in what ought to be called the main rectangle rather than the main square has a permanent exhibition of twentieth-century Czech painting, some fine ceilings, doors refurbished with intricate copies of the original silver hinges, and a unique collection of relief marquetry from the seventeenth and eighteenth centuries, with religious and mythological themes. From any angle—from the top of the castle tower, or from one side of the square or another—the roofs of the town present a striking picture: pitches of varying steepness; two, three and even four lines of dormers, some glazed and some gaping open for the benefit of pigeons so fat on the crumbs of biscuits and *oplatký* that they can barely fly up to even the lowest level; wayward chimneys, and a clash of colours. Nearer to ground level, there are some attractive bay windows, especially those of the house known as Špalíček.

A little way north of Cheb is the third of the better known spas, Františkovy Lázně, or Franzensbad. Its mineral waters were known at least as early as the fifteenth century, and in 1526 Paracelsus made some tests on them; but detailed analysis had to wait for Berzelius, studying them at the same time as the Karlovy Vary waters. Although Františkovy Lázně is much smaller than its two famous colleagues, it is attractively set in woods and parkland, sheltered by the Ore Mountains. One of its springs has the highest known concentration of Glauber salts, and its bath treatments depend on rich peat deposits.

South of the spas, along the border strip from Tachov to the environs of Volary, lies what used to be the Chodsko patrol region. Taking their name from the Czech word for walking, the Chods guarded the frontier passes and trails and kept them in good repair. Their symbol was that of a dog's head, and in return for their faithful protection of the important trade routes from Bavaria to Prague and the Golden Trail or Salt Trail through Prachatice they were granted special privileges by successive monarchs. The most prized of these was freedom from the usual obligations of serfdom. When the Habsburgs reimposed serfdom on defeated Bohemia, they automatically included the

Chods. Smarting under the tyranny of the foreign lord set over them, Wolf Lamminger of Albenreuth, or Lomikar, the freemen produced their royal charters in court and demanded that they should be honoured. Their pleas were rejected and they were commanded henceforth to preserve 'eternal silence' on the subject. Armed rebellion broke out. There are many romantic legends about its dashing guerrilla leader, Jan Sladký-Kozina, who was executed at Plzeň in 1695 after the defeat of the rebels as a warning to all who might wish to emulate them. Kozina's last words are said to have been a threat that one year from that day Lomikar would stand beside him for judgment before God; and just a year to the day, Lomikar collapsed at a banquet and died.

Capital of the territory over which the Chods kept vigil was Domažlice. Here they had their own free court within what is still proudly inscribed as the 'stout wall of the fatherland'. The castle museum contains copies of the old charters, and related historical and folklore exhibits. There is more folklore in the museum of Jindřich Jindřich, an artist who collected local costumes, furniture, pottery and paintings. The distinctive costumes are seen at their best, not just as museum pieces, during the annual summer festival, when the streets are filled with dancing and the sound of the bagpipes, and the equally distinctive dialect buzzes under the arcades of the town square. The only comparable events are the folk festivals of Stražnice in Moravia and the Vychodná amphitheatre in Slovakia. Domažlice is a state protected reservation, so its old gateways and the Renaissance and baroque beauties of that long town square are safe for the foreseeable future.

The glassworks of the neighbouring Šumava region having flourished for only a comparatively short time, superior resources and techniques in the north and north-west established what are now the main sources of Bohemian glass and porcelain. Kaolin deposits near Karlovy Vary supplied the porcelain makers of Stará Role on the outskirts of the town. Close by are the creators of the beautiful Moser glass. Finely set in the Lusatian Mountains, Nový Bor is the undoubted aristocrat of the industry. Its crystal tableware, ornaments and chandeliers have long been a major export, and the museum of glasswork in the main square is as important to the history of the town as any of its more immediately attractive houses. In a forest outside the town are the graves of those who fell during the Rumburk revolt, one of the many demonstrations against the Habsburgs during the First World War. Further east below the slopes of Krkonoše, the Giant Mountains, are more colonies of manufacturers, large and small. Even after the Second World War the crafts of the glass maker and cutter remained very much a cottage industry, carried on beside individual forges close to the quartz deposits of the mountains.

Krakonoš was, and maybe still is, the mischievous giant of this twenty-five-mile range along the Polish border, its main peaks reaching almost five thousand feet. On the whole he is amiable, preferring to reward the virtuous and punish the wicked, which is not always the nature of resident ogres. On one occasion he took pity on an old woman who, carrying a basketful of glass to market, slipped and smashed the precious work of many weeks. Commanded by Krakonoš to pack the pieces back into her basket and take them home, she found when she got there that they had been transmuted into gold.

It is significant that glass should play such an important part in the legend. Other, similar tales deal with the region's other long-established occupation—weaving.

At Kamenický Šenov, which has been famous for its crystal since the seventeenth century, was established the first glassmaking school in the country. Turnov has its state school of jewellery, and is known for its grinding and setting of Bohemian garnets and other semi-precious stones from rich deposits in a hill ten miles away. Jablonec, specializing in costume jewellery, has become the marketing centre for glass and jewellery produced in the region, and has a technical museum with an unrivalled collection of examples from various centuries.

Železný Brod, on the river Jizera, was an ore mining and smelting town in the fourteenth century. During the devastation of the Thirty Years' War its ironworks were destroyed, and it turned to glass production. As well as cut glass, it has fostered a characteristic and easily recognized line in coloured bowls, vases and figurines. The town's main hotel is appropriately named the Cristal. An exhibition in the local college of glass technology is open to the public. Even more fascinating, though, is the museum displaying scale models of the old timbered houses which are such a feature of the district. Several full-size examples have been preserved in the town itself, but modern intrusions have inevitably marred their true proportions and ambience: to appreciate the full spread of their façades in juxtaposition one with another, we must enter the stylish doll's-house world of the museum.

Paths, neatly signposted as usual, lead out of Železný Brod into the hills. One or two display what at first sight look like multi-coloured mosses or diminutive flowers. Closer inspection reveals a scattering of tiny glass beads and offcuts dropped by some carrier from one of the little factories on the slopes.

The most attractive walk through the woods is that following the Jizera for seven or eight miles to Semily. Slopes and forests steepen, a lovely hush descends on the world, broken only by the rustling of leaves and a whisper of water; and a few times a day a train rumbles eerily along the far bank, sheltered over certain stretches by props and roofing to stop chunks of cliff falling on the line. Semily is an undistinguished but cheerful little town with a toy factory whose trains, trucks and games often appear in English shops: no great goal in itself, but a pleasant marker buoy about which to turn, perhaps making the journey back to Železný Brod by another system of paths or by one of those trains which rumble above the river.

In the Giant Mountains above are ski resorts almost as popular as those of the High Tatras. Skis were first brought here from Norway at the end of the last century by the lord of the manor, Count Jan Harrach. He ordered copies from the local sawmill for the use of gamekeepers on his Harrachov estate. The village of Harrachov, originally a small glass-making community, has now become one of the main resorts and maintains an artificial ski run for practice all year round. Slightly smarter, set in a deep saucer rimmed by glittering peaks, Spindlerův Mlýn was once a silver-mining town but now makes its profits from tourists and sportsmen. With its shops, tennis courts and other facilities it is an ideal place to stay at any time, whether you are the energetic type or not. Mountain walks and drives lead away above dizzying vistas, and rest and refreshment huts along the whole range make it ideal country for the walker.

Some miles south of the border mountains is an intermittent outcropping of weird rock formations. Starting in what the Czechs like to call their Bohemian Switzerland, these 'rock towns' continue across another romantically named region, Český Ráj, the Bohemian Paradise. Great pillars, labyrinths, chapels, castles, and groupings like organ pipes have been shaped from Cretaceous sandstone, their tortured flanks and brows wrinkled by volcanic action. One mighty arch sixty feet high, Pravčická Brána—the Pravčice Gate—offers views over the rocks and walls of the western area, with names like Wilhelmina's Wall and the Robbers' Castle. One can walk, or, rather, scramble over ten or twelve miles of these strange conformations; and rock climbers can pit their skills against jagged pillars and chimneys. If you find this too exhausting, a boat from the village of Hřensko will take you along the Kamenice stream through the gorges and ravines of the sandstone maze. The landscape softens around Mácha lake, named after the poet whose lyrical *May* has become a Czech classic.

Rocks in the Bohemian Paradise also have some imaginative names: the Leaning Tower, the Countess's Lookout, the Brotherhood Chapel, and many more. The Prachovské skály— meaning, simply, sandstone rocks—have in their time really served as towns: there are signs of Stone Age habitation, when the overhangs and battlements must have served as a natural defence against enemies and the weather. And here and there, man-made castles such as that of fourteenth-century Trosky on its two spires of volcanic basalt, known as the Maiden and the Grandma, are in the distance indistinguishable from the ancient handiwork of nature.

If the rock towns are petrified monuments of prehistoric cataclysms, many of the villages and towns dotted across the northern fringes of Bohemia echo with human conflict.

Chomutov, now a mining and industrial town, was built upon an old border settlement which once fell into the hands of the

Teutonic Knights. This German influence made it staunchly Catholic, for which it suffered when the far-ranging Hussites reached it in March 1422. Hundreds of Taborites had recently been massacred after surrendering to one of Sigismund's commanders on a sworn promise not to harm them; a promise not honoured because the commander felt one did not have to keep one's word to heretics. Now it was time to settle the account. All the men of Chomutov were killed; and most of the women, too, died—at the hands of the Hussite women.

Teplice has been known as a spa since Celtic times, in general treating rheumatic and circulatory diseases, and has had many distinguished patrons including Goethe, Beethoven and Wagner. It has an interesting baroque church with paintings by Reiner and Brandl, remains of a Benedictine convent founded by Queen Judith, and Matthias Braun's Holy Trinity plague column. Better known to history as Teplitz, it was for some time headquarters of the allied armies against Napoleon. After his victory at Dresden in 1813, Napoleon's forces came within a few miles of Teplitz, but fell back after the capture of their commander. Napoleon contemplated leading a further attack himself, but called it off because of the difficulty of getting his artillery over the mountain roads.

Duchcov echoes with more recent strife. A memorial plaque recalls a skirmish between miners and armed police in 1931, during a period of widespread unemployment, wage cuts, strikes and demonstrations. Relic of a more romantic age, the château of this mining town was Casanova's home during his last years, when he worked in the Valdštejn library. Here he wrote his Memoirs, and here died in 1798. Many personal belongings and associated material are displayed in the château, and he is buried in the church of St Barbara.

Litoměřice endured the Hussites and the Thirty Years' War. Strongly Catholic, it denounced adherents to the Chalice and drowned many of them in the river Labe, or Elbe. When Žižka turned his attention towards them, the townsfolk were so alarmed that even before his troops appeared they had sent messengers to Prague to arrange an armistice. At the end of the Thirty Years' War, debts and the compensation demanded by the victors from many boroughs added up to a crippling sum, but Litoměřice seems soon to have recovered and thenceforth attracted admirers rather than contestants. The Czech linguist Jungmann and the poet Mácha lived here, and Mácha was buried here in 1836. When the Nazis occupied the region, the poet's remains were disinterred and taken by protective admirers to Prague for burial in Vyšehrad cemetery.

In the Gothic town hall, now a museum, is an altar-piece with fine sixteenth-century panel paintings by the Master of Litoměřice. The town archive treasures a Utraquist hymnal noted for two portraits of John Huss within. Among the striking houses on the town square, one proclaims its builder's faith: it is topped by a cupola in the shape of a chalice.

An annual summer trade fair, mainly of local glassware and textiles, is held in Liberec. Its museum has permanent exhibitions of glass and textiles, and some fine medieval Flemish tapestries. Many of the town's houses have a distinctive stucco decoration depicting religious and mythological themes, a sort of large-scale pargeting, from which the style of building has come to be known as the Liberec (or Reichenberg) house. A more sinister museum is that of Nazi Barbarism, in the villa which once belonged to Henlein, the Sudeten German leader; though Cheb has the unenviable claim to have been the real centre of the Sudetenland Nazi movement.

North of Liberec rears up what appears to be a true fortress rather than a mere château with a few ornamental battlements. Built around an original keep, Frýdlant was for twelve years Valdštejn's main command post. After his fall it was confiscated by the Emperor and later presented to the imperial general, Matthias Gallas de Camp, whose family continued to live here until 1945. Between 1645 and 1647 the fortifications were strengthened and given their present appearance by the commander of the Swedish forces in Bohemia.

If Frýdlant was Valdštejn's military headquarters, the spacious, colourful town of Jičín was his true capital. In 1623 he sold off his Moravian lands because anti-Catholic guerrilla raids and peasant disturbances were becoming too difficult to control, with all his other commitments. He bought estates around

Jičín and set about organizing the entire region to his liking, so that jealous rivals soon came to see the town as the capital of a private kingdom within the kingdom. The burghers were given lavish loans on the understanding that they rebuilt their houses to conform to their lord's tastes. He founded a Jesuit school to which all those in his employ had to send their children, built his own church, and along the whole eastern side of the main square laid out his luxurious palace. After his death the rich estates he had built up were confiscated and sold off by the Emperor to foreign supporters who made a fortune out of them; but the palace, the church of St James, the massive gateway and many other features in the town provide a lasting memorial to Valdštejn's splendour. Here in 1813 came the Emperor Francis I to take personal charge of his armies, massed outside the town, against Napoleon; and in the conference hall on the first floor of the palace the treaty of alliance against Napoleon was signed by Austria, Russia and Prussia.

The Austrians and Prussians did not remain friends for long. When Bismarck's ambitions for a greater Germany led him to challenge the imperial power, there was a terrible confrontation near what is now Hradec Králové and then was Königgrätz. The town, set where the rivers Labe and Orlice meet, grew up on the site of a Slav settlement on trade routes from the Danube to Poland and the Baltic. It became a royal town in the fourteenth century, when its unique red-brick Gothic cathedral of the Holy Ghost was built, miraculously escaping the usual subsequent cycle of restoration and revision. In the eighteenth century the Austrians transformed the entire town into a virtual fortress, tearing down many irreplaceable buildings to provide material for their fortifications. On 3 July 1866 Bismarck's forces attacked the main Austrian army between Königgrätz and the village of Sadowa, or Sadová. It had been a rainy night, and in the morning the mud hindered the progress of the Prussian artillery. Hand-to-hand fighting raged through hamlets and farmhouses until the Prussians had forced the imperial troops back into woods around Sadowa. In the final terrible engagement in the village of Chlum, more than ten thousand Austrian officers and men were killed in twenty minutes.

There is now a commemorative look-out tower on Chlum hill.

The house known as U Špuláku on Hradec Králové's main square was once a meeting-place of the Bohemian Brethren. This evangelical sect, also known as the *Unitas Fratrum*, sprang from the Hussites but was so extremely Protestant in its views that many Utraquists condemned it. When Utraquists and Catholics ultimately united to end the strife of the Hussite wars, they mutually denounced the Brethren. In 1508 the sect was banned by royal decree and many of its members fled abroad to escape imprisonment or rough justice—or injustice—at the hands of anti-Protestant mobs. Further persecutions in the reign of Ferdinand I drove out even the hardiest, though some managed for a while to survive in Moravia and, with the tacit sympathy of anti-imperialist nobles, quietly continue their observances as the Moravian Brethren. Complete proscription of the sect came after the Habsburg victories of 1620; but it reappeared in Saxony, from where its austere beliefs spread in due course to small communities in England and America.

If we follow the winding Labe south, we come to Pardubice, an old town which, like many in England, owes its present character to the prosperity brought by railway development in the last century. At about the same time its racecourse became the venue for a major annual steeplechase, and there is a motorcycle track where regular contests are held. The town square has not, unlike so many of its counterparts, become the Square of the Red Army or of Klement Gottwald or anyone more recent, but retains its dedication to William of Pernštejn, the Czech nobleman whose family owned the town and castle for some seventy years. A street also called after the Pernštejns is largely made up of Renaissance houses set upon older Gothic foundations. Many more of these would have survived if it had not been for the Swedes, who set fire to a large part of the town in 1645. The castle fared better. Incorporated in its western wing is the fourteenth-century childhood home of Arnošt, first Archbishop of Prague. William of Pernštejn added a château, ramparts and bastions, with an attractively arcaded courtyard. Inside, there are some intricately inlaid parquet floors and lavish murals. The castle museum displays a remarkable collection of stuffed birds. Its moat, now dry, was part of the Pernštejns' enlightened watercourse system, used not only to defend the castle but to drive watermills and hammers. The contours of this moat were responsible for the odd positioning of the houses in Kostelní ulice (Church Street).

Here the river turns due west, and writhes beside the railway line to Kolín. We can follow a roughly parallel road, or veer slightly south to visit Čáslav, where a statue of Žižka dominates the main square, and Žižka's body lies in the church. Or so we are told. A legend current shortly after his death claimed that he had given instructions for his body to be flayed and for a war-drum to be made from the skin; and many people claimed to have seen this drum before it was seized by Frederick the Great as booty during his wars with Maria Theresa. But there are other, better authenticated records of his having been first buried at Hradec Králové and then, because of the disapproval of the local anti-Taborite priest, removed to Čáslav, scene in the past of two great Hussite conclaves.

From here it is only a few miles to what was once the second most important town in Bohemia. By the end of the fourteenth century it was famous all over Europe for its silver mines, largely worked by German settlers under Czech royal protection. Kutná Hora—Kuttenberg to its immigrant miners—supplied the mints of several neighbouring countries, and was also allowed to produce its own distinctive gold and silver coins, designed by Italian craftsmen. Wenceslas II refashioned his palace to accommodate these designers, so that it came to be called the Italian Court. It is now the town hall, with a coin museum in which from time to time demonstrations of old minting techniques are given. In the courtyard of the castle museum are displayed medieval tools and machinery for extracting ore from the silver mines.

The patron saint of mining is St Barbara, and it is to her that the most striking building in the town is dedicated. Driving in through the industrialized outskirts, one catches repeated glimpses of three soaring, spiked tents of stone—an inexplicable blend of steeply pitched oast-houses and Byzantine pavilions. Set above a steep valley of terraced gardens, the cathedral was begun in 1388 by the Peter Parler workshop as a rival to St Vitus' cathedral in Prague. When the Hussite wars broke out, only the chapels and the outer nave had been completed. The roof and its three upswept cones were not finished until the middle of the sixteenth century. When the Jesuits took over they made many alterations to the interior and eventually modified the roof also in baroque style. A thorough restoration was undertaken at the end of the last century and the beginning of this, with a completely new western front. Within, the mining theme is insistent: coats of arms of the guilds; murals in the miners' chapel; and a statue of a miner in the nave. Minters and coiners are also honoured in a chapel and murals.

Kutná Hora is a cheerful place in itself, with its steep, twisting, plunging streets—rather in need of some paint and plaster —and its bustling main square. St James' church, deceptively English in appearance at first glimpse, is older than it looks, another creation of the Parler workshop. The tall fluted columns of its lofty nave make it seem too tall for its length. More familiar in its ornate baroque style is the church of the ubiquitous John of Nepomuk. The painter Peter Brandl is buried in the church of Our Lady, whose altar-piece representing the Visitation of the Virgin appears to have been derived from a Dürer woodcut. The cross-fertilization of the various craft workshops of Europe at this time is an unending and tantalizing study in itself.

To the north is Poděbrady, where we rejoin the river Labe. The spacious gardens of this spa, which specializes in the treatment of heart diseases, have a statue of Smetana, appropriate enough in an environment resonant with orchestral concerts and light music; but the statue most symbolic of the town is that of the Hussite king, George of Poděbrady, standing in the square not far from the castle. Thrusting up from the river bank, the original palace is all that remains of the stone fort built by Otakar II to guard a strategic route across the Labe, together with part of the northern wing. King George was born here in 1421, but would probably not recognize his home now: the Habsburg Ferdinand I and Rudolf II carried out extensive alterations, and in the middle of the eighteenth century the entire château was rebuilt. Visitors during the summer months can join spa convalescents for a season of plays presented in the castle courtyard.

Now we are on our way back to Prague. A diversion to the south will take in Průhonice; to the north-west, the river leads on to Mělník.

Průhonice *ought* to be worth a visit, but in all honesty one must make some reservations. A Renaissance château somewhat severely mauled in the late nineteenth century is now the main administrative building of the National Museum's botanical section. Set in parkland in the English style, its turreted tower looks over the trees to a six-hundred-acre spread of rock plants and shrubs, with rare alpines and flamboyant rhododendrons. There are walks beside the lake and through the shadows of the arboretum. It is a delightful place to spend a leisurely day. Yet last time I was there, large tracts seemed to have gone quite literally to seed. In general ambience and in detail it ought to be able to compete with, say, Wakehurst Place; but it doesn't. I can only hope that I saw it during what was, for some unknown reason, a bad time, and that on some future visit it will show itself in its true colours.

As to Mělník, I have no reservations whatsoever. It is a gem. Church and château stand high above the confluence of the Labe and the Vltava, with vineyards climbing the steep slopes to the very walls of the town. Viewed from the terraces or the château's excellent wine restaurant, the two rivers are often blurred by a shimmering heat haze—or that, at least, is how I invariably picture them. From below, apparently out of the cliff face itself, a racing skiff will glide forth; and exploration of the towpath reveals a large club boat-house and little cottages with their own moorings. A melancholy hoot in the distance announces a barge approaching lock gates on the Vltava. Traffic on the two waterways is so brisk that signals are necessary at the junction.

There was a Slav encampment here in the ninth century, and it is said that nearby Říp Mountain was the vantage point from which the chieftain Čech surveyed the Bohemian landscape and decided to settle. The name most closely associated with Mělník is that of Princess Ludmila, grandmother of St Wenceslas. It was perhaps in their sainted memories that Charles IV designated Mělník the dower town of queens of Bohemia in perpetuity; and he encouraged the planting of vineyards whose finest produce is bottled under the name of Ludmila. The annual wine harvest ceremonies are ritually dedicated to him. Vladislav II showed less respect for Charles' memory: in spite of the imperial decree he mortgaged the dower town. After passing through the hands of several noblemen, including the Valdštejns, it came in 1753 into the possession of the Lobkovic family, who held it until 1938. Whatever the failings of successive lords, they did conscientiously maintain the vinicultural standards, and the vintners' guilds became the most powerful in the community. The massive barrels in the château cellars are an awesome sight but a pleasing one. Equally pleasing is the sight of lorries toiling uphill and into a town street to discharge great heaps of grapes down yawning chutes, feeding the process which will refill those barrels. An exhibition of the vintner's craft is on view in the castle museum, next to a picture gallery in which Dutch paintings accompany the works of Reiner, Brandl, and the baroque master Karel Škréta.

Smetana married his second wife and composed parts of some of his operas in the tranquillity of a neighbouring village; and in this same village another Čech, the author Svatopluk Čech, also lived and worked for some time. Like so many of their fellow artists they were both consciously nationalistic in their work, using local and patriotic themes with a fervour which has long been unfashionable in English music and literature. Some may find these tendencies distracting, even distasteful. But for the Czechs and Slovaks such emotions and ideals are inextricably bound up with everyday life and thought, and therefore with art. When I discussed this present book with a doctor friend in Moravia and said I intended it to be non-political, his wife was not sure she had heard me aright. 'How can any serious book be non-political?' she asked in genuine bewilderment.

If we look at a few representative writers and composers in the next chapter we will soon find how impossible it is to study their work in isolation, unrelated to the centuries-old Slav struggle for identity and independence.

Words and Music

During the years of Austrian domination, writers and musicians prospered only in proportion to their willingness to use the German language, follow the imperial fashions of the era, and avoid the crudities of 'peasant' and 'servant' language and melody. Yet, thanks to a few scholars and to those country folk so despised by the largely foreign aristocracy and gentry, the tunes and rhythms of Czech speech and song continued to pulse below the surface.

The first recorded use of the Czech language is in early hymnals and translations from Latin histories and legends, followed early in the fourteenth century by a patriotic chronicle known as Dalimil's Chronicle. Charles IV wrote his memoirs in Czech, and John Huss's reformed orthography provided a more flexible literary medium. Huss's ideas were carried on by Petr Chelčický whose radical ideas were a formative influence on the practices of the Bohemian and Moravian Brethren. In their town of Náměšt' nad Oslavou the Brethren had a printing press, one of the first in the country, and in 1533 they issued the first Czech grammar. It was only a matter of time before a thorough translation of the Bible was made, and between 1579 and 1593 this was undertaken and printed at Kralice, not much more than a mile from Náměšt'. The Kralice Bible Museum has many examples of early printing, including some works by Jan Amos Komenský, or Comenius.

Born in 1592 to parents who belonged to the Brethren, Komenský was in due course to become the last bishop of the *Unitas Fratrum*. He was one of those teachers who believed in a philosophical unity of science, religion and what today we

11 Mělník, home of the 'Ludmila' vineyards

would call sociology, so that education must be a matter of communal building from the ground up and never the study of artificially separated subjects. He produced the first book aimed at teaching children by means of pictures; endeavoured to start a pansophistic college in London; and was invited to Sweden to reform its whole educational system. In his *Panergesia* he wrote:

> In truth Europe is separated from Asia, Asia from Africa, Africa from America, and between empires and lands lie mountains and valleys, rivers and fields. One Earth, however, bears and nurtures us all, the same air quickens and embraces us, the same heavens rise above us, the same sun lights us all in our turn; we all live in one common habitation, one breath of life inspires us all. We are all citizens of one world: what then prevents our gathering in one community, under the selfsame laws? People were formerly scattered over the earth; now they gather together in larger and larger bodies. What then prevents us from hoping that we may all one day be one well-ordered unity, permanently joined by bonds of science, law and religion? For one and the same thing is natural to all people; one system of the senses, reason, will, and all vital forces.

All citizens of one world . . .! Komenský's faith must have been sorely shaken more than once. Pastor of the Brethren's school at Fulnek in Moravia at the time of the battle of the White Mountain, he was driven out by Spanish mercenaries and had to go into hiding for a few years before sadly leaving his country for good. His home and library had been destroyed; in exile, his wife and children died of the plague; and as bishop of the Brethren in Lesno, Poland, he suffered once again when the Swedes sacked the town in 1656 and burnt his house and library. Finally he settled in Amsterdam.

The Brethren's meeting-house in Fulnek is now a state-protected Komenský Memorial, and here and in his birthplace of Uherský Brod are examples of his vast output of books and pamphlets, including some rare editions in foreign languages.

Komenský was only one among many to be driven from his homeland. With the refugees went most of what was promising in Czech literature. Writing in the Czech language was almost non-existent until, at the end of the eighteenth century, Dobrovský and Jungmann set about the long task of reviving it and restoring it to its proper place.

Even when Czech nationalism had taken a good hold of the

12 Telč, preserved as a town reservation
13 Pernštejn castle in the Bohemian-Moravian highlands

popular and intellectual imagination, many authors continued to use German. The intensely nationalist composer Smetana had to make a considerable effort to familiarize himself with Czech rather than stick to the German on which he had been brought up. But between 1836 and 1867 František Palacký, leader of a faction striving for the eventual union of Bohemia, Moravia and Silesia into a federal kingdom, was writing his *History of the Czech People* in Czech. Czech plays had been staged at rare intervals from the end of the eighteenth century, but the dramatist Josef Tyl was beginning to make his mark. In December 1834, at the theatre now named after Tyl, though known to Mozart and his contemporaries as the Nostitz, his play *Fidlovačka* received its first performance; notable mainly for the introduction of a song by František Škroup, *Kde domov můj?*—Where is my Home?—which reappears in Dvořák's overture, *My Home*, and was to become the basis of the Czechoslovak National Anthem.

The first woman to write and become a best seller in the Czech language was Božena Němcová, born in 1820. She scandalized some folk with her behaviour, Bohemian in every sense of the word, as if she aspired to become a Czech George Eliot or Georges Sand; but her books were tender and observant studies of simple people, in the vein of Mrs Gaskell. The most successful and enduring was *Grannie*.

Also dealing with ordinary people in everyday life was Jan Neruda, whose sketches of his friends and neighbours in the Little Quarter give added savour to one's appreciation of the still recognizable taverns and houses. Edith Pargeter's translation of these tales ought long since to have been taken into some publisher's series of classics, paperback or otherwise.

Alois Jirásek, born in 1851 in the Eastern Bohemian town of Hronov on the river Metují, wrote historical novels of a stirring, romantic nature, and survived until 1930 to see the reality of an independent Czechoslovakia. He was laid to rest in a sumptuous modern tomb in Hronov, and the theatre named after him has become the centre of an annual amateur dramatic congress and contest. On the outskirts of Prague the Renaissance hunting lodge of Hvězda, the Star, by the ill-omened White Mountain, also enshrines a memorial to his work and in particular to the cycle of novels covering the Hussite era.

The region around Hronov seems to have been quite a forcing-ground for writers. Božena Němcová worked for some time at Červený Kostelec, and Karel Čapek was born nearby at Malé Svatoňovice in 1890. He became a journalist and then for a while stage manager at a theatre in Prague's Vinohrady, marrying a well-known actress of the day, and in 1920 was the first author from the new Czechoslovakia to win international acclaim for his play *R.U.R.* or *Rossum's Universal Robots*. Here in the old Czech tradition of Rabbi Löw and his Golem was a modern tale of artificial creation, this time with a pseudo-scientific gloss which has provided subsequent writers of science-fiction with a theme of which they seem never to tire. There was an element of dour fantasy in all Čapek wrote, including the successful *Insect Play* on which he collaborated with his brother Josef, and *The Makropulos Matter*, again a tale of artificiality—this time the artificial prolongation of the life of the ravishing Emilia Marty by a chemical elixir until the sheer boredom of immortality makes her glad to accept death. Around this story Janáček built one of his most moving operas. Karel Čapek completed his last play, dealing with the evils of dictatorship and war, shortly before Hitler's rape of Czechoslovakia, and died on Christmas Day 1938. His brother Josef, less fortunate, lived on to be imprisoned by the Nazis, dying in Belsen in April 1945.

Two novelists born in the same year, 1883, grew up to become representative writers of their country and to mint pictures from the same metal, though exhibiting opposite sides of the coin. One was a German-speaking introvert of Austrian Jewish parentage; the other a slangy, drunken, mischief-making Czech extrovert who wrote fitfully and without discipline, and lived in much the same way.

Franz Kafka was driven into neurotic mental seclusion by a father who despised his literary interests Taking a doctorate in law because he felt this would allow him more leisure time for writing, he became an insurance clerk and then, retreating more and more into himself, threw up this job and devoted himself to the creation of strange allegories and fragments of nightmare.

He planned to marry but, as recent publication of his letters has shown, he kept the poor girl on a twisted string and reacted to her as tortuously as he reacted to every challenge from the outside world. Isolated from that world of ordinary mortals, he spoke of writing as 'a form of prayer' which must not be interrupted by the 'false hands which reach out to one while one is writing'; and seemed to wish those prayers to remain forever secret, since he instructed his friend and executor, Max Brod, to destroy all his manuscripts unread after his death. Brod refused to carry out this request and set himself instead to fit the disparate chapters of various works into the order he believed their author intended.

The Trial and *The Castle* must rank as two of the most prophetic novels in the twentieth century—prophesying not material advances and inventions such as penicillin, atom bombs and trips to the Moon, but the impersonal, irrational terror which was so soon to cloak Europe and spread its shadows across the whole world. A man arrested, interrogated, and implicitly condemned on a charge which is never put specifically enough for him to refute: how many tragic autobiographies of our time have told of this nightmare—and how many have told it with such nightmarish truth as Kafka's clairvoyant fiction? The tuberculosis which killed him in 1924 may, as with Keats and D. H. Lawrence, have heightened his awareness and raised the pitch of his writing, or may have been just one element among many that tortured his mind and vision. It is the truth of his pessimism which is so frightening: a verifiable truth of implacable organizations which torment the ordinary individual without explanation or excuse.

A curious reminder of Kafka's career is to be found in the Týn church: although Jewish, he had for some time a study with a window which looked directly out over a side altar of the church, its curtain now drawn half back as if to persuade us that the brooding author is still there peeping from behind it and making his bitter prognostications.

Jaroslav Hašek was no recluse. He spent most of his time mixing boisterously with his fellows, neglecting his work, hoaxing and drinking and listening. From his earliest schooldays he showed signs of indolence and waywardness. He played malicious jokes on his friends and took part in anti-German riots in Prague for the sheer sake of smashing things. Instead of pursuing studies at a commercial college he took to the road in the company of tramps and gipsies; then, having managed to get a respectable job in a bank, almost immediately walked out and went wandering again. Thinking that the supposedly free and easy hours of a writer's life would suit him, he became a contributor of short pieces to newspapers, but could not make an adequate income from them. He joined the anarchist movement and made inflammatory speeches which brought him to the notice of the Habsburg police, who perhaps took him more seriously than he took himself. Several times he was sent to prison. Even when he fell in love and finally persuaded doubting parents to let him marry their daughter, he proved incapable of holding down a job and leading an ordinary life. With the help of a friend he became, of all unlikely things, editor of an animal-lovers' magazine; but was dismissed after hoaxing readers with articles about spurious creatures he had invented. Throwing himself off the Charles Bridge from the very spot where St John of Nepomuk had traditionally been thrown, he was sent for a while to a mental home; and early in the First World War spent a few days in prison after pretending to be a Russian spy.

But in the middle of all his excesses he did not lose his retentive memory. Policemen, lunatics, bureaucrats and the Austrian military—he saw, heard and remembered them all. In 1911 he published in a humorous paper a number of stories about a character known as the Good Soldier Švejk. Called up eventually for military service in the war, he used everything he encountered as material for further adventures of this classic shirker. Švejk is the scrounger, the artful dodger known in every army in the world: dishonest, disreputable, incompetent, dodging work and danger, but always ready with cunning answers which reduce his superiors to impotent bewilderment. In the last resort the only charge that can be made to stick is that good old disciplinary standby, dumb insolence. But although a universal figure, Švejk has always had a special significance for his own countrymen, who throughout so many centuries and so many successive overlords learned the technique of passive resistance one day, the pricking of pomposity the next, sly sabotage the next.

Towards the end of the war Hašek found himself in Russia. Having been captured and imprisoned by the Tsarist forces, he had joined the Czech Legion to fight the Germans and Austrians, was ordered after the Russian Revolution to fight the Bolsheviks, and finished up as a member of the Bolsheviks himself. For some months he was actually commissar in a small Russian town. There is every indication that his cynical eye was selecting for future use the follies of war and human behaviour which best accorded with his style of writing. At the end of 1920 he returned to Prague with a mistress he had picked up on his travels, and with two women, a son and an implacable thirst to support, set about recording the wartime adventures of the Good Soldier Švejk. He originally visualized this saga in six volumes, but hard drinking and rowdy company dragged him down, and he was still working on the fourth section when he died in January 1923. His ghost, arm in arm with that of Švejk, still haunts U kalicha, both trying to make themselves heard through the unending din.

Translating Hašek's bawdy slang and finding an English equivalent for ungrammatical everyday twists of Czech phraseology has until recently put major stumbling blocks between Švejk and the English reader. An English edition which circulated for some years was shortened and heavily censored. But in 1973 an unexpurgated version appeared in a translation by Sir Cecil Parrott, once British Ambassador to Prague. Sir Cecil explains and apologizes for the difficulties in catching Švejk's tone of voice and in unravelling other linguistic problems; but has in fact produced a splendidly convincing, rumbustious book —no mere pedantic exercise but a labour of love, resulting in a story which at last stands on its own, or perhaps Švejk's own, two sturdy feet.

The emergence of distinctively Slovak writers was a more painful process. Although Czech as a language had been humiliated for many years, it was gradually allowed to creep back into its own. Slovak was treated badly from the start, and worst of all at just the time when Czech was reasserting itself. No Slovak books were permitted in Magyar schools, and any child caught reading one was liable to expulsion. Circulation of newspapers was frowned on. In many regions the only written Slovak permitted was that on calendars or in prayer-books. A few priests and teachers tried to keep the language alive in spite of the official imposition of Magyar in all schools. Anyone with an ambition to write creatively in Slovak found it more prudent to leave the country: one much admired short story writer, Bencúr-Kukučin, lived abroad for thirty years and returned only after the foundation of the new republic.

Even in that new atmosphere there could be no immediate flowering. When the Komenský university opened in Bratislava, most of its early professors were of necessity Czech. Writers and musicians, feeling their way, concentrated for a time on ethnographic studies, recording regional ballads and folk-song.

Among the stubborn nationalists who, under the most unfavourable conditions, preserved and utilized every loophole to expand the language were the philologist Šafařík, who died in 1861, and the militant Ludovít Štúr who, in producing a patriotic newspaper, fashioned the Central Slovakian dialect into a new literary model which others could follow and adapt. After liberation from the Magyars, young writers in search of a modern style came at first under strong French and English influences. It was some time before creative work with an individual flavour began to come through, most of it with a direct national appeal. Many wrote about the war which had recently finished; and all too soon found another war upon them. The generation writing after 1945 have even grimmer tales to tell of barbarity, with only the somewhat repetitive figures of heroic partisans to strike a more optimistic note.

There would be little point in listing authors and titles of books which have not been translated into English. At the same time there is a danger that the few translations issued by British and American publishers or in English-language editions by Artia in Prague have been chosen because of hoped-for international interest rather than specific relevance to life in their country of origin. Some authors, too, are for various reasons no longer in official favour—which rarely has anything to do with the intrinsic literary merit of their books.

In *Death is called Engelchen*, the Slovak author Ladislav Mňačko tells a largely autobiographical story of partisan operations in Moravia towards the end of the war. The highland village scene is brought movingly to life, darkened by the shadow of an approaching S.S. detachment under Otto Skorzeny— whose recent death was accorded a favourable obituary in *The Times*, remembering in the best sporting spirit his flamboyant rescue of Mussolini and forgetting his record of cruelty to less dramatic figures. Death and darkness are repetitive in the themes drawn from those deadly years: *Romeo and Juliet and the Darkness* . . . *Diamonds in the Night* . . . and Rudolf Jašík's *Dead Soldiers Don't Sing*. In this latter a young Slovak writer, who died before finishing the novel, gives a disturbing insight into life in the Slovak puppet state operated by the Nazis, building up towards the time when the pretences are stripped away and the people are ripe for revolt. The same background, same mood and same menace were conjured up by Ladislav Grosman in his *Shop on the High Street*, which in 1966 became an Oscar-winning film.

The autobiographical element is strong in the short stories and film scripts of Arnošt Lustig, who was sent at the age of sixteen to the Jewish ghetto of Terezín. In the volume published in English as *Night and Hope* he links incidents from the histories of children, adolescents, doomed adults and predatory guards within the enclosed town where every pretence of normality could collapse at any moment into the reality of the gas chambers and Hitler's 'final solution'. Lustig survived Terezín, Auschwitz and Buchenwald; but his father went to the gas chambers in Auschwitz. He married a girl who had also been in Terezín, and in a novel published in 1962 (in England in 1966), *Dita Sax*, showed with his usual bleak honesty how impossible it was for any who had been through such experiences to adjust to the falsely comforting routine of ordinary existence.

Yet even the most appalling wars fade in the memory, and new writers take over to deal with present conflicts. Some of their enthusiasms and some of their strictures would mean as little to the English reader as a television play on the social problems of Knightsbridge flat-dwellers would mean to a Czech or Slovak audience. But, as with Kafka's work, there are some themes which send out far-reaching ripples. Milan Kundera's *The Joke* tells of a young man, an inveterate hoaxer—shades not just of Kafka but of Hašek!—who sends his rather earnest girl friend a flippantly treasonable postcard . . . and sees his career in ruins. And then in the same nihilist mood he seduces the wife of the man who engineered his downfall. A political novel; and at the same time a story of any small office or big business. Kundera's play *The Owners of the Keys*, full of equally disturbing questions, was produced at the Belgrade Theatre in Coventry in June 1967.

Then there is Václav Havel, who plunges us right back into the Kafkaesque nightmare of bureaucratic obfuscation. His play *The Memorandum*, presenting the trials of a man who needs to interpret the meaning of an important message in an officially authorized Newspeak, as George Orwell put it, but can learn this essential language only by putting in an application written in that very language, was shifted effortlessly in a B.B.C. television production to an implied British business setting, in which it was all too convincing.

The temper sounds at worst grim, at best rather sour. But to set against these serious probings there are the more light-hearted successes of Czechoslovak cinema and stage: Trnka's delightful puppets, films such as *A Blonde in Love* and *Intimate Lighting*, the experimental theatres and satirical cabarets in the side streets of every city, and The Magic Lantern with its ever-changing blend of live theatre, film and music.

Always and everywhere in this land there is music.

The influence of Cyrill and Methodius gave early Czech liturgical music a Byzantine flavour, but after the collapse of the Great Moravian Empire it was the Roman usage which predominated. One of the earliest surviving plainsong chants is named after St Wenceslas. Later the Hussites went in for forceful unison singing of melodies not far removed from plainsong, though some had folk-song elements with characteristic rhythms and intervals. The fifteenth-century Hymnal of Jistebnice records over seventy of these. Of later hymnals, the most influential was published by Komenský in exile in 1659 and smuggled in large quantities into Bohemia.

As the Habsburg grip tightened, large numbers of Czech composers and instrumentalists left the country: some to escape political and religious persecution, others to find wider scope for their talents in less restricted conditions. Settling in the small courts and dukedoms of Europe, they spread the reputation of Bohemian musicianship until Johann Christian Bach in London could solemnly assure Dr Charles Burney that, given conditions as favourable as those enjoyed by the Italians, the Bohemians could certainly outclass them; and in his travels Dr Burney discovered for himself that their homeland was indeed 'the conservatoire of Europe'.

Adam Michna of Otradovice produced hymnals with tunes often indistinguishable from folk music. A two-way traffic is also apparent in his transcriptions and orchestrations of Czech carols, some overheard and noted down and some obviously his own original work. Michna's St Wenceslas Mass was one of the first compositions in the form of what we would now call a cantata. Born in 1600, he lived through his country's tragedy and in due course left to take up a post in Mannheim.

A composer who stayed was Vejvanovský, but then he kept the right company: his patron was the rich prince-bishop of Olomouc, a cultivated and powerful man who could protect and nurture the talents of those who served him well. Vejvanovský poured out dance suites and serenades for string and wind ensembles, and was especially vigorous in his music for brass, with a strong whiff of Monteverdi's sumptuous ceremonial style.

Černohorský worked for a time in Padua and Assisi, and had Tartini among his pupils. In 1735, seven years before his death, he returned to Prague as organist and choirmaster of St James' church, whose modern choir still feature his motets in their recitals. A great quantity of his choral and organ music was destroyed by fire in the church, but enough examples survive to make us regret what must have been lost.

One of the most influential performers of his time was Jan

Stamic, or Stamitz. He was born in 1717 in Německý Brod, now Havlíčkův Brod, where his father was organist. The original name of the town testifies to the predominance of German miners in the region—'Německý' simply means 'German'—and the church itself was founded by the Teutonic Knights. Stamic must have felt perfectly at home with Germans when in 1742, having caught the attention of the Elector Palatine while playing at the Emperor Charles VII's coronation, he was lured to the court of Mannheim. As first violinist and director of the orchestra there, he composed more than forty symphonies and established a style of interpretation which was to affect orchestral playing all over Europe. Attempts were made to get him to Stuttgart as *Konzertmeister*, but he remained in Mannheim until his death. His brother Anton joined him, then later became a priest. There were also two sons to add harmony: Carl, born in Mannheim, served for a while as second violin in the orchestra before setting off for Paris with his younger brother Anton and becoming an even more prolific symphonist than his father.

Another musical family was that of the Bendas. At one time there were no fewer than four violinist brothers in the court orchestra at Berlin. The most gifted of them was Jiří, or George, who left in 1748 to conduct the Duke of Gotha's orchestra. He spent some time in Italy in the ducal service and returned to Gotha fired with determination to write musical melodramas in competition with the Italians. These semi-operas are unlikely to be revived; but Benda's symphonies sound as fresh and exhilarating as the day they were written, and among frequent recordings is one which claims to be the shortest in the world, lasting only about seven minutes.

František Benda remained second leader of the Berlin orchestra for almost a quarter of a century after his brother's departure, until at last he was promoted to *Konzertmeister*. His own compositions lack the panache of Jiří's, but remain extremely agreeable: perhaps the excellence of his flute concerti owes something to Frederick the Great's partiality for that instrument.

Some musicologists tend to lump these composers and many

of their contemporaries together into the loose category of 'Czech baroque' as though this were some sort of stereotyped sub-Haydn amalgam. Nothing could be more misleading. The Bohemians did not so much work according to the trim fashion of their time as create that fashion. Less luxuriant than the Italians, they were also crisper and more direct. There are few obvious nationalist elements in their compositions, yet some of the rhythmic swagger and tunefulness of traditional folk songs undoubtedly conditioned their approach to formal phrasing.

A miller's son was to become one of Bohemia's most admired exports. After studying music with one of the Benda family still in Prague, Josef Mysliveček left in 1763 for Italy, where his operas soon earned him the title of *Il divino Boemo*. In 1770 he met the fourteen-year-old Mozart, the beginning of a friendship which meant much to the younger genius both musically and personally. Under the influence of Mysliveček and that of the Dušeks, the pianist-composer František and his wife Josefina, a distinguished singer, Mozart was already prejudiced in favour of Bohemia before the time came for him to visit Prague.

A so-called National Theatre had been established in Prague by Count Nostitz. By 'national' was implied only that the theatre should leaven the current rage for Italian opera with some German material: the question of Czech was not even considered. Even as it was, the manager was an Italian impresario, Pasquale Bondini; and when, largely due to the urging of the Dušeks and Mozart's Viennese patron Count Thun, *Le Nozze di Figaro* was staged in December 1786, it was naturally performed in Italian. Intrigue and delays in Vienna had left a wretched aftertaste. In Prague there was instant success, and a great clamour for the composer himself to appear in the city. Mozart arrived on 11 January 1787 and stayed in Count Thun's palace. He was overwhelmed by his reception:

> At six o'clock I drove with Count Canal to the so-called Bretfeld ball, where the cream of Prague's beauties are wont to gather. . . . I looked on with the greatest pleasure while all these people skipped about in sheer rapture to the music of my *Figaro* arranged as contredanses and waltzes. For people here talk about nothing but *Figaro*. Nothing is played, sung or whistled but *Figaro*. No opera is drawing like *Figaro*. Nothing, nothing but *Figaro*.

Mozart himself was persuaded to conduct a performance of the opera. Boys in the street whistled his tunes. A strolling harpist devised such excellent variations on one aria that Mozart composed a special piece for him, which the harpist played from one tavern to another until his death in 1843.

Mozart also presented the city with an immortal gift. Having composed a symphony in D shortly before setting out, he now conducted its first performance at the Nostitz, since when it has been known as the Prague Symphony; and improvised so dazzlingly at the piano that he was called back time and again for encores.

To add to his joy, at a time when Vienna was proving chilly towards him and he was seriously in need of money, just before he left for home he was commissioned by Bondini to write a new opera. The theme was chosen by his finest librettist, Lorenzo da Ponte: at one stage referred to as *The Stone Table*, it became *Don Giovanni*. When Mozart set out once more for Prague the opera was still incomplete, though the première was scheduled for 14 October to honour the visit of a royal honeymoon couple, Prince Anton of Saxony and the Archduchess Maria Theresa. Mozart and his wife stayed at an inn with da Ponte lodging across the street so that they could shout from one window to the other when ideas occurred to them. Then the Mozarts were invited to use the Dušek villa on the outskirts of the city, in what is now the industrial suburb of Smíchov.

The Bertramka, set in an attractive hillside garden which even today is not overwhelmed by the clatter of neighbouring factories, was rumoured to have come to Dušek's wife as a result of her liaison with the handsome Count Clam-Gallas. Mozart himself seems to have been half in love with the lady, but his time at the villa had to be spent in hard work rather than dalliance. The stone table in the garden is the one at which he used to sit. Legend has it, though, that the last notes of *Don Giovanni* were set to paper indoors—in a locked room. The final pages were in fact those of the overture. There had been all kinds of trouble at rehearsal, Mozart had written and rewritten arias and ensembles on the spot; and still the first night had to be postponed, one of the leading singers having fallen ill. The evidence for the overture having been finished and copied two nights before the performance is pretty strong, but most of us prefer to think of Mozart being shut away and refused his release until the job was complete—or perhaps of the alternative version in which his wife Constanze shared the room with him and told interminable stories to keep him awake.

Whatever its birth pangs may have been, the new opera was a success. Mozart was invited to stay in Prague and write another, but had to return to Vienna, where he was soon to be given the post of Court Composer after Gluck's death. He did not see Prague again until 1791, when he was urgently invited to write a festive opera in connection with Leopold II's coronation. With *Die Zauberflöte* and the *Requiem* still unfinished, he hastily fitted in this new commission and produced *La clemenza di Tito* within a few weeks. It was not a success, and Mozart left Prague ill and dejected.

When he died in December of that year, Vienna accorded him a pauper's funeral, attended by a small group of mourners. In Prague, the news plunged half the city into mourning. The huge church of St Nicholas in the Little Quarter could not hold those who wished to attend the memorial service, at which Josefina Dušková sang in the *Requiem* which had played so sombrely on Mozart's mind during the closing months of his life.

Today, reversing the old tendencies, most operas at the National Theatre and its subsidiaries are performed in Czech. But every now and then performances of *Don Giovanni* are given in Italian at the theatre which saw its first production. The first time I attended one such, it was as a matter of curiosity. I felt that it would be a worthwhile experience to see and hear the work in the small theatre for which it was commissioned, even if the singing were not of the highest quality. To be honest, the wide vibrato of those Czech sopranos can sometimes be a trifle dispiriting: I prefer singers who can hit the note rather than average it out. But I take this opportunity of apologizing for any initial doubts. The performance was then, and at a repeat performance some months later, the most scintillating I have ever seen or heard. Atmosphere . . . sentiment . . . nostalgia? I fully understand the scepticism; and refute it.

In 1974 the Tyl theatre, still with the Nostitz name along one side, was renovated and repainted outside in a pleasant green and cream, with its gates and railings smartly repaired.

As with language and literature, so the history of indigenous Czech and Slovak music is linked with the patient work of village schoolmasters. They taught in school on weekdays, and played the organ in village churches on Sundays and holidays. Without them there would have been no grounding for the books that waited to be written or the music that Bohemians were to carry out into the world. Without them, the two million Slovaks who emigrated to America during the most soul-destroying decades of Austro-Hungarian repression would not have been able to argue so convincingly in the cause of a cultural and social independence for Czechoslovakia.

One such was Jan Jakub Ryba, born at Přeštice in 1765. Son of a schoolmaster, he studied philosophy in Prague but felt obliged to come home when his father fell ill and asked him to take over the village school. Ryba's first love was music, but having experienced the wider world he tried to make all of it real to his pupils, encouraging them in the study of agronomy and horticulture, and adding hygiene and physical training to their somewhat limited curriculum. At the same time he worked on a musical dictionary and a treatise on musical theory which was to run to four volumes, and composed a great deal; but he is rarely accorded more than a passing mention in the encyclo-pedias and dictionaries of our own time, and while alive was conscious of his remoteness from the mainstream of Bohemian creativity. His affection for his own environment led him to publish a volume of songs in Czech, which was no way to win official acclaim. Even less likely to endear him to the authorities was his *Christmas Mass*, approximately following the ordinary form of the mass but commenting freely in everyday Czech on each section. One might try to discern a parallel in Benjamin Britten's *War Requiem*, with its interpolations of poems by Wilfred Owen; but by 1962 the English language was not, even by musi-cal snobs, proscribed in its own country as the Czech language was in Ryba's musical environment. The exultant opening of the Kyrie, 'Hej, Mistře, vstaň bystře'—'Hey, Master, get up quickly'—must have come as quite a shock to any solemn pundit who condescended even to listen to the work of this rural recluse. The work is full of joy, the orchestral parts full of scurrying vitality. But in 1815, disillusioned and oppressed by his lack of contact with artists of his own stature, Ryba committed suicide in Rožmital.

Probably unknown to Ryba, the same course had been followed by a Moravian-born composer in Slovakia. Edmund Pascha from Kroměříž entered a Franciscan monastery at Hlohovec in Western Slovakia, studied philosophy and theology, and became fluent in several languages. He preached and both played and taught music in a number of monasteries, including those at Prešov and Žilina. It was in the Žilina monastery library that his *Harmonia Pastoralis* cycle, lost for many years, was rediscovered in the 1930s. The manuscript includes a *Christmas Mass* built around the ordinary form of the mass but with the Latin pared away to allow long pastoral interjections in Slovak vernacular. Slovak religious music had a stronger folk element in it than that of the Czechs, and certainly far more than we are used to—though perhaps the little bands of musicians who played in church organ lofts as late as Thomas Hardy's day added a rural tang which we have too readily forgotten. In the remote areas of the Slovakian and Moravian-Slovakian hills, Christmas carols had for centuries rung with the same directness and naïve clarity as the primitive altar-pieces and carved nativity scenes we have grown to admire. Pascha's Mass is full of these Slovak cadences, bagpipe sounds, buzzing flutes and dance rhythms, all set within a barely conventional baroque framework.

But innovations in ecclesiastical music, no matter how inspired, were not enough. National pride demanded a truly national creator of that most fashionable of all art forms, opera. The first truly Czech opera was *The Tinker* by František Škroup, first performed in 1826, courageously defiant of convention in its elevation of a poor Slovak tinker to the rôle of hero. This was the same Škroup whose incidental music to *Fidlovačka* was to provide the country's National Anthem His attempts to repeat the success of *The Tinker* in subsequent operas failed.

14 Mikulov, pearl of Southern Moravia

In musical quiz games on radio and television we are often presented with jokey translations of composers' names. So far I have not come across any mention of Frederick Cream, and hope I shall be forgiven for introducing the real begetter of Czech opera thus flippantly.

Bedřich Smetana was born on 2 March 1824 in Litomyšl, in the foothills of the Bohemian-Moravian highlands. His father was a brewer who, marrying for the third time, brought his wife and their two daughters, together with surviving daughters of his second marriage, to live in the brewery of the Valdštejn château here. It is recorded that on the morning of Bedřich's birth, his father was so overjoyed at the appearance of a son that he had a barrel of beer rolled into the courtyard and invited everyone to join in the rejoicings.

Litomyšl was, and still is, a beautiful proportioned town redolent with history. Growing up around a tenth-century border fortress, it was granted a town charter in 1259 and was created an episcopate by Charles IV. The easternmost bishopric in Bohemia, it lost its bishop overnight in April 1421, when news of Žižka's approaching armies drove him post-haste into Moravia. The foundation stone of the present château was laid in 1568, and the building completed almost twenty years later. After a fire at the end of the eighteenth century the interior was enhanced by decorative stucco, and a theatre was installed. This was also the period when the brewery was built. Rooms in the Smetana home have been refurbished in the style prevailing during the composer's childhood, and concerts are given in the courtyard and the park.

Wild roses growing in the woods are said in local legend to spring from tears shed by members of the Bohemian Brethren fleeing the country, holding their last sacrament in a clearing and then burying the chalice. Young Smetana must have known this and many other tales from local history; and acquired more when the family moved to Jindřichův Hradec, and even more when his father retired to an estate near fabled Blaník Hill. František Smetana was an accomplished amateur violinist and encouraged the boy's musical leanings, though when Bedřich began serious studies in Prague at the age of nineteen there was

15 Folk costumes at a local festival

little money to spare. There were, however, plenty of ideas to spare. Czech nationalism was in the air, the younger generation talked of little else, and when Smetana prepared to set out on his first concert tour in the hope of achieving fame and wealth, his uncle warned him that to succeed as a German virtuoso would be to betray his Slav inheritance and renounce that national recognition which was more valuable than gold. Perhaps the final jab of the spur came during a visit to Liszt in Weimar, when a well-known Viennese conductor insultingly commented that the Czechs produced fine fiddlers but were unlikely ever to come up with a composer capable of writing intrinsically Czech music of any consequence. After a spell in Sweden running a music school and giving piano recitals including many of his own pieces, Smetana returned to Prague in 1861 determined to win one of the prizes offered by Count Jan Harrach for the best comic and historical operas on Czech themes.

The result was *The Brandenburgers in Bohemia*. Because of the intrigues of a conservative cabal, it won only a grudging 'conditional' prize; and Smetana was also passed over for the appointment of opera director at the new Czech Provisional Theatre, established pending the creation of a permanent National Theatre. The man chosen in his stead was in no hurry to stage *The Brandenburgers*, and its first performance did not come until January 1866. Its immediate success must have been more of an embarrassment than a triumph to the clique in charge of the theatre.

While waiting for his first opera to see the light of day, or at least the footlights, Smetana had been working on a second one, quite different in character. Instead of a grandiloquently heroic theme he chose one dealing with love and laughter in a little village. He was so sure of his ground that he finished the overture before his librettist had even started the main story: a far cry from *Don Giovanni!*

There are several places in *The Brandenburgers*, such as the chords leading into Ludiše's aria in the first act, where we are 'reminded' of something which in fact had not yet happened. Then all becomes clear: the whole cast of the music, in spite of its martial solemnity, is preparing us for the joy and relaxed assurance of *The Bartered Bride*.

The version of this performed in May 1866 was different from the one we know so well today: it had only two acts, and lacked some arias and dances. Even so it achieved an even greater success than its predecessor, and the cabal could no longer deny Smetana his claim to the full prize or to directorship of the opera.

As well as conducting and establishing an adventurous repertoire he went on to write further operas in both moods: histories and legends in heroic vein such as *Dalibor* and *Libuše*, and comedies such as *The Two Widows*. Then, at the height of his career, he had to relinquish his official positions and for a while felt he would be unable to compose again. In 1874 he had begun to complain of pains in the ears, and in spite of various medical treatments and visits to specialists early the following year, he went deaf. To make it worse, though he heard nothing of the outside world or his own music, he was plagued by shrieks and thunderings and shrill whistles within his own head. Forced by increasing poverty to leave Prague, he went to live with his married daughter in a small hunting lodge in the woods at Jabkenice.

In spite of these afflictions he completed the cycle of *Má Vlast*, attended the long-delayed première of *Libuše* although he could not hear a note, and poured his heart and memories into the string quartet in E minor, *From My Life*. He even ventured on further operas. The last of these, *The Devil's Wall*, took two and a half years to complete because of advancing illness. Although it had been intended as a comedy, Smetana injected something darkly sardonic which gave it a flavour quite unique in its time. A story of the thirteenth-century Lords of the Rose, set in their castle at Rožmberk and on the Vltava near Vyšší Brod monastery, it tells of the devil's attempts to thwart the builders of the monastery by creating the rocky dam of the Devil's Wall and diverting the river. Below its pastiche of church rituals and mockery of romantic chivalry there runs, however, an almost despairing undertone of Smetana's love for his country and its traditions.

The first few performances were a disappointment. 'They want nothing else from me!' lamented the composer. He was now beginning to behave oddly, forgetting names, sometimes finding himself incapable of speech, sometimes shrieking repetitive monosyllables. Defying doctor's orders not even to think about music, let alone write it, he managed to finish his second string quartet and was fumbling with ideas for a new opera when in April 1884 he had to be taken away to Prague lunatic asylum. He died three weeks later. The autopsy showed the cause as syphilis.

One of the viola players in the theatre orchestra for eleven years, some of these under Smetana's baton, was Antonín Dvořák, who came to this job after a spell in a restaurant ensemble. Throughout these years none of his fellow instrumentalists knew that their colleague was devoting every moment of his limited spare time to composition.

Born in September 1841 at Nelahozeves, the boy was the eldest of nine children of the village butcher and innkeeper. He was apprenticed as a butcher and expected to take over his father's business, but the village schoolmaster urged that his musical talent should not be wasted and managed to have him sent to Prague Organ School. While playing in the theatre orchestra he composed a great deal of choral music and two operas, as well as two of those first four symphonies which disappeared for some years from catalogues of his work and so confused the numbering. In 1873 he left the orchestra and took a post as church organist so that he would have more time for his own work; and in 1874 applied for a state grant available to needy composers, presenting his second and third symphonies to support his case. Fortunately one of the judges on the panel was Brahms, who at once recognized Dvořák's talent and was to be his friend and admirer thereafter: two years later he persuaded a leading Berlin publisher to bring out the Moravian Duets, and this publisher then commissioned Dvořák to write a set of Slavonic Dances for piano duet and in an orchestral version.

His use of folk song, country dances, village brass band sounds and leaping rhythms within fairly conventional concert-hall forms appealed to a wide international audience. His *Stabat Mater* was a great success in England, and he visited the country many times to conduct his own works. In June 1891 he was presented at Cambridge with an honorary degree of Doctor of Music. Between 1892 and 1895 he was director of the National Conservatory of Music in New York. It was here that he wrote his ninth symphony, *From the New World*. Many a programme note refers to the inspiration he received from negro spirituals of the time, but Dvořák himself denied 'all that nonsense about my making use of original American national melodies'. The work is in fact full of Czech themes and nostalgia for his home-land; an emotion even more lavishly displayed, and then disci-plined into an undoubted masterpiece, in the Cello Concerto.

In spite of success in the capitals of the world, Dvořák re-mained a country lover. The little museum in his family home at Nelahozeves is a perfect memorial: in sentiment he was never far from the village on the Vltava, and it is appropriate that the yellowing grey château should also have a museum of musical instruments. A little way to the east is the baroque château of Veltrusy, with its park and summerhouses and little ruined follies, and with an oval central dome like Ickworth in minia-ture. From this he derived the inspiration for his opera, *The Jacobin*. In the opposite direction lies Zlonice: Dvořák gave the title of *The Bells of Zlonice* to his first symphony, perhaps in memory of the schoolmaster-organist there who did so much for him, and who also appears in *The Jacobin*. His overtures and much of his chamber music are full of Czech gaiety and Czech patriotism. His melodic gift was prodigious. But Stanford wrongs him in saying, 'He is a child of nature who did not stop to think, and said on paper anything which came into his head'. The melodies and rhythms of his country may have come bubbling up spontaneously, and sometimes he went on at great length; but his craftsmanship and his control of his material were never in question, save perhaps in his disappointing attempts at opera, none of which worked out satisfactorily.

A great advocate of the nationalist songs and choral works of Dvořák and other composers was Leoš Janáček, born on 3 July 1854 in the Moravian village of Hukvaldy. On the face of it

Janáček might be thought to have led a strictly academic life, suitable for a critic rather than for a creative artist. His father taught in the village school; Leoš studied music in a monastery school in Brno and then went on to a teachers' training college and to Prague Organ School; and was himself the founder and administrator of Brno Conservatoire and Organ School. As an avid collector of folk songs, many of them from the Wallachian region in which he was born, he could have been simply a worthy scholar enriching the store of material available for historical study. But, like Smetana and Dvořák, and even more like the later Hungarian, Bartók, he found his own imagination fired by these songs and dance music. He was quite apart from any of his contemporaries, and indeed from most of his successors, in his use of everyday speech rhythms in vocal music: Moravian and Slovak dialect and turns of phrase dictate the shape even of much of his orchestral music, replacing the classical development of themes by a strange counterpoint of concise, often abrupt little motifs. The full flowering of his unorthodox genius comes in his operas, where speech and song and orchestra are one. It is worth noting that even when deeply involved in the operas of his mature period he was still collecting, arranging and publishing cycles of folk songs for choir and solo voices.

Of the nine operas, the first two were somewhat predictable and folksy, and could be performed today only as historical curiosities. The third, in contrast, is a work of overwhelming power and conviction, and is performed more frequently than any of the others, all over the world. *Její Pastorkyňa*—'Her Step-daughter'—is usually known under the name of that step-daughter, *Jenůfa*. The girl lives in a village in the Javorník valley in Moravian Slovakia, and the story of the rival step-brothers who love her, of her illegitimate child and her puritanical step-mother known disparagingly to everyone as 'the church-woman', is a savage rural tragedy which it would be all too easy to parody. But this dark obverse of a sunlit village comedy such as *The Bartered Bride* is, like so many of Janáček's themes, based on truth—a truth transfigured and raised to a new plane by the composer's own commitment to the place and the people.

It seems incredible now that at first Prague National Theatre refused to stage the work. The first performance took place in Brno in January 1904, after which Janáček burnt the original manuscript and prepared a revised version. A large part of the work was written during the fatal illness of his daughter Olga, who foresaw her own end and insisted on his playing through the score a few days before she died. The tragedy which pulses through the music is echoed in the beautiful piano pieces written after her death, *Down an Overgrown Path*, where the owl hoots more and more insistently its prophecy of that death.

Real-life incidents in the real, observable countryside continued to draw Janáček. His song cycle, *The Diary of a Man who Disappeared*, was inspired by his reading in a Brno newspaper of a farmer's son who had vanished from his village with so little apparent reason that foul play was suspected. Then a diary found in his room revealed, in a sequence of poems, that he had secretly been in love with a gipsy girl who had borne his child and whom he must now follow. And what other composer has ever based an opera on a newspaper strip cartoon? For this is virtually what led to *The Cunning Little Vixen*.

Late in life Janáček had fallen in love with an attractive woman, Kamila Stösslová. It could have been an absurd romance, the last sentimentality of a man losing his powers; instead, it released from him a great flood of his finest music. There must have been some personal motivation in his choice of Čapek's *The Makropulos Matter* as the basis for an opera, with its theme of immortality and continuing passion. The same theme gave rise, in a different mood, to his musical tribute to the little vixen who had for some time been appearing in a cartoon strip about a forester's life. Janáček left the city and set to work in his country retreat in the woods. The story of animals mingling with human beings, of a captured vixen who walks on her hind legs when she wishes to play the fine human lady, and then reverts to a wild creature when hungry or in courtship, could be the sickliest sort of Walt Disney whimsy. But here again, Janáček escapes the obvious. The whole opera is a hymn to the brotherhood between man and nature, reaching an exquisite climax in the forester's final reminiscence . . . with a brief, skittish closing moment when a little frog sums up the whole meaning of the work in his denial that the forester has seen him before: 'No, not me, that was my grandpa—he used to tell me about you'.

In the last year of his life Janáček wrote, mainly at the village of his birth, Hukvaldy, his second string quartet. At first he dedicated it to Kamila as *Love Letters*, but then modified this to *Intimate Pages*. 'I am not', he said, 'opening my heart to idiots.' Again the Moravian idiom is strong, with melodies supported and interrupted by fragmentary little formations. It is full of passion and an incredible confidence—the work of a young man rather than one near death's door, and not merely self-pitying autobiography but a summation of all the things Janáček had worked towards throughout his creative career.

Other Czech composers such as Foerster, Suk and Fibich have been heard to a limited extent outside their own lands, but only the specialist would be able to say much about their work. One who travelled, figuratively as well as literally, was Bohuslav Martinů. Born in Polička in Eastern Bohemia on 8 December 1890, he spent his early years in an apartment high up in the church tower. These rooms have been renovated to look just as they did when he lived there. Martinů himself attributed the academic, neo-classical cast of his music to the remoteness he always felt in his eyrie: the view, he later explained, miniaturized people in the streets below, and he preferred to look out into the light and spaciousness of the countryside beyond the town. He studied violin and organ at the Prague Conservatoire, but without making any great mark. As a composer he was largely self-taught. For over ten years he worked off and on as a violinist in the Czech Philharmonic Orchestra, and then in 1923 went to Paris. French influences are clear in much of his work, and his dream-world opera *Julietta*, with its haunting bistro accordion theme, is based on a French play. Yet he returned home frequently, and there are folk music elements and references to Czech fairy tales and customs in many of his compositions, growing stronger as time went on. In 1940 he and his French wife fled to the United States, and in 1952 he became an American citizen; but he could never break the ties with his homeland, and among his vast output—he was one of the most prolific composers of this century—are a *Memorial to Lidice*, a lovely folk cantata called *The Opening of the Wells*, and many orchestral and piano pieces using Czech dances. In spite of his own comments on his dispassionate outlook, he wrote his sixth symphony in such an irregular and free-flowing style that he named it *Fantaisies Symphoniques*, and was delighted that it should be associated with Charles Munch and the Boston Symphony Orchestra, since 'I like Munch's spontaneous approach to music —the music takes shape in a free way, flowing. . . .'

Until 1918 Slovak music suffered the same official restrictions as the spoken word. The ablest scholars, few as they might be, were subjected to the greatest harassment and frequently had to emigrate. It was impossible to form orchestras, choral societies or chamber groups, since any social gathering of Slovaks was forbidden on the grounds that a rebellious conspiracy might result. Anyone gifted enough and stubborn enough to compose music would find neither audience nor players. Even the singing of Slovak songs aloud in public could result in dismissal from a job and even, if political implications were suspected, in imprisonment. The first Slovak opera, *Wieland the Smith*, was begun by J. L. Bella in Kremnica in 1880, but he found himself compelled to leave the country, and finished the work not to a Slovak text but to a German one—by Richard Wagner. The first performance in Bratislava took place only after the creation of Czechoslovakia. This same determined composer wrote a dramatic oratorio, *The Marriage of Jánošík*, based on ballads of a popular folk hero in the dashing outlaw tradition, which would have stood little chance of performance in its country of origin.

Still the old ways were not allowed to die out altogether. Slovak melodies and rhythms crossed the border into Moravia and Bohemia, and struck sympathetic resonances there. For those forced to remain at home, the native music was sung only in private or, at best, at remote village celebrations where it could be considered quaint and harmless. Here, as in Bohemia during the worst times, much indigenous lore was kept alive by village priests and schoolmasters. One schoolmaster-organist and his wife, herself a pianist, were the first teachers of their son

Eugen Suchoň, born in 1908 at Pezinok in the wine-growing region of Western Slovakia. By the time he grew up there was freedom to sing and study and compose. After studying composition and the piano at Bratislava Academy he went in 1930 to Prague, and in 1933 returned to Bratislava as professor of composition. The following year he wrote an overture and incidental music to a play by Stodola, *King Svatopluk*, seeing its possibilities as an opera but feeling himself not yet equal to the task.

In 1941 a modern Slovak novel about love and violence in a mountain community caught his attention, and this time he had the confidence to start. Conditions were hardly more propitious for creative work than they had been under the Magyars, and the opera was not completed until after the defeat of the Nazis. Its first performance was in 1949, soon after which it won a state prize, acclaim in Prague and in Austria, and was recorded. *Krútňava*, 'The Whirlpool', has in its portrayal of village life and drama all the intensity of Janáček, and several parallels in the plot. Again we have a pregnant step-daughter and again two men jealously vying for her hand. Again there is a murder. Again a fatalistic reconciliation at the end. But the use of speech rhythms is different, and the orchestral timbre quite fresh. Suchoň spreads himself far more in intricate ensembles than was usual with Janáček. The most riveting part of the opera is the third scene, in which a Slovak wedding ceremony is carried through against the sexually fraught ritual and dancing, with mounting turmoil in the music and mounting tension on stage, all focused on the bedecked bride at the centre of the whirlpool.

Now Suchoň went ahead with *Svatopluk*, turning from rural to historical drama just as Smetana had once turned from historical to rural, then back again. The story is that of the Great Moravian Emperor who banished Methodius' pupils and collaborators and invited Latin priests in to take their place, treated with a freedom which brings it closer to legend than to known facts. It ends with the ruthless monarch facing the knowledge that there are others more ruthless than he, and dying as his own sons come to blows before him. Filled with re-creations of old chants, bagpipe music and blends of other ancient instruments, the opera asserts the immortality of the Slav character and ethos. It seems, on a few hearings, to lack the cohesion and intensity of *Krútňava*; but one would need to hear it many more times, and to see it in a worthy production, before blundering into a possibly false judgment.

Of modern Czech, Moravian and Slovak composers, few are heard in this country, and it is hard to detect any developing pattern. The best way to listen to them is in their own country. There is no way of guaranteeing that a visit to Brno or Bratislava will coincide with an interesting concert; but there is always something interesting going on at the Prague Spring festival, and all year round there is the chance of stumbling on something new, unexpected, and provocative.

Moravia

'My mother told me never to have anything to do with Czech girls', recalls a Moravian friend of mine. 'She said all the Czechs are an unfeeling, aggressive lot.' Nevertheless he married a Bohemian girl, and when I last saw him appeared to be bearing up tolerably well.

Among their Bohemian neighbours the Moravians do have a reputation for taking things more easily and of being more naturally relaxed and sociable. Their emotional climate is warmer, their hospitality more instinctive and immediate. Generalizations on such a subject can be risky: a dozen contradictions will be offered in as many seconds; but having at one time travelled at a leisurely pace through parts of Moravia with a Czech friend much addicted to Southern Bohemia, and watched him falling reluctantly under the spell, I will add my testimony and take the consequences.

Moravia is enclosed and sub-divided by a number of linked and intersecting mountain ranges, often higher than they seem when approached over gently rising, undulating country. To the west it is divided from the Bohemian plain and river valleys by the Bohemian-Moravian Highlands, a lumpy plateau rising at its highest point to a heavily wooded ridge. The rivers Sázava, Svratka, Jihlava and Dyje all rise in these uplands, and although the soil has always been too poor to support extensive agriculture this has its advantages to the holidaymaker in the provision of mile upon mile of unspoilt forest and vale, a wealth of rich trout streams, and plentiful game. Since the Second World War a number of small communities have been built up into brisk industrial centres, but without creating too many eyesores.

Continuing on a north-eastern arc we come to the much higher Jeseníks—tempting walking country, with marked paths up slopes and over ridges, mountain chalets and inns, lookout towers and peaks which are lookout towers in themselves. Gradually the slopes sink across the Odra Hills and then rise again to the broken ranges of the Beskydy Mountains and the Javorníks, roughly enclosing the region of Wallachia. The border between Moravia and Slovakia runs down here and on through the White Carpathians until picked up by the valley of the river Morava.

Smaller ranges and outcroppings cut across the centre of the province. One of the most interesting geological phenomena is the confused stretch of cliff, cavern and water running for fifteen miles or so through the Moravian Karst north of Brno. Within this labyrinth are small grottoes and vast cathedrals with columns of limestone and intricate stalactite chandeliers. The Catherine Cavern is a good hundred yards long, and between sixty and a hundred feet high. Steps and corridors slope and twist from one vault to another, more ornate than the most extravagant baroque church. Emerging suddenly below a precipice we are at the bottom of the Macocha gorge, a hundred and forty yards below its sheer edge. This cleft is in fact a colossal ruined chamber, all that remains of a cavern whose roof fell in during some prehistoric upheaval. Further tunnels and galleries lead to the underground river Punkva, along which boats glide to a sequence of widening lakes. Near the lace-making centre of Sloup are more holes and caves, and below a ruined castle near Ostrov is the so-called Dungeon Cave which in the grim past really was used as a ready-made dungeon.

For all the leisurely charm of its people, and the extent and variety of its rural scenery, Moravia contrives at the same time to be one of the most prosperous industrial regions of the entire country, with its own Black Country around Ostrava and Vítkovice, extensive factories at Gottwaldov, new developments in what could once have been called the backwoods, and of course the chemical and engineering works of Brno, home of the Bren gun.

It has become a platitude to speak of Brno as 'the Manchester of Czechoslovakia', largely because of its rapid eighteenth-century expansion as a textile centre. I trust Mancunians will not be too offended if I say that this does Brno an injustice. Thickets of factory chimneys and trailers of smoke may give a forbidding impression at a distance, but the centre of Brno is bright and spacious, with tree-lined streets, wide boulevards, market squares of invigorating breadth and airiness, a pedestrian shopping precinct, and an all-pervading sense of prosperity. Gardens and shrubs around the modern theatre are trim and not informally straggling, as in the Bohemian tradition. Nothing is cramped. Even in the most populous suburbs, old and new, there is room to breathe. Many cafés and restaurants have terraces and colourful awnings in the Italian, French and Danish style.

Human settlement in the Svratka valley and in caves of the sheltering hills has been traced as far back as the Stone Age. Celtic and Teutonic tribes had homes and burial grounds in the environs before the Slavs began to establish their Great Moravian Empire. A fort to protect trade routes was built on what is now the cathedral hill of Petrov, later captured by Polish invaders who wrested all Moravia from the Přemyslides until Břetislav I managed finally to turn the tables. Břetislav constructed a royal castle; but in the time of Otakar II the strategic superiority of Špilberk hill was recognized and a new castle arose here, the site of the old one being presented to the Church. In the time of Charles IV the more recent building was the residence of his brother, who planted orchards and vineyards on the flanks of the hill.

But Špilberk's associations are mainly with unhappier matters than fruit and wine. Bravely resisting Hussites, Turks, and then the Habsburgs, it fell eventually to the latter and began its career as one of the most feared prisons in all the Austrian dominions. Swedes captured during the sieges and battles of the Thirty Years' War were flung into its dungeons. Criminals mingled with Hungarian rebels and other political opponents of the Habsburgs. Napoleon's troops captured the castle and levelled its fortifications, but it still served as a prison. Nineteenth-century Italian and Polish patriots spent their time between dank cells and torture chambers. In the First World War, Czech radicals took their turn. In the Second World War the Nazis used it as a staging post on the way to their extermination camps.

Now Špilberk is a chilling museum of torture implements and macabre history. Here men were fettered to die under the maddening drip of water; here was the rack; here a memorial hall to the Italian *carbonari*; here the cells where women were bricked up; and here the guillotine chamber which the Nazis were preparing for mass executions when the end of the war put an end to their schemes. I was shown round by a man who could point to the wall against which he had been chained for an eternity, not knowing from one hour to the next whether he would suddenly be added to the indiscriminate death list. His philosophical attitude could have arisen only from his deep pleasure in being still alive.

In one room there is an exhibition of grotesque photographic montages showing Hitler, Goering and their associates in absurd postures and juxtapositions. They were the work of Helmut Harzfeld, a German who during the First World War changed his named to John Heartfield in protest against his country's campaigns against England. A fervent communist, he produced films for U.F.A. after the war, travelled in the Soviet Union, and in 1938 settled in Prague. At the time of Munich the Nazis asked for him to be handed over; but he managed to escape to England, and did not return to Germany until 1950.

It is a relief to turn one's back on the monstrous gaol and look out from its walls over the city; or to take the taste away in its excellent wine restaurant.

The older town of Brno grew up between the cathedral hill and the church of St James. Work started on the church and on conversion of the Romanesque basilica of SS Peter and Paul simultaneously in the thirteenth century, and there is a legend that the builders had a bet as to who would finish first. St James' won the race, so its master mason set up the statue of an angel with its back turned contemptuously towards Petrov.

The cathedral was badly damaged by fire during the Swedish attack on the town, and its numerous restorations have left it with a generally baroque ambience, plus an overlay of early twentieth-century Gothic, emphasized by the two towers. Tales of the Swedish siege include one of a bell-ringer who, having heard that the frustrated enemy commander had vowed to call off the operation and go away if he had not forced the town to surrender by noon on a certain day, rang the midday peal an hour early and just averted an all-out assault on the starving inhabitants.

St James' church has the highest tower in Brno, and three high naves soaring to floridly reticulated vaulting. This dates from a Gothic restoration early in the sixteenth century. The church escaped the addition of baroque trimmings, so that its interior retains clearer outlines and proportions than we are used to in this part of the world: instead of the heavy columns, gilt, and confusion of saints in a dark setting, the altar is backed by a white reredos which lights up the whole place. There are gleaming, polished pews with elaborately carved ends, and the stone pulpit is carved with reliefs of the Nativity, Christ preaching in the temple, and the Ascension. A remarkable organ in black and silver is mantled in a fine lacework of black tracery, falling in folds like a mantilla.

Both the Old Town Hall and the New Town Hall have been formed from an amalgamation of different buildings from different periods, offering the student of architecture a wonderful opportunity to identify each constituent and trace the joins. In the same way, a bishop's palace and chapel have been linked with the palace of the Dietrichsteins to create the Moravian Museum, with exhibitions of natural history and archaeology, and a picture gallery containing works by, among others, Rubens and Cranach. A one-time Institute for Ladies houses a representative collection of Moravian folk art. Within the museum courtyard is the baroque Mercury fountain, and in the market-place beyond the Dietrichstein palace a resplendent fountain by Fischer von Erlach representing Cerberus and symbolic figures of the continents grouped about a rock—four continents, since Australia was not yet known.

In the older town below Špilberk is the Augustinian monastery, almost unspoilt since it was founded in the fourteenth century, which Gregor Mendel entered as a monk in 1843. He taught science in the monastery school, and carried out experiments in the crossing of peas and other plants, and of bees, and propounded his now famous laws of heredity and determinant genes. When he became abbot he had no time to pursue his researches, and it was not until after his death that other researchers along the same lines discovered how much he had already established.

It was in this same monastery that Janáček first studied music. He, at least, has suffered no posthumous neglect. The Brno opera house is named after him, and there is a Janáček academy of music and drama in what used to be the German gymnasium.

The permanent trade fair grounds bring thousands of foreign businessmen to the city. This international atmosphere and the provision of guidebooks and signs in a multitude of languages makes it easy—if tiring—to find one's way around. A quick survey of the fair buildings is easiest from the spiral stairway and gallery of the glass tower. There is a Czech Grand Prix every August around a track with more than thirty hairpin bends, and during the winter months ice skating and ice hockey matches take place in the Winter Stadium.

From Brno a comprehensive round tour of Moravia could well begin in a south-westerly direction, heading into the valley of the river Dyje beyond its confluence with the Svratka.

The first important town is Znojmo, an industrial centre retaining enough of its historic core to merit protection as a state reserve. It is also a good point of departure for the holiday region of the hills, the river, and the great Vranov reservoir. Archaeological finds indicate human settlement on this spot from very early times, and it is known that substantial fortifications existed in the time of the Great Moravian Empire. Břetislav installed a royal castle, and there are still some impressively solid remains of medieval ramparts and bastions. Znojmo has a fine range of Romanesque, Gothic and baroque churches and chapels, including the eleventh-century rotunda of St Catherine in which a rare cycle of frescoes was uncovered and restored after the Second World War, comprising contemporary representations of various members of the Přemyslide dynasty. In more recent history a local man laid claim to have invented a lightning conductor a few years before Benjamin Franklin. But the town's most widely known product is the sweet-sour pickle. Of all its canned and bottled foods this is the one most frequently seen on any Czech plate. Small and larger gherkins are sliced to garnish plates of ham or to provide a cool accompaniment to some hot dish; twisted into rosettes, they sit in the middle of an array of salami; nudge aside a sliver of cheese, and there will be a smudge of the familiar green beneath it. It is difficult to imagine any meal, in a private home or in a restaurant, without the tang of the young cucumber as an ingredient.

Vranov castle occupies a precipitous upthrust of rock above its dam lake. This crag has been an obvious refuge from the twelfth century on, but earlier strongholds have been softened over the years by piecemeal conversions to a residential château. The most enduring influence is that of the Viennese baroque master, Fischer von Erlach. Seen from the waters below, the predominant feature is the oval hall which, surging forward like the blunt prow of a ship, seems detached from the rest of the complex physically and in spirit. Within, it has sequences of murals on mythological subjects.

The reservoir was constructed in the 1930s, drowning the village of Bítov. A new village of that name was substituted in the vale of a little tributary. Bítov castle was safe from the waters, as it has been safe from many other threats since Břetislav built it in the eleventh century. Like Vranov, it stands on a dizzying headland, but this one is if anything more impressive: the river cuts round it on three sides in a tight hairpin bend, so that the only approach is through the woods along the promontory. Even so, fear of the encroaching Turks in the sixteenth century led to a heavier fortification of walls and towers, upon which a neo-Gothic transformation was imposed in the last century. Boats ply the length of the reservoir from Vranov to Bítov, and there are holidaymakers and well-rewarded fishermen in clusters along its beautiful banks.

Another state reservation town is Slavonice in the Bohemian-Moravian Highlands, close to the Austrian border where for centuries it guarded a trade route between Vienna and Prague.

Its Renaissance frontages are decorated lavishly with mythological painting and ornamental graffiti of great intricacy, as if each were in artistic competition with its neighbour. The characteristic tunnel-like entrance with barrel vaulting, and usually an inner staircase leading up to the first floor, is known as a mázhaus.

There are many more of these entrance halls in the loveliest of all such reservations a few miles on where, set within a girdle of ponds limpidly reflecting its towers and spires and glowing colours, is Telč.

The long, uneven main square is incomparable. On three sides it has extended vistas of graceful arcades surmounted by Renaissance upper storeys, white and green and ochre, with ornamental mouldings and sculpted and castellated gables and cornices. Behind these sumptuous burghers' houses are courtyards and gardens, and a protective outer ring of smaller dwellings fringing the water. The fourth side of the square is closed off by the Rožmberk château and two churches, one a former Jesuit foundation, the other the parish church of St James, from the late fourteenth century.

Telč was a royal town early in the Middle Ages, protected by linking its surrounding ponds into a wide, meandering moat. Within this was a girdle of town walls and bastions, of which a fair part still survives. In 1339 the Vítkovci Lords of the Rose acquired the royal estate from John of Luxembourg and remained here until 1604. It was not until the sixteenth century that the castle took on its present dimensions, expanding around the original feudal stronghold. Instead of a fort it became a well-furnished palace, with some of its walls and ceilings flamboyantly decorated to rival the external graffiti of the town's façades. Today one enters by way of an arcaded courtyard with a gallery above; and beyond, through an ornamental iron gateway, is a trim Renaissance garden with an attractive cloister along one side.

The surrounding countryside with its meres and woods provides a worthy setting for Telč. There are the usual marked trails, bordered by a profusion of wild flowers such as we rarely see in England now that zealous crop sprayers have done their worst. And here, as in many other locations, you will find your-self lured off the path by wild raspberries and wild strawberries.

North of Telč is the industrial town of Jihlava on the river of that name, with a little suburb of summerhouses beside the water. At one time it had the richest known sources of silver in Europe, and minted its own coins until the time of Wenceslas II, who granted a monopoly to Kutná Hora. With the rise of Kutná Hora, and the destruction of its own mines by an earthquake, the townsfolk turned eventually to textile manufacture. Today Jihlava is noted for its Army ice hockey team, the best in Czecho-slovakia. The Czechs are proud of their position as one of the top three European countries in this sport, and the team which they enter for international tournaments comes mainly from the Jihlava players.

In these uplands there are still scattered hamlets of wooden houses in the old style, when living conditions on the infertile slopes were harsh and a family's furniture, crockery and cloth-ing were usually hand-made on the premises. Local craftsman-ship has still not died out. But among such communities are several which in recent decades have changed their way of life and prospered from industry and tourism. The most striking example is Žd'ár near the source of the Sázava, which flows westward from here to join the Vltava between Prague and Slapy. Since the end of the Second World War its population has increased more than tenfold. The old town, centred on the church of St Prokop and the town square with its Renaissance town hall and plague column, retains many of its timbered houses; but it bustles with the very twentieth-century life of its foundry and engineering works. The castle was built on the ruins of a monastery razed during the Hussite wars, and adapted to the baroque taste by Giovanni Santini early in the eighteenth century. It has a book museum with collections of hymnals and illuminated manuscripts, and examples of printing techniques from Gutenberg to modern times.

We can take in two far more grandiose castles on our way. Pernštejn rears up in a jumble of sheer walls and steeply pitched roofs, angled buttresses and balconies and overhangs, segments of building packed in at every angle and on every level. For more than three hundred years it was the home of the Pern-štejns, who began with a round tower on the easily defensible rock in the thirteenth century and then packed inner and outer baileys and watch-towers around it. For several generations they held official rank equivalent to that of governor of the province, and acquired comfortable and more accessible residences in many towns under their sway; but the castle seems to have been favoured as their true family home and not merely a baronial refuge in time of strife. Gradually they inserted more civilized living accommodation into its defences. Today it displays collections of weapons and hunting trophies, and furniture of various periods.

Bouzov has the appearance of one of the more outrageous Rhine castles or a film set, and in this case first impressions are not too wide of the mark. Once one of a defensive chain of fortresses which passed through the hands of many noble Czech families, it was acquired in 1699 by the Order of Teutonic Knights. This crusading brotherhood, originating in the twelfth century, had long since lost its religious character and been re-fashioned into a sort of masonic order. Napoleon tried to suppress it, but it lingered on, and one may assume that its hazily sentimental character was responsible for the sentimentally picturesque trimmings added to Bouzov at the end of the last century and the beginning of this. Candle-snuffer towers, dog-tooth gable and copper cupola invite the eye and mind to picture mail-clad knights galloping splendidly over the bridge and through the gateways to a rapturous welcome and perhaps a carillon from behind the clock; but they didn't go in for that sort of thing at the turn of the century, except in the play-acting of wistful imagination. Still, if Bohemia can have its make-believe Windsor at Hluboká, why shouldn't Moravia allow itself a cosy little Neuschwanstein here?

There is a grimmer parallel with Bohemian history close at hand. The village of Javoříčko, like Lidice, was razed to the ground, and most of its men were massacred. A monument, usually heaped with flowers, stands on the edge of a square with a tranquil background of woodland and rising hills. Paths through the trees lead to caves discovered just before the war.

Other people executed in the district were scores of suspects rounded up during the seventeenth-century outbreak of witch-hunting hysteria. Accused of practising the black arts in the Jeseník hills, they were brought before inquisitors in Šumperk and burnt at the stake. Today Šumperk, a busy textile town, is a favourite point of departure for trails over those same hills. Peter's Rocks, supposed venue of many a witches' sabbath, can be reached by car trip to the inn below the summit, followed by a five-mile walk.

There are several beautifully situated spas in the region. Alkaline springs were discovered in the woods of Karlova Studanká at the end of the eighteenth century, today used mainly by workers from the Ostrava mines. Jeseník was known as Gräfenberg when German settlers exploited its ore mines, and five miles away Bad Gräfenberg grew up as a spa early in the nineteenth century, founded by a local farmer with a strong faith in nature cures. Another farmer with similar views established Dolní Lipová spa, and there are sulphur springs and a convalescent centre for polio victims at Velké Losiny. All these attractive places look even more attractive if one is in good health and capable of exploring the interwoven trails and successive ridges, tinted in the distance with varying intensities of cloudy green shading almost into blue. The forestry warden for the region was at one time the composer Dittersdorf, who divided his time between outdoor duties and the composition and performance of light operas and chamber music in the ducal service at Javorník. The castle in whose small theatre many of these works were first heard now has a museum in his memory.

The northern sector of Moravia should, strictly speaking, be referred to as Silesia. This much disputed territory has changed hands many times in its history, and the rich coalfields and ore mines on both sides of the Moravian–Polish border have always been a coveted prize. An integral part of Poland in the eleventh century, it later seceded and was split into several dukedoms, which welcomed German settlers and then accepted Bohemian suzerainty in the fourteenth century. When the Habsburgs took Bohemia they included Silesia among their winnings, but lost a large part of it to Prussia in 1740. The part remaining in Habsburg hands was included in the new Czechoslovakia after 1918, while the Prussian section was restored to re-born Poland. The border between the two countries seems too obviously a political rather than a geographically natural one: if there is a barrier, it is the one formed by the Odra hills to the south and, curling in around the south-east, the much higher Beskydy ranges, cutting Silesia off from Moravia rather than from Poland. One town, Těšín, has a foot on either side of the frontier.

There are lovely stretches of pine and birch woods, and a region of primeval forest in the region, caves and trout streams, some health resorts, and lingering echoes of folk song and dance such as Janáček caught in his *Lach Dances* and *Songs from Hukvaldy*; but it is as a region of heavy industry that we usually think of it. Ostrava, founded by a thirteenth-century bishop of Olomouc to guard the northern approaches to Moravia, grew rapidly after the discovery of huge coal deposits and is now the third largest city in the republic. In fact, like so many industrial conurbations, it spread out so haphazardly and so fast that many of its streets went beyond the pit workings, whose mounds of slag now thrust up like blackened Aztec temples from the middle of housing estates and shopping areas. Engineering plants, two huge iron and steel works, and all the clutter that goes with such things have been rammed or tipped in around the mines.

There is lighter industry in Opava. Textile and food processing factories do not produce such dark clouds as those of gasworks and coking plants. But the centre of this pleasant town, clean and bright as it is, retains only a few relics of its past, much of the original character having been trampled under by the destructive fighting of 1945. The museum was destroyed and then rebuilt after the war. Of the town hall, only the clock tower remains. Opava was the administrative capital of Silesia under the Bohemian crown, and later, as Troppau, of the dukedom which remained under Austrian control. The Diet used to meet in a former monastery, and it was to this building that the rulers of Austria, Prussia and Russia came in 1820 to confer with Metternich on joint measures against radicals and revolutionaries. At this meeting it was solemnly agreed that no concessions should be made to commoners who impertinently wished to restrict the power of kings.

As with several Yorkshire industrial towns of similar size, escape into the countryside is swift and easy from here. The Moravice valley is tempting, and within its parkland setting the château of Hradec is in comfortable walking distance. On the site of an earlier Přemyslide castle, now an enclosed residential rectangle with an oddly detached neo-Gothic tower, it is much visited by local couples because of its attractive wedding hall.

Nový Jičín has a very specialized trade of its own. Its main factory makes hats, and in the castle is a museum displaying the hatter's craft and examples of headgear and hair-styles through the ages.

There appears to be a plentiful supply of two other commodities hereabouts: talent, and wooden houses.

Janáček was born at Hukvaldy; Sigmund Freud at Příbor; Mendel at Hynčice; and Palacký at Hodslavice, where his old home has become the Palacký Memorial. It stands close to a timbered church, typical of the rural communities on whose terrain the only thing not in short supply was wood. In Štramberk, below the slim beacon of the tower rising from the castle ruins, narrow streets carry a jumble of largely timbered houses up the hill. Velké Karlovice has another church in the same style and several other buildings. Rožnov and Valašské Meziříčí have open-air museums and ethnographical collections preserving examples of folk art and a variety of wooden, shingled cottages, town houses and farmhouses—even a complete town hall—collected from the Wallachian region and reassembled on site in the manner of the better known Scandinavian prototypes. Valašské Meziříčí also has a finger or two in another old craft: its textile plant specializes in repairing old tapestries and creating new ones to special order.

In the neighbouring hills, rich in tales of Robin Hood outlaws and brigands, a cable car takes one to Pustevny, where some of the brightest wooden buildings are to be found: painted verandahs vie with sunburst gable decorations and incised roofs, some topped with shingled spires and flourishes reminiscent of Chinese temple spires set on a Swiss mountain chalet. Attractive as they are, these are artificial re-creations by an architect at the end of the nineteenth century.

Other legends of the hills include that of Radegast, a god of the primitive Slavs to whom sacrifices had to be made on Radhošt mountain. A scowling statue has been set up on the supposed site of his altar, but his influence has been cancelled out by a chapel higher up the slope dedicated to SS Cyrill and Methodius.

For those interested in more recent artifacts, Kopřivnice has a museum of veteran and vintage cars as well as the modern Tatra automobile factory, and near the railway workshops of Studenká is a museum of railway coaches. At Rožnov, in addition to its folklore collections, there is an astronomical observatory.

Vsetín, a busy industrial town with good road and main line railway connections to the west and into Slovakia, may be of no great historic or picturesque interest but is a good place from which to set off into the hills or out on to the Haná plain; and it has an admirable modern hotel of which I have the most agreeable memories. One delightful train ride can be taken along the branch line through a string of timbered villages and hamlets in the Becva valley, ending at Velké Karlovice.

If we travel instead towards the plain, we find a place associated with a national delicacy which has not so far been mentioned in these pages. At Vizovice is the best known distillery for the commercial production of slivovice. This fiery, fruity spirit, made from plums and smelling unmistakably of rotten plums the moment you open the bottle, is indigenous not only to Bohemia, Moravia and Slovakia but also to Yugoslavia and other regions across this segment of Europe. Legally or illegally, every grandmother has her own pet recipe, and I have been treated to many a glass of bathtub slivovice superior to the mass-produced brands. Addicts can grow as angry in their discussion of relative merits as do the connoisseurs of Scotch whisky. Whatever the source, it is not a drink to be steadily swilled in large quantities: it goes down best at the beginning of a meal with a glass of chilled mineral water on the side.

A few miles on, and we are approaching a widespread stain of red brick: red brick housing estates with little gardens, a red brick hotel, a red brick hospital, the interminable red brick wall of a red brick factory. It is all part of the well-equipped domain of the employees of Svit, the huge local shoe complex once known as Batá; the town is Gottwaldov, once Zlin. Batá was a self-made man who, starting in his own small workshop, built up the boot and shoe combine until by the mid-thirties it was turning out a couple of hundred thousand pairs a day. Following a tradition established before the First World War by Johann Liebig, a textile worker who became a millionaire while at the same time caring for his family of employees with company houses, sickness benefit, discount shops and social activities, the Batá organization attracted people from the country into industry by offering enlightened working conditions and the chance of life in what could truly be called a garden city. The factories have expanded to take in manufacture of tools and machinery needed in the footwear trade; there are tanneries, and makers of other leather goods. Batá himself was killed in an air crash, and the trade name still used in the West has been abandoned on its home ground. With such a flourishing business, Zlin had its own prewar airfield, but the climate was so misty that after the war it was decided to move the runways to Holešov.

Klement Gottwald, after whom the town was re-named, was born not so many miles away in the bright little town of Vyškov, where today a statue of Lenin stands on the spot which in similar provincial communities is often occupied by a crumbling, neglected saint.

From Holešov we can climb back up the hills or browse along the valley ending in the straggling little village of Rusava. This, like its cousins in the Rožnov direction, was once noted for its wooden cottages; but now most of them have been modernized and the timber is smart, varnished, gleaming. Holiday chalets cling to the forest slopes. A poor region within living memory, it is now a place of new houses and bright colours, with well-kept gardens full of flowers. Camp sites and parking lots nestle in the clefts of miniature mountain ranges, varying from clearings in the trees to large enclosures with huts sleeping up to four people, complete with kitchenettes, showers, and a communal restaurant.

Below these untilled slopes lies one of the most fertile expanses in the land, the Haná plain. Watered by the river Morava, this has always been a rich producer of grain and sugar beet, feeding the local mills and sugar industry. It had the most prosperous pre-war farms and, I was assured by an envious friend, now has the most prosperous farm managers. From early days a pious Catholic region, its vast fields are dotted with little churches on hummocks—as if our own Fens were to sprout an onion dome or perky spire at every slight rise of ground, a wayside shrine at every crossroads. Closer inspection reveals many of the church towers sporting little balustraded galleries near the top. Harvest festival is celebrated every year in full folk costume, with a special ceremony in the amphitheatre at Náměšt' na Hané, whose castle also has a regional museum and a collection of ornate coaches once belonging to the wealthy prelates of Olomouc.

Olomouc and Kroměříž are the two most lavishly endowed towns of the plain. Today Olomouc is kept alive by its machine tool works, salt and sugar mills, and food and chocolate factories; but its historic centre is protected as a town reservation. A bishopric established in 1063 later was elevated to an archbishopric. There are Romanesque remains of a Přemyslide castle and others of the same period embedded in the walls of the heavily restored cathedral of St Wenceslas. Beethoven's Mass in D, the *Missa Solemnis*, was written for the installation of an archbishop in this cathedral. Everywhere we find noble fountains with mythological subjects, cheek by jowl with traces of the sumptuous ecclesiastical past—churches and a monastery, bishops' and canons' residences, and the archbishop's palace. The church of St Maurice, seeking some unique splendour, had a colossal organ installed in the eighteenth century with a veritable plantation of pipes: some authorities estimate more than two thousand, some say about ten thousand; but I confess I have not counted them. Secular history has left its usual clumsy marks on Olomouc. The last Přemyslide, Wenceslas III, was assassinated in the deanery while assembling troops for his campaign against a Polish usurper. For long the capital of Moravia, the town relinquished that privilege to Brno in the same year that the Swedes descended on it and captured it. Hitler's bullies were here, and during the fighting in 1945 the sixteenth-century astronomical clock on the town hall was so badly damaged that years of painstaking work were needed to get it going again, after which it was redecorated by a modern Czech painter, Svolinský. The old university was transferred to Brno in the eighteenth century, but there is now a Palacký University named in honour of the historian and statesman who spoke out on behalf of 'the lands of the crown of Wenceslas' when the Austrian court fled to Olomouc and he, with other members of the Austrian parliament, settled down in Kroměříž to thrash out a new constitution.

Soon after the suppression of the 1848 riots in Prague, Windischgrätz had had to turn his attention to a far more serious rebellion in Vienna. The decision of the absolutist monarchs at Opava not to countenance liberalism in any shape whatsoever was being flouted. Nationalist feeling ran hand in hand with the call to abolish repressive feudal laws. The feeble-minded Emperor Ferdinand was hurried out of Vienna by his advisers and taken to Olomouc, then known as Olmütz. He was persuaded to abdicate, and in the archbishop's palace handed over power to his young nephew Franz Josef. Reformers had great hopes of their new ruler at first, especially as there was talk of his pacifying the Czechs by having himself crowned king of Bohemia in Prague—talk which came to nothing. And while the imperial court was at Olomouc, the recently elected Constituent Assembly was also ordered to leave strife-torn Vienna and continue its deliberations on a new constitution at Kroměříž, or Kremsier.

Ironically, the man so revered today for his advocacy of Czech nationalism, Palacký, was at no stage in favour of complete independence. Rightly concerned about the growth of a German empire which would use the influential German population of the Czech lands as a lever to take over those lands in due course, he saw a strong Habsburg confederation as the best safeguard. What he sought was greater autonomy for different national groups within that sprawling, insensitive autocracy; yet from time to time even he had to realize that this involved a contradiction in terms. Many of his own colleagues disapproved of such sub-divisions, not wishing the 'three gems in the crown' of St Wenceslas—the gems of Bohemia, Moravia and Silesia—to be splintered and shared out among infiltrating Germans, Poles or anyone else. On the other hand, delegates representing a minority as powerful as the Germans were not keen on submitting to a direct Czech administration.

In the end the draft constitution managed to declare itself in favour of strong imperial authority while at the same time asserting, 'All political rights emanate from the people'. This was announced at the beginning of March 1849. A few days later, on the orders of the Prime Minister, Schwarzenberg, soldiers were stationed in the assembly hall and in the streets. Word reached the assembly that those of its members who were suspected of having played any part in the Vienna disturbances were to be arrested; whereupon many of them fled. The cynical Schwarzenberg produced an alternative constitution, which was of little merit in itself and in any case was hardly needed now that the revolutionaries were being successfully brought under control. The new emperor and his counsellors favoured a return to absolutism. On 31 December 1851 it was decreed that the Kroměříž constitution, which had never actually been implemented, was null and void.

Kroměříž still has a most opulent air. Its main square is large enough to permit the visitor a slow, 360-degree turn to take in a radiant panorama of patrician houses, flowers in large ornamental urns, clock tower, copper spire, baroque dome, and erratic rooftops. Towering above one corner is a square outpost of the château, and behind it, set slightly askew, a square tower topped by an octagon and then topped yet again by a bulbous flourish in copper.

The whole town was in the fief of the bishops and, later, archbishops of Olomouc. After widespread destruction by the Swedes during the Thirty Years' War, including the firing of the cathedral and the castle, Bishop Karel of Liechtenstein summoned Italian masters from Venice to build him a new palace. As work progressed a large park was also laid out, showing traces of English influence and some of Versailles. It contains a rondel of formal flowerbeds divided by cropped miniature hedges, fountains and pools, a music pavilion set at the convergence of paths through the grounds, and beside the flower garden a long colonnade lined with statues of mythological figures.

Over the years this residence has been occupied by sixty bishops and twelve archbishops. As loyal supporters of feudal monarchy they were granted wide-ranging privileges, and became the wealthiest lords in Moravia. Until 1870 the tenants working their lands had to serve in their militia when called on to do so. They collected paintings and engravings and books, and Bishop Karel was so rich that he could outbid the emperor himself. Much of the library was looted during the Swedish campaigns, and some by devious means found its way into the Vatican library; but collecting was resumed in 1694 by the indefatigable Karel, and this has largely survived in spite of another fire in 1752, this time not due to enemy action. In 1945 the Nazis set fire to the tower.

Many distinguished visitors have stayed here: among them Charles IV, Maria Theresa, and Tsar Alexander III. Hospitality must always have been bounteous, and the setting worthy of it. A rococo reception room is hung with Bohemian crystal chandeliers and has a fine five-part Venetian mirror. Scores of stuffed heads stare out from the walls of the hunters' room. There are florid murals, and one entire ceiling is a sybaritic fantasy by Maulpertsch, who was also responsible for the famous ceiling of the Philosophers' Hall in Strahov monastery, Prague. The hall of the Feudal or Vassals' Court is walled in artificial marble, with the bishop's throne in the centre of one side facing an ornamental dock with a single chair in it. Inlays of parquet flooring differ between one room and another. In the picture gallery is the most valuable painting in Czechoslovakia, Titian's *Flaying of Marsyas*. There are works by Cranach, Veronese and the Brueghels, and copies of Rubens and Titian. Some pictures, including Van Dyck's study of Charles I and Henrietta Maria, were bought from Oliver Cromwell when he sold off the contents of certain English royal residences.

South-west of Kroměříž, beside the river Litava, is the small town or large village of Slavkov. Its approaches are lined with clean little cottages, most of them only single-storey. They all look too quiet and humble to support the large baroque château, or even the imposingly classical white church with its Greek portal and Corinthian pillars. This church of the Resurrection is in essence a very formal, high, dignified hall in white stone and plaster, its frontage crowned by a life-size relief of the dismissal of the apostles. Inside are six stone reliefs set in large niches in the north and south walls. High above the niches, six large windows shed light into the otherwise enclosed interior. There are three pulpits, altars in red Salzburg marble, and on the main altar a cupola supported by eight columns.

Behind the church a modern housing estate is tucked discreetly away. To one side, as we cross the road, we come under the shadow of a once proud château slightly humbled by the entrance to a wine tavern in one wing, and a fruit and vegetable store in its vaults. The mansion was built for the Kounic or Kaunitz family during the early part of the eighteenth century. Its original plan was amended as work progressed, and it finished up rather like a Celtic cross with a thoroughfare cut through the centre of its two short arms. When open—the word *adaptace* featured prominently when I was last in the vicinity—it offers a good picture gallery and one among many local exhibitions of Napoleonic material. For it was here that the Holy Roman Emperor Francis II, Emperor Francis I of Austria, stayed on the night before defeat and that Napoleon came to dictate his terms after victory in the Battle of the Three Emperors.

His plans for an invasion of England wrecked by the battle of Trafalgar, Napoleon had turned his full force against opponents on the Continent and, determined to force a direct confrontation on the Russians and Austrians, by late November 1805 reached the Moravian hamlet of Kandie. Here he spent a few days working out his tactics. On 1 December an opening skirmish in the village of Telnice was the prelude to a battle next day near Slavkov, then known and still best known to most as Austerlitz.

While Francis slept, Napoleon is said to have spent much of the night before the encounter studying the lie of the land from

Žurán knoll, marked today by a stone cube with a diagram of the battlefield. A chapel of the Holy Virgin was demolished to make way for trenches and gun emplacements, and rebuilt in 1832. The view from the ridge has probably not changed much since that bloody day. Wide fields roll down a long, smooth slope; a few snug villages nestle in little declivities as if wary of raising their heads too high; a line of spindly trees is ghostly in the distant haze.

The Russians and Austrians attacked Napoleon from both sides in the hope of a quick decision. Napoleon breached their centre on Pracký hill and took them from the rear. After the opening moves, fighting went on along the ridge and down into the villages until its effective conclusion in the afternoon at Újezd, where a chapel of St Anthony of Padua was gutted but, unlike the human beings who fell here, was restored to life in 1863. No farmer or cottager in the neighbourhood could even now be ignorant of the battle and its consequences. French, Russians and Austrians buried where they fell are commemorated in small Calvaries. Bones still turn up in many fields, and the most minor building project yields its share of buttons and fragments of uniform. There were mass graves on the main battlefield and in Kobylnice, Blažkovice, and other villages. A wall in Sokolnice still bears marks of French cannon. On the 160th anniversary of the battle in 1965 the people of Slapanice set up a small memorial. The old posting-station in Pozořice, where Napoleon rested after his victory, is preserved by the state, together with several related sites.

Human remains unearthed nowadays are usually transferred to a crypt under the Cairn of Peace. This huge representation of a Slavonic tumulus, narrowing upwards to a copper crown bearing the Slavonic cross, was the brainchild of a Prague architect, Josef Fanta. When completed in 1912 it was presented to the nation. The sculptor Vesmík set four figures leaning on shields, one at each corner, to represent the three armies and the spirit of the Moravian battlefield itself. Inside is a chapel, with the burial chamber below. The slope immediately below the memorial is landscaped with hedges and shrubs; behind is a small museum of weapons, coins and other relics recovered

16 Bratislava seen across the Danube

over the years, relief plan of the battle with a layout of toy soldiers, and portraits of some of the personalities involved. The museum in Slavkov château supplements this exhibition with further weapons, uniforms, engravings and documents.

Unless we propose to return directly to Brno, any side road will take us into villages of bright little cottages with porches, pergolas, compact gardens, and beds of roses along the pavements. Křenovice is one such; and there is Šaratice, giving its name to a well-known local mineral water. If we are tempted along the route into Moravian Slovakia, two rich mansions and one hilltop castle lie within easy reach.

At Bučovice an Italian Renaissance architect built a moated château right against the edge of the little town, allowing himself room only at the rear for fine ornamental gardens. From outside the impression is somewhat blank and austere; but hidden away within the rectangle of the wings is a courtyard where severity gives way to a most graceful arcaded ground floor and balconies.

Buchlov was meant as a fortress, and unlike many it continues to look like one. Its towers and high walls rear up over a steep woodland slope, visible in tantalizing snatches from the roads below, framed between trees and then lost among them, only to reappear from another angle. A thirteenth-century royal castle, it started with the two heavy square towers joined by a wall and sheltering a small palace. Residential quarters were extended gradually, but in the sixteenth century the builders had to concentrate on further fortifications to guard against Turkish invasions. Much of the collection of weapons, porcelain and rare old glass was assembled by the wealthy Berchthold family in the nineteenth century.

This same family also owned Buchlovice, a few miles away: a most appealing confection, with a beautifully proportioned red and cream arc, backed by an octagonal cupola, facing a balancing arc across a courtyard and rondel of flowerbeds. There are ornamental gardens in the park behind, and an arboretum of rarities from many parts of the world. Early in this century Buchlovice was a residence of Count Leopold Berchthold, who in 1912 became Austro-Hungarian Minister of

17 Vrátna vale in the Low Tatras
18 Štrbské Pleso, a mountain lake in the High Tatras

Foreign Affairs—a foppish playboy whose petulant blunders in dealing with Serbia were largely responsible for the outbreak of the First World War.

Here we are already setting foot in that quite individual, fascinating region known as Moravské Slovacko, Moravian Slovakia, because of its blend of neighbouring yet distinctive cultures. When we step further in, it will be to find enough additional influences to warrant an even clumsier portmanteau name.

Moravian Slovakia

When so many historical records of the rise and fall of the Great Moravian Empire have been preserved, it seems odd that the location of its royal capital should still be in doubt. Historians and archaeologists have been indulging in speculations, contradictions and hopeful assertions for a long time. Now, however, it appears that an answer may be forthcoming.

The capital is referred to in various chronicles as Veligrad, and in one as 'the indescribable fortress of Rostislav'. Some theorists identified this with Velehrad, a place of pilgrimage on the Moravian plain to which Cyrill and Methodius came on their first mission. But opinions veered towards Staré Město, a suburb of Uherské Hradiště, where tombs furnished with bronze, silver and gold ornaments were found. Fragments of an ancient church were uncovered and restored. Uherské Hradiště itself was a royal town of later date, built around a thirteenth-century fortress. Its museum has collections of material from archaeological sites in the district, and also some lovely examples of local and Slovak folk costume.

But even the gold and jewellery of Staré Město paled in comparison with discoveries at Mikulčice, in the Morava valley some distance to the south-west. In 1954 a shard was turned up on a farm, and archaeologists were at once called in to assess its significance. The state ethnological authorities are very strict about sealing off potentially important sites the moment anything of this kind is revealed; and there are sly jokes about lazy farmers who are always hoping to run their plough into an ancient beaker or dagger so that they can stop work and claim compensation while investigations proceed. Digging at Mikulčice started immediately, and within a year the foundations of some impressive buildings began to show. A line of earthworks followed the curve of what had once been an arm of the Morava. Widely spaced excavations indicated a more extensive settlement than had at first been visualized.

A wooden fortress had been established some time in the late seventh century within a palisade. Remains of a workshop for treating gold and iron were identifiable, and a number of iron and bronze spurs made it clear that there had been a military force here, possibly a royal one. Another fortress, this one with stone ramparts, grew up in the eighth and ninth centuries, covering some fifteen acres. The surrounding five hundred acres had been occupied by a sizeable community. By the time a sixth of the castle area had been investigated it had already yielded the foundations of a palace and five churches, one of them a large three-naved basilica. In the outer defences five more churches were found, the most impressive being a wide rotunda with two circular apses, decorated with coloured frescoes, in the centre of a burial ground. From the graves and from vaults which clearly belonged to noblemen and possibly to the royal family were taken chased gilt bronze spurs and buckles, necklaces, gold earrings, ornamental buttons, ceremonial swords, silver and lead crucifixes, and coins minted in the time of that Byzantine emperor who sent Cyrill and Methodius to this land. Medical and social diagnoses could be made from some of the skeletons: one had a deformed spine; one had a broken leg badly re-set; and one skull was that of a negro slave. Examples of Cyrillic script have been found, and on some bricks is the mark of the Roman XIVth Legion. Seeds of grass and fruit trees have provided valuable pointers to the agrarian economy of the community. In 1967, two long oak dugout canoes were found perfectly preserved twenty feet down, where they had lain for more than a thousand years.

The remains of two of the churches and a number of the grave finds have been roofed over to form part of an imaginatively planned museum, very much in the style of Fishbourne, with chronological displays of discoveries and copies of the more valuable material which has been sent to Brno. Paths lead to exposed foundations of various other churches and chapels, in surroundings reminiscent of English water meadows, with park-land beyond. Away from the river banks it was not always as verdant as this. The prairie character of stretches of Southern Moravia threatened at times to turn the whole region into a desert until, in the nineteenth century, a forester with more eco-logical foresight than his fellows urged the systematic planting of trees to hold the place together, and got his way. Even now, the lowlands and the shallow slopes which provide such splendid conditions for vineyards can offer only spasmodic protection to the traveller on a sunny day, and drought is all too common. The heart of the region used to be known as 'the land without shadows'; and even today the shadows are sparse and gauzy.

Turning in towards that centre from Mikulčice we pass through a strange twentieth-century plantation. Jabbing up from orchards and fields around Lužice, over rooftops and strad-dling the very back gardens of the village, is a small forest of oil production rigs. But oil, desperate as the modern need for it may be, can never compete in local esteem with the noblest produce of this corner of Moravia: wine.

Moravian Slovakia is so called because of the close resem-blance of its dialect, customs, costume, music and folk art to those of Slovakia. Borderlines between two peoples are indistinct here. These southern and south-western frontiers are the only ones in Bohemia or Moravia without the sketchiest protection of hills or mountains: 'the soft under-belly', as it has often been called, is exposed to invasion and infiltration by many a nation and notion. Austerlitz on its northern fringe was by no means its only battlefield. Tatars, Magyars and Turks have all been here. During the Thirty Years' War the land was fought over so often and so often laid waste that in the circle of vignerons' villages around Čejkovice, Bzenec and Hodonín only seven in-habited houses remained. Yet some who had come to fight stayed to add new strains to the already mixed blood, or, as is the way of armies, at least left a number of children behind. There are many descendants of the French who were here dur-ing the Napoleonic campaigns. It is surely not too fanciful to think one sees French features in some of the vineyards; and with the characteristic countryman's blue beret, many could be transported in a second to slopes beside the Rhône without arousing any comment.

This is not an obvious tourist area: its scenery is not spectacular, there are few of the great castles and mansions we find elsewhere in Czechoslovakia, and there are no architecturally rich townships; but for anyone with the time and inclination to relax in one place for a week or so and allow himself to be taken over by it, the rewards are immeasurable. Wine, warm hospitality, and the warm Moravian-Slovakian temperament go inextricably together. Come to think of it, I have rarely encountered a surly or embittered wine grower, in spite of all nature's hazards and dirty tricks; and here folk seem especially mellow and sociable.

Vineyards and a whole street of wine cellars start a few yards from the doorstep of the isolated hotel below Bořetice. This hotel is a 'JZD' establishment, meaning that it is operated by an agricultural cooperative. An unpretentious modern building, its frontage has been enlivened by a wide ribbon of paintings like some *faux-naïf* cottage fresco. In this band and in other panels are intertwined grape and vineleaf motifs. The hotel dining room has rural scenes painted by a local vigneron. Only a few minutes' walk away is the artist's wine cellar, its exterior in no way conspicuous among so many along the row of huts, but the interior a revelation of exuberant primitive decoration. The little caves driven into the hillside and then enclosed by small stone chambers give the appearance of a village street, a satellite of the village on the ridge: simple squared-up buildings each with its heavy door and its steps down into the chill vault where the barrels are kept. Behind, each has a narrow strip of vineyard climbing the hill. Within, walls and barrel ends are embellished according to the owner's fancy. The most ambitious, that of our friend who decorated the hotel, has rural scenes carved out of the plaster of walls and ceiling, and, in a separate room at the back, pseudo-classical and mythological scenes with plump cherubs swooping over the ceiling and even plumper, full-lipped, corybantic women offering fleshy delights which would have made even Rubens marvel.

A stroll along this rutted track can be dangerous. A door will open, you will be invited to taste a glass of Sauvignon or Müller-Thurgau drawn from the barrel; and the moment you start sipping, a neighbour will pop his head round the door and tell you not to waste your time but to come and try *his* wine. The glass is small, but will be implacably refilled. 'You shouldn't drink wine', runs the expert advice: 'drink a litre and a half, and you may be drunk . . . just *taste* it, and you can manage three or four litres before it begins to show.'

These strips of land are usually a one-man concern. Each grower is entitled to a hundred square metres for private use, giving an average annual yield of about ten to twelve hecto-litres—that is, something in the region of two hundred and fifty gallons. When the grower has filled his casks the excise officer comes to calculate the duty owing. Once this is paid, the owner can do what he likes with the contents of his barrels: he can sell to a state enterprise or local cooperative, sell to his friends or passers-by, or drink it all himself. Some decide to amalgamate with neighbouring vineyards and form a small cooperative of their own. One particular vineyard supplies only the President and an especially privileged wine restaurant in Prague. It is common practice for the agricultural cooperative of a village or closely-knit group of villages to lease a restaurant in one of the main towns and cities, engage its own staff, supply the food and wine, and thus have an outlet for its produce and an income from which to balance its commune budget.

A cooperative supplied by individual growers in this district is at Čejkovice, once the property of the Knights Templar. They built extensive cellars under the fortifications, and one of the current blended wines is labelled 'Templar'. Later the little town became the centre of a barony. Its last Czech owner was a Hussite, so the Jesuits collected it among their spoils from the Thirty Years' War and continued the wine-making tradition until 1773, after which the cellars fell into disuse. In 1936 the passages were dug out and adapted again for wine making and storing. The largest vat in the bowels of the hills holds eighteen thousand litres. There is an 'archive' vault in which samples of the best wine from year to year are kept; and one section of interlinked cellars and intimate alcoves has been turned into a restaurant.

Like several of its kind, the Čejkovice plant is part of a wider agricultural complex. Some producers operate with old-fashioned equipment and methods as a sideline to the main farming output, to some extent subsidized by fellow workers who like the product and still rather envy its mystique. Both state wineries and local cooperatives distribute in much the same way, but can compete in selling to shops and restaurants and in particular to the best-known chains of stores, state and co-operative. Residents of Prague sometimes assert that the cooperative chain, by dealing more flexibly with suppliers in different regions, can get smoked meats and other local delicacies from the country more readily than the unwieldier state enterprise.

Until 1971 all Čejkovice's output was sold to the state enterprise at Hodonín, but since then it has extended its own bottling operations. Hodonín, a few miles away through thin birch plantations and slivers of woodland on the fringe of the 'no shadows' land, was the birthplace of Thomas Masaryk; his parents had a cottage in Čejkovice, and Masaryk was for a time usher to the headmaster of the local school.

Hodonín is much more of a modern factory than that at Čejkovice, but is built around similar basic plant. 'It's always untidy', apologized our hosts during a visit in 1975, 'because we're always expanding.' These apologies were unnecessary: so long as the end product maintains its present quality while quantities increase—so that one day we may even taste these wines in England—there are no grounds for complaint. Splendid casks so old that the staff are afraid to risk repairing them are giving way to concrete cisterns set in high walls, linked by a network of glass tubing. The old 'pots', as they are condescendingly referred to, can no longer cope with modern production. 'Pot' is also used colloquially to refer to tiny wine plots in the back gardens of local houses.

Hodonín buys from a number of smaller cooperatives—'which aren't all that small nowadays'—with about half its purchases coming from other parts of the country and from abroad for blending. A sample taken from each supplier's consignment is numbered and put aside. Experts taste it without knowing the origin; and when it has been approved and used, further numbered samples are tested at bottle stage. Calculations of output are rarely made in terms of bottles but of 'waggons', each waggon being the equivalent of a hundred hectolitres. Although this factory system and terminology seem far removed from the loving personal care given to each tendril and each small cask by the individual grower out in the countryside, that indefinable instinct which is just as important as scientific quality control is evident here also, and Hodonín boasts that it has never failed to carry off a gold or silver medal from any major exhibition.

Individual growers in the Břeclav district submit their choicest vintages to an annual competition, as amiable and as fierce as the jam-making competition at an English village fête, but on a larger scale. After judges have awarded their points a catalogue is printed, listing names of the growers, the classification of their wine or blend, and the points awarded. Eager friends, rivals and visitors queue up to buy the catalogue, a small glass, and tickets entitling one to taste the wines in hundreds of bottles laid out in a hall above a Břeclav restaurant: the number of tickets you buy depends on the state of your purse and your estimate of your own capacity. On posters around the room a government health slogan, 'Eat more fruit, it's good for you', has been altered for the occasion to 'Eat more grapes, they're good for you . . . liquefied.' Men stand about the room in groups, sipping and chewing the wine and arguing; or sit at tables marking their catalogues and agreeing or disagreeing. Some, used to wearing their hats all day in the sun-baked fields, still wear them. Others take them off to reveal a clear line between white brow and deeply tanned face. The waiter in our hotel, seeing us return with the catalogue, diffidently confessed that he was an exhibitor but had not had a chance of going along to see how his entries had fared. He was a bit hurt by one marking which he felt was lower than his wine merited.

Břeclav is a key railway junction, standing as it does close to the Austrian border at a confluence of lines from Prague,

Vienna, Bratislava, Budapest and Warsaw. One line, hugging the border, goes to Valtice, Mikulov, Znojmo and beyond; and although this strictly speaking takes us out of Moravian Slovakia, the wine belt runs on so naturally that it seems equally natural to include a few near neighbours in our itinerary.

Until 1919 Valtice was part of Austria proper, and for centuries the main residence of the Liechtenstein family. They possessed in all ninety-nine estates. If they had ever been greedy enough to acquire a hundredth, this would have rendered them liable to maintain a standing army in the service of the Austro-Hungarian emperor, so they managed to restrain themselves from this further grab. Their thirteenth-century fortifications at Valtice have long since been swallowed up below the vast surrounding park, and the present château preserves the largely baroque appearance imposed on it by Karl Eusebius Liechtenstein. This lord of the estate, having spent five years abroad, returned full of new ideas for the reconstruction of his mansion. He and his successors were accused by envious acquaintances of suffering from—or, more likely, enjoying—a 'building obsession', and were forever altering Valtice and their summer residence some miles away at Lednice. Karl Eusebius watched over his designers and craftsmen, interfered and revised plans as he went along, and may well have been responsible for a collapse of nerve in his Italian architect, Tencalla, which led to the collapse of his badly conceived church. From his experiences Karl Eusebius culled theories for writings on art and architecture, declaring it the duty of wealthy men to invest their time and money in the creation of immortal edifices: such monuments would forever symbolize the glory of a noble family, its name and its wealth, provided there was no tinge of false pride.

The château has 365 windows, a great succession of painted ceilings, tarsia flooring inlaid with stars and polygons of mixed hues, and some splendidly ornate woodwork in the gallery, doors and pews of the high baroque chapel. In the ballroom, artificial marble carries musical motifs in relief, and there are Bohemian crystal chandeliers in the Venetian style, gilded in 18-carat gold. In some rooms the original rococo wallpaper has survived, but many pictures and pieces of furniture were brought from other places to create as nearly as possible the original ambience.

From the time of their earliest settlement here the Liechtensteins cultivated the grape. A family cellar laid out in 1430 ran right under the moat, and is still subject to seepage. The columns supporting the roof have in our day been reinforced with concrete. Against the walls are old beam presses and imposing rows of barrels, one bearing the motto: 'Leave girls alone and stick to wine—girls deteriorate with age, wine improves.' In 1640 a cruciform cellar was added, nearly four hundred feet long and three hundred feet along the crosspiece, with barrels and tanks now holding about a million litres. At one end is a special section for the cherished 'archive' wines.

These cellars are now used by the Valtice winery, which is unique in that it draws almost exclusively from its own vineyards, running right on to the Austrian border, with one large stretch on a slope directly adjoining the factory and feeding grapes straight into subterranean tanks. Only a small quantity of grapes is bought from state farms, and nothing comes from abroad: indeed, Valtice is one of the few wineries with a fairly brisk export trade, sending a few wines to England, some rosé to Japan, and some white to Switzerland and Canada. Output is about three million bottles a year. One wonders that such a small township could provide not merely an adequate labour force but also an adequately trained force. Supervision of the thirteen essential points in production of a worthy bottle of wine, including purity, colour, bouquet, taste, analytical values, sugar and sulphur and so on, has to be acute: one small error by one operative, and at any one time as much as ten thousand pounds could go literally down the drain. But Valtice can draw from its long-established Wine Technical College, the only one of its kind in the Czech sector of the republic: there is also one in Slovakia. Prentice work from the college, when up to standard, is often sold in local shops and supermarkets. Do the staff, one wonders, take advantage of their training and the knowledge acquired in the winery to go off to better-paid jobs in city restaurants? 'Very few', I was assured: 'they prefer to stay here and drink *good* wine.' Certainly there is no substitute for these pure, living, untreated and unblended wines drunk on the spot. Valtice plans to produce a limited quantity of fine vintage wines for exclusive use in wine restaurants which it operates in Prague, Opava, Brno, and some Interhotels. They will be worth looking out for.

The brand names of some Valtice blends are encountered on the walk to Lednice, all ten miles of it through land once belonging to the Liechtensteins. The route from one of their châteaux to another is marked out by temples and follies—the Rendezvous, Gracie (The Three Graces), and Apollon among them, all to be found on Valtice bottle labels. Ten miles may seem a deterrent to anyone not passionately devoted to walking, but the paths are on the level most of the way, and weave through appealing countryside and little tracts of woodland. The first wood encloses the incongruously massive marble arch of a temple to Diana built in 1813, with rooms up the sides and across its top. A couple of miles on is a sandstone chapel built in honour of another figure associated with the chase—St Hubert, patron saint of hunters. This open, pinnacled triangular erection has odd echoes of the Albert Memorial, but dates from 1855. The Three Graces, carved by Martin Fischer out of one block of stone, stand between the extended arms of a semicircular colonnade with statues by Klieber in its niches, in a clearing not too remote for cyclists and picnickers at weekends and during summer holidays. Half a mile on is the colonnaded wall of a huge farm built in Empire style in 1809, almost Italianate in its form and colouring, Danish in its spaciousness.

Approaching the outskirts of Lednice we come to a nature reserve incorporating a system of wide, rush-lined meres alive with wildfowl. Still there is a long walk around the lakes, gradually curving behind a temple of Apollo, also with sculpture by Klieber.

Set in an extensive park landscaped in the English style, Lednice château also looks as English as Hluboká, though in a different vein: it might well be a nineteenth-century neo-Gothic Cambridge college. The Liechtenstein obsession with construction and reconstruction ran unchecked here. The medieval original was converted into a Renaissance mansion, rebuilt in the late seventeenth century to designs by Fischer von Erlach, rebuilt in classical style in the late eighteenth century, and then given its present second-hand and second-rate appearance in the middle of the nineteenth. One of the wings of the earlier fabric is the present church. The mansion itself scarcely merits a visit, but its greenhouse of tropical plants, its gardens and ornamental trees and shrubs, and the convoluted lakes and channels luring one on are quite a different matter. Each water-side path leads to some artfully placed folly. There are engaging little grottoes, a crumbling aqueduct which never was, and framed between trees across an expanse of lake the most remarkable folly of all: the largest minaret outside the Muslim world. It seems that a nineteenth-century Liechtenstein wished to build a church on this spot, probably as a landscape feature rather than a focus of devotion. When Lednice burghers and clerics expressed disapproval, Liechtenstein defiantly said he would erect a minaret instead; and did so.

The cross-country path from Valtice to Lednice starts beside the railway station. Those who prefer taking to a train rather than to their own two feet could well continue along the line to Mikulov, incontestably the most beautiful town in the region. It is best surveyed from the stony path past chapels and shrines on the adjacent 'Holy Hill'. The castle was another Liechtenstein possession, but they sold it to another noble family, the Dietrichsteins. On its hummock above the Austrian border lowlands it was an important stronghold for centuries, reinforced in the seventeenth and eighteenth. Hitler's S.S. used it during the war, and many sequestrated valuables were stored here, including costumes of the Vienna State Opera. When it grew obvious that Germany had lost the war, the S.S. tried to blow up the entire castle. They did extensive damage, destroying most of the interior, and their explosions threw fragments of valuable porcelain all over the roofs and streets of the town. Many a house still has a jagged souvenir of the occasion.

In the cellars, which suffered least, is a mighty beam wine press dated 1751, and the largest wine vat in central Europe, so huge that it needs as many buttresses as a small chapel to hold it in place. Built in 1643, it took more than eight months to make. About twenty feet long, it is bound by twenty-two iron hoops each weighing over nine hundred pounds, and holds over 22,000 gallons. One may draw one's own conclusions from the fact that this was the receptable for the manorial tithes which the owners took from vineyards on their estates and used or sold off as it suited them.

Nobody manufactures such superb monsters today. The large Mikulov winery on the outskirts of the town is a gleaming federation of tile, concrete, steel and glass. Completed in 1969, it is the most modern and most streamlined of all the wine producing concerns in Czechoslovakia, turning out twelve million bottles a year and with a storage capacity of seven hundred waggons. Pressing and fermentation is usually carried out in village cooperatives and the wine then sent here for clarification and, where appropriate, blending. The growers in the neighbourhood claim to be among the best paid in the world, in that the ratio between the price paid for a kilogram of grapes and the price of the finished bottle is the lowest recorded.

The two largest cooperative suppliers are those of Dolní Dunajovice and Dolní Věstonice. This latter is the site of remarkable excavations which in 1950 uncovered a great cache of ivory and mammoth bones left by hunters in about 20,000 B.C., necklaces of shells and animal teeth, and figures used in ancient magical rites. There were also unique examples of figurines fired from clay and powdered bone, some of the first known ceramics in the world. The most famous is the Věstonice Venus, a grossly exaggerated female shape in which all other features are subordinated to those conveying a ritual fertility symbol. She has given her name to a sparkling wine, Venuše, produced in Mikulov by the *méthode champenoise*, employed in only one other winery in the country. In this department there is no mechanization whatsoever: everything is done by hand. Yeast cultivated in a research institute at Bratislava is kept working here, and the process of adding this to the fined (or clarified) wine, bottling, turning regularly, disgorging and liqueuring is carried on in the accepted tradition. Only three hundred waggons a year are sold—at a loss. To charge an economic price would be to price the wine out of the market, but subsidies ensure that that same accepted tradition is not allowed to die out. Workers in the sparkling wine department notice one odd side effect: they develop a much more zestful appetite than their colleagues on other processes. One man put on more than two stone and had to be ordered to diet, drinking nothing but milk. The sight of this daily dose made his workmates feel ill, and the poor fellow had to go outside and take his medicine where nobody could see him.

There are other problems in other parts of the plant. Of the two hundred and more employees, half are women. Girls are taken direct from school and trained, and in the bottling plant fifty women work two shifts a day, turning out on average thirty thousand bottles a day. One shift is made up of older women, the other of newcomers up to the age of twenty-five. This was not laid down by the management: it just sorted itself out that way. Unfortunately it causes the very tolerant management a lot of headaches. Members of the younger shift tend to get married and have babies, thereby creating far more problems on the younger shift than on the older.

In the bottling plant and elsewhere there is quite an international atmosphere: the latest production line was made in Austria, the filtration plant is French, a number of workers are Croat settlers . . . and the herbs used in many of the aperitifs produced here come from Italy.

On a visit to Mikulov I had the good fortune to be shown round on a day when tasting samples of exhibition wines had been left uncorked, and I was allowed to make my way through some of the most exquisite Sauvignons, Neubergers and Traminers I have ever tasted. 'Once it's been opened, you know, it won't keep', I commented. My companions had never heard the Flanders and Swann song, so the remark fell a bit flat; but it was the only thing on the premises which did. Mikulov, like Valtice, has plans to issue classified vintage wines to sell at a realistic price in shops and restaurants which will have to prove their ability to store and handle the wine properly. The general public taste, it has been established, is for sweetish wines, which hurts the connoisseurs in the building. Some years ago, blending what they hoped would be a well-balanced seller of about three

hundred thousand bottles a year, they found themselves confronted by a demand for a million. Now this blend, called
Romance, accounts for half the entire Mikulov output.

Being less wasteful than we are, the Czechs can return their
wine bottles as we return beer and many cordial bottles. Some
made in 1950 still go to and from Mikulov. Lighter bottles are
now being manufactured because of employment regulations
which forbid women working in factories or shops to lift crates
or other containers weighing more than fifteen kilos.

On a circuitous drive back to Břeclav, or returning there by
train from Lednice, one sees an unmistakable declaration of
other ethnic influences in the region: a local village and railway
station are signposted The New Croatian Village.

Scholarly attempts to sort out all these strands are being made
in and around Strážnice, a pleasantly untidy old town sprawling
within the fragments of old fortifications, the most substantial
remnants being two gateways with oval drum towers. Just outside is a patch of land on which, after five or six years' preparation, intensive work began in 1974 on an open air museum
devoted to houses and workshops of the region, dismantled and
re-erected to form, in the end, a community of living history.
So far the site has acquired some old thatched homesteads, a
reconditioned blacksmith's forge, some wine cellars, and a few
of the tiled cottages known as 'haystacks' because of the steep
pitch of roof above the narrow building.

The great local expert on such matters is Heřman Landsfeld
of Strážnice. An inveterate digger, he has unearthed 123,000
archaeological specimens from different centuries, and has these
catalogued, bundled up, stored in marked boxes, or displayed
in glass cabinets in his crowded home. When a critic said that
he must have exaggerated the number of his finds, Landsfeld
invited the challenger to visit him—and after some awe-struck
calculations received an apology. His instinct is like that of a
dowser: he knows where to dig, and knows what he is likely to
find, though he has had some very agreeable surprises from time
to time. In his collection are Roman relics, fragments from the
great Moravian days, and a large amount of sixteenth and seventeenth century work. Among great numbers of stove tiles are

some from about 1650, partly charred: these can be identified
as coming from a workshop known to have been damaged by
fire in 1663 when the Turks were making forays into the area.
On other tiles, metal traces such as zinc in the pigment have
lost their colour and reverted to their original state. There are
pottery moulds and matrices in all manner of designs, including
one of a podgy baby, for baking loaves and cakes for wedding
feasts, christenings, and other ceremonial occasions. Landsfeld
is delighted with one item in his hoard: one of the earliest examples of a chamber pot, introduced into the country in the sixteenth century. He also has black milk pots marked with a cross
against witches who might turn the milk sour, and a witch's
cauldron—not the iron cauldron we are used to seeing in paintings or on stage in a production of *Macbeth*, but one in pottery,
painted green for luck, to guarantee the success of the potions
brewing within. The witch's fire had always to be made with
fungus collected from trees, which produced a vast quantity of
smoke: all very dramatic, but liable to choke the witch herself
to death.

One of the most mystifying sections of this home-made
museum is that devoted to relics of the Habáns, an austere
Calvinistic sect which kept itself so much to itself that few
authentic records of its practices have survived. Wishing as little
contamination as possible from the outside world, the community trained its own tradesmen and even relied on self-taught
physicians. Trade was carried on with outsiders, but there was
no social mingling and no intermarrying. Among the domestic
goods which Heřman Landsfeld has assembled are knives, including one with an antler handle, moulds, and a number of
religious emblems and small objects whose significance is now
unfathomable. The Habán cottages are recognizable by their
double ceiling, within which prohibited books were kept wrapped up, away from the prying eyes of inquisitors. Driven out
by relentless persecution, the more stubborn members of the
sect went on into Slovakia before being finally dispersed; but
there are thousands of their descendants in the lowlands.
Heřman Landsfeld is officially authorized to dig for Habán
ceramics and to add them to his collection. When he finds

duplicates, he sells them to the Ethnographical Museum at Strážnice.

As if all this activity were not enough, Landsfeld makes his own porcelain nativity scenes, bright with peasants and musicians in local dress, helped over the years by his wife and two daughters; collects pipes from all over the world—just to fill in the time—and now has about four hundred, including some highly decorated porcelain military pipes; lectures on archaeology, ceramics, and painted furniture; and organizes exhibitions, most of them for the benefit of the local museum, who in 1975 were empowered to set aside a large sum to purchase items from his collection and facilitate his future work.

The museum and the offices of the Institute of Folk Art are in the château of Strážnice, once a border fortress in Otakar II's defence line against Hungary. A thirteenth-century castle was reconstructed by one of the Kravař family in the middle of the fifteenth century, and then later pawned. In 1501 it came into the possession of the squires of Žerotín, who remodelled it as a Renaissance mansion. After the battle of the White Mountain the estate was presented to Count Franz von Magnis, who had fought with the imperial armies in that battle, and remained in the family, used mainly as a hunting lodge, until 1945: the two last male members of the line fought with the Germans at Stalingrad and were both killed there.

The present appearance of the château dates from renovations round about 1850. Of the original building, which used to be moated and linked with the river Morava, the only part remaining intact is the library, in which collections of prints and manuscripts from other Magnis estates were eventually centralized. In the various rooms today are the occasional exhibitions mounted by Heřman Landsfeld and other researchers, permanent exhibitions of folk art and old musical instruments, and a display of hunting weapons, some the work of a celebrated armourer in nearby Kyjov.

Ethnographical studies in the institute concentrated at first on costume and folk architecture. In 1946 a folk song and dance festival was held in the park, and encouragement was given to local villages to resume the traditional festivals which in some cases had lapsed because of wartime conditions or sheer indifference. Many a village did not need this prod: old traditions had been maintained between the wars and could be revived without effort. People still lovingly painted their Easter eggs—*kraslice*—as their ancestors had done; wedding ceremonies still followed an old symbolic ritual; singing and dancing came spontaneously. It was understood from the start that nothing should be forced on reluctant or self-conscious people. There has been none of the mincing archness of many a well-meaning but artificial jollification around an English village maypole. Once prompted, young people threw themselves into the re-creation of old songs and dances. In regions where the rhythm does not seem to come as readily as in others, festivals are organized only once in every two or three years; but this does not mean that many groups do not have their own informal sessions throughout the year.

Even when families move to new developments, including the inevitable tower block suburbs around larger towns, they often take their village customs with them and try to observe these native rituals even if only on a small scale. Some fade as customs change, die out of their own accord, and cannot be artificially revived. Others are tougher. But for how many generations can old rural observances survive this urban transplantation? It is still too early to say.

The most comprehensive folklore festival is held every July in Strážnice. I was delighted to find that the director who showed me round the château was no purely academic organizer: a couple of evenings after our meeting I saw him on stage in Brno, part of a male ensemble singing a splendid drinking song. Velehrad also has a festival in July. At Vlčnov and in Hluk the Parade of the Whitsun Kings symbolizes the old ceremony of young men going to the wars. In Kobylí the event of the year is the celebration of St George's Day—the Czech lands having the same patron saint as England.

Kobylí is a little town of two thousand five hundred people. From a distance its houses seem to slide downhill, to a meeting of other slopes in a valley serrated with orchards and strips of vineyard. Light sparks from greenhouses where seeds, shoots and grafts are carefully developed before transfer to nurseries. Many local vineyards buy their seedlings from here. In a predominantly white wine area, Kobylí is one of the few producers of red wine. On the outskirts of the town you can walk more than a winding mile through avenues of peach blossom, with clouds of it clinging to stepped terraces like some Celtic earthwork. There is nothing picturesquely ancient in the streets, but many a house is built on old foundations, and in some cellars are traces of the Habáns, establishing their construction before 1620 when the sect was ordered out of the country.

St George's Day begins early with young men in white shirts, black jackets and black trousers, all decorated with colourful floral embroidery, strolling through the streets to invite people to a feast. A small band leads the way, and the youths following carry wine carafes and glasses which they offer to passers-by or to giggling girls in cottage doorways. Kobylí needed no encouragement to revive its festival: it has been held without interruption for as long as there are any records.

After church, attended by dozens of older women in wide, brightly coloured skirts and thickly woven shawls with thick, swinging fringes, there is a lull during which everyone repairs to a wine cellar—his own or a friend's—and prepares for the long afternoon and evening. Once again the band is on the march. This time its immediate followers are the girls of the village, supposedly coaxed out by the knock at their door and the young men's offer of wine. In fact the dozen or so chosen maids have been getting dressed for hours. There is keen competition to see who can manage to wear the largest number of crisply starched petticoats, covered by elaborately patterned skirts and blouses with lacy sleeves, embroidered streamers, and floral headdresses. Once attired for the occasion, they cannot sit down until the stiff skirts and petticoats are taken off. The senior maidens of the village—not old maids in our sense, but rather late teenagers—have the most dazzling headdresses, while their slightly younger attendants have simple headscarves.

The procession reaches the little fairground, where swings and roundabouts are already busy, and where another orchestra is waiting. Sun beats down on a permanent circle of concrete about a maypole as high as a ship's mast. The boys put their wine flasks at the foot of the pole, then ceremonially take a partner and begin to dance. For thirty minutes they have the dance area to themselves, stopping every now and then for a glass of wine. Stifled in their bulky armour, the girls grow pink, and find it advisable to take only a ritual sip at the wine rather than risk collapse. After half an hour, the public are invited to join in.

From time to time groups of young men from villages near and far enter the arena, introducing themselves with a characteristic song. The orchestra of fiddles, cembalom, clarinets and perhaps an accordion knows all these tunes off by heart, and picks up the theme after a mere couple of chords. No jazz musician could be swifter at recognizing a tune and a key and plunging straight in at the right tempo. Even without the music, the inhabitants of Kobylí would know where their guests came from by the cut of their shirts, jackets or trousers—such as the bright red, tight trousers of youths from the Podluži region— or the decoration of their hat-bands.

There is the pleasure of greeting friends, arriving unexpectedly. A few evenings ago I attended a rehearsal of the thirty-piece Zavádka song and dance ensemble in Čejkovice—a vigorous, warm-hearted, terrifyingly energetic team who could race non-stop through a couple of hours of solos, duets, choruses, leaping and swirling dances that made even a rehearsal seem as vivid as a brightly lit stage—and here they all come: the theme song, the formal introductions, the dancing, and then a hospitable invitation to what in England would be the beer tent but here, predictably, is the wine tent. From within a cool interlacing of pine branches and vine tendrils we look out at the tireless girls, accepting one partner after another, keeping it up until twilight comes and the fairground lights cast different glows, different shadows. Still it goes on, round and round the maypole. And it will all be taken up again tomorrow morning and go on through another day. Next year perhaps the older girls will be married, and their attendants of this year will be the ones to wear the floral crowns.

One ritual which must be observed on the arrival of visiting youths is the handing over by the village girls' squires to the guests. Each Kobylí squire leads his girl to a newcomer, and they dance together. One wonders how many marriages between families from different villages start this way.

Though weddings are not necessarily celebrated in full folk costume, much of the traditional procedure is still followed today. The bridegroom's friends, fortified with hot wine, proceed early in the day to the bride's home. The gate, even if only a modern front gate or just a front door, is locked. The men all knock loudly and sing appropriate local songs. At last they are allowed in and entertained. Then they ask to see the bride, to ensure that it is the *right* bride. First an old woman, probably the grandmother, is brought forth: 'No, not this one.' The principal bridesmaid is presented: she is complimented on her beauty, but she won't do. The third time the right bride is produced. In the presence of the visitors she asks her parents their pardon for leaving them, and for their blessing. In the case of an orphan who has been brought up by others, this can be a very sentimental moment.

The party then proceeds to the register office and, if the couple wish a religious ceremony as well, they all go on to the church. Afterwards the reception is held in the bride's home.

Now the bride's parents test the bridegroom to see if he is worthy of their daughter. It seems a bit late to do this, and I have been unable to obtain a straight answer as to what would happen if they belatedly discovered he was unworthy.

A loaf of bread is set before the bridegroom, with a wooden knife. He must prove his manhood by cutting the loaf. A real man puts the wooden knife aside and takes out his own knife to cut it. What would Freud have to say about that? Then a length of knotted wood is brought, and he must show that he can chop it in two with an axe.

It is the bride's turn. A piece of crockery is smashed on the floor and she must show her ability to sweep it up properly.

These formalities duly concluded, the feast begins. Traditional dishes are chicken with noodles, and baked and roasted meats. Eating and drinking go on until about four o'clock in the afternoon, when it is time to start 'throwing into the cake'. A round cake with a wide hole through its centre is put on top of a large crock. The principal bridesmaid takes charge, chats with the best man, and both of them pour out old saws and sayings to encourage the guests in order of seniority to throw money and gifts into the pot through the hole in the cake. Each item is accompanied by songs related to the relationship of the donor, and each donor must say his or her formal piece. When everyone has contributed, the contents of the pot are poured into the bride's lap by the bridesmaid, who wishes the bride, 'May you have a son or daughter within the year.'

'One of those lovable old customs', observed a wry local to me, 'designed to get money out of the wedding guests.'

Throughout all this the bride has been veiled and seated. Beside her she has a wine bottle with a wreath of flowers about its neck, from which she pours only for her mother and father. If she is wearing the local costume, she will have a sumptuous wedding headdress. Now this must be removed; and a married woman's bonnet is set on her head. This custom is dying out in most places, but some traditionally minded families still observe it.

Echoes of this ritual are to be found in the tense third scene of the Slovak opera, *Krútňava*, mentioned earlier. Music, dialect and everyday customs echo and re-echo across the border between Moravia and Slovakia here, where no hills bar the way and it is possible to cross the dividing line without being aware of it. A straight road, a scattering of villages, some wine cellars like little white chapels decorated with garlanded frescoes and stylized roses, and before we know it we are approaching Bratislava.

Slovakia

In the days of Marcus Aurelius there was a fortified Roman camp on the Danube known as Posonium. The Slavs arrived in the fifth century, and under Břetislav the town became Bratislava. When it fell to the Magyars they adapted Posonium to Pozsony, and for some time after the capture of Buda by the Turks it was the capital of Hungary: between 1563 and 1835 ten Hungarian kings and eight queens were crowned in the cathedral of St Martin. At the same time the large number of German settlers called it Pressburg, a name confirmed when the Habsburgs took over. Finally it reappeared in 1918 as Bratislava.

Its history and situation, almost at the junction of Austria, Hungary and Slovakia, have given it a cosmopolitan air, to which the busy Danube traffic contributes. It was probably even more marked when there were larger admixtures of Germans and Magyars than there are now. After it ceased to be the capital there was a period of stagnation until it became the administrative centre of Slovakia in the Czechoslovak republic; though it is just about as far as could be from the geographical centre. Between the two World Wars the population doubled to about 130,000, and since the second has doubled again. There are engineering and chemical industries, paper and textile mills, and a big trade in food and wine from the surrounding countryside. The oil refinery was connected by pipeline with the Ukraine oilfields in 1962.

The oldest parts of the town, about the castle hill, are under state protection. The castle itself was the prime cause of Bratislava's existence, defensively fortified by a succession of overlords. Its general shape was dictated by Sigismund, but to relieve its four-square heaviness a small tower was placed at each corner in a Renaissance conversion. These give it the appearance of a chest-of-drawers turned upside down, with four squat legs in the air. Burnt out in 1811, it appears in early photographs as a gaunt shell with its corner towers splintered and misshapen. Serious reconstruction was not attempted until after the last war, since when the grounds have become a favourite promenade and rendezvous, with an amphitheatre for concerts, plays and displays.

Below it, old mansions and twisting lanes of tightly packed houses cling to the hill. The cathedral in St Martin's Square was built during the fourteenth and fifteenth centuries, its high tower being originally part of the town fortifications. At its pinnacle is a replica of a cushion bearing the Hungarian crown of St Stephen, reminding one of all those coronations within its walls. There is an old town hall which now houses the main sections of the city museum, and a Jewish town hall in the old ghetto quarter. Imperial diets were held in the Landhaus from 1802 until 1848. The building now forming the municipal art gallery, close to the town hall, was once the palace of the primate of Hungary, in whose hall of mirrors the Treaty of Pressburg was signed a few weeks after the battle of Austerlitz: Austria ceded Venetia, Istria and Dalmatia to France, and recognized Napoleon as king of Italy; while sovereignty was granted to Bavaria and Württemberg as a reward for the support they had given Napoleon.

The wine taverns, especially those serving 'green', fresh wines straight from the barrel, are filled with music, most of it spontaneous. 'The Czechs like to argue politics and football while they're drinking', observed a friend some years back: 'the Slovaks like to sing.' I have known, too, a couple of visiting businessmen who find Bratislava more relaxed in this and other ways than Prague. But let us not start another Czech-Slovak conflict!

A Magyar university founded here in 1465 was the first on Hungarian soil. It was transferred to Pécs after 1919, when the Slovaks established their own Komenský university. In those early days of the republic there were dissensions regarding

Slovak education. Some felt that Czech professors at the new university were preaching exclusively Czech ideas rather than working for the expansion of Slovak language and culture, and that schools and the university were not offering sufficient openings for Slovak teachers and teaching. This was a recurrent grumble in the formative years, along with complaints that industrial developments were being allowed to lag behind those of Bohemia and Moravia, and that representation in the Prague parliament was inadequate. One sad result of this was the willingness of certain elements to believe that collaboration with Hitler and a unilateral declaration of independence would achieve a truly national, healthy state. (Almost forgotten now is the fact that Great Britain promptly recognized this so-called independence with an exchange of consuls.) After 1945 the old arguments were thrashed out again on a more tolerant basis. In 1968 a federal system of government was instituted, with further adjustments in 1971.

Before establishing their fortifications on the Bratislava castle hill, the earliest Slavs had a settlement a few miles away at Stupava, under the eastern edge of the Little Carpathians. Here, too, came the refugee Habáns from Moravia before their final dissolution. Their ceramic designs have been adapted by modern potters in the region to establish a characteristic local ware.

Stupava is an ideal spot from which to set out into the hills with their paths, chalets, romantic ruins and streams. Among the wild life can sometimes be seen a bird which has long since ceased to breed in England: the great bustard. To the north, over to the far side of the range, Smolenice castle raises its tower and turrets from thick woodland to survey the lowlands around Trnava. It is very romantic in the nineteenth-century manner, on the site of earlier fortresses, and since post-war renovation has become a country retreat and conference centre for lucky members of the Slovak Academy of Sciences. Writers also, both in these and the Czech lands, have a number of country houses and estates set aside where for a nominal sum they can rent rooms in which to work untroubled by the clamour of family or city traffic.

Near Smolenice is the underground labyrinth of the Driny

dripstone cave, with its colourful frozen waterfalls and convoluted stalactites and stalagmites.

A little way to the north is Brezová, scene of a Magyar-Slovak clash in the heady revolutionary year of 1848. A month after Kossuth's declaration of an independent Hungary, Ludovit Štúr, who gave his countrymen a distinctive literary language in his newspaper written in an adapted central Slovakian dialect, led a deputation asking the new régime for a more liberal constitution: in a free Hungary there must surely be freedom for Slovak customs and the Slovak language? Mass meetings were held to back up the petition. English history books have taught us to regard Kossuth as something of a hero, if a rather inept one. To the Slovaks he was a worse oppressor than any they had so far encountered. Magyar troops set about crushing every whisper of possible insurrection. Gibbets known to the Slovaks as 'Kossuth gallows' or 'trees of liberty' were set up all over the land for summary execution of Slovak leaders or suspected leaders. In September a volunteer army under Štúr met Magyar forces at Brezová. After a gallant fight the Slovaks were defeated and forced to flee into Moravia, while their country was put under martial law. Disillusioned, the rebels decided to aid the Austrians in their suppression of Kossuth's short-lived state, hoping that after victory the new emperor would show some tangible sign of gratitude. The victory won with their assistance gave them, in fact, nothing. Franz Josef, more concerned with appeasing the large Magyar population once he had restored order, virtually handed the Slovaks back to them.

From the heights of the Little Carpathians we see the wider stretch of the river Váh valley, opening out after its dramatic journey from the Tatras and the Fatras. What the Vltava is, historically, scenically and emotionally, to Bohemia, so the Váh is to Slovakia. A journey up its ever narrowing, ever steepening gorges from the Danube to the great mountains is an unforgettable experience, with every mile bringing more and more startling, wilder and wilder vistas. And of course one should go up-river rather than down: the other way round, it is simply a decline from the superb heights to the comparative dullness of the Danube plain.

The Váh and the Nitra join and run into the Danube—in these parts, the Dunaj—at Komárno. This shipbuilding town, producing passenger and small cargo vessels for the Danube and other river traffic, stands on the site of an extensive Roman camp. It remained an important fortress well into the times of Hungarian domination, when vast underground defences were dug—a sort of Magyar Maginot line—to stem the Turkish thrust across the river. On one bastion is carved the defiant motto *Nec Arte nec Marte*—neither by skill nor by force. The Danube museum has some valuable prehistoric and Roman exhibits, but little else before the baroque age: a large part of the town perished in earthquakes, one in 1767 and a worse one in 1783. St Andrew's church was built on the site of an older church destroyed by the tremor, and incorporates a fair amount of stone from the ruins of older Roman buildings. The town's most celebrated son was Franz Lehár, son of a military bandmaster, who trained in Prague as a violinist and then found his real *métier* in operetta, basing much of his music on Slovak tunes cunningly transformed into a Viennese idiom.

Following the Váh by road, we find long stretches where road and rail run parallel with the river, sometimes with slopes running right down to the opposite bank, sometimes a sequence of shallow steps towards the foot of the hills. Small thoroughfare towns and villages are strung out along the banks, with geese splashing in the gutters and frequently meeting for a conference in the middle of the road. Wooden houses are fewer than of old, and many of those which remain have been lumpily plastered over. But those which survive are accompanied by new brick and stone houses which follow the traditional shapes and, like the older buildings, are almost invariably set with the gable end to the street, the main doors facing one another across secretive alleys. In the broader stretches of the valley, farmlands climb low slopes and then peter out; we come to an expanse of marshland or scrubby heath, defaced by gravel pits, cement works, electricity stations and a rank of pylons; the fast-running water is disciplined by dykes, and a web of channels has been created to control its occasional floods when the Tatran snows melt.

Piešťany stands just north of the Slňava lake into which the
river widens, suddenly fussy with pleasure boats. On 'Bath
Island' are spa buildings among trees on the water's edge. The
sulphurous mud here has been known since Roman times,
squeezed up by ancient volcanic action to form soft, steaming
deposits in which medieval patients immersed themselves to
cure gout and rheumatic complaints. Today this radioactive
mud is made up in the form of compresses; and when the patient
shows signs of recuperation he is sent off on walks to the west up
the slopes of the Inovec mountains. Piešťany has frequently been
flooded, and Turkish invaders at one time destroyed the entire
spa; but its curative properties have, as it were, repeatedly
restored it to life.

Further north, on the western bank of the river, stand the
toothy grey ruins of Čachtice, some fragments of which date
from the thirteenth century. A bailey was added later by one of
the many local barons who at one time or another claimed to
be Lord of the Váh valley. The most famous, or infamous, resident was Elizabeth Báthory, wife of Count František Nádasdy
but more often remembered as a sort of Countess Dracula. It
was whispered in the locality that she tried to preserve her youth
by bathing in the blood of murdered young girls, and even the
callous authorities grew concerned about the number of maidens
who had disappeared. In due course it was established that she
must have killed several hundred, and in 1611 she was imprisoned in the gaunt tower of Čachtice, where she died three
years later.

The whole valley reeks with melodrama and the memory of
villains, mountebanks, and outsize warlords. Like the Rhine,
the river is frowned on at every twist and curve by some heap of
jagged stone: rocky eminences and pillars, clawed at by vora-
cious trees and lichens, rear up from either side with harsh edges
interrupting the pattern of the trees, and suddenly there comes
a conglomeration which is no mere geological outcropping but
a man-made castle, more dizzy and improbable than any
natural phenomenon.

By the end of the thirteenth century, robber barons were
seizing and exploiting large areas under the nose of a weak and

bewildered Hungarian king. One of the most ruthless was Matthias Čák, who grabbed his neighbours' lands, demanded fealty from them as if he had himself been of royal blood, and in 1299 took Trenčin castle and from there proclaimed himself Lord of the Váh and the Tatras. In time he was master of nearly all Western Slovakia. It was his influence more than any which set the son of Wenceslas II of Bohemia on the Hungarian throne; but other nobles jibbed, and in the end young Wenceslas went back to his own country and to assassination at Olomouc in 1306. Bereft of his royal nominee and patron, Čák continued his quest for supremacy. His private armies attacked the royal residence of the new monarch at Buda, and it took the support of German settlers before the arrogant baron met defeat at Rozhanovce, near Košice. Still he remained paramount in his own self-contained kingdom until his death in 1321.

The foundations of his stronghold were laid in Roman times. An inscription carved into the rock commemorates the victory in 179 of Roman legions over the Germanic Quadi tribe. Later a medieval stone castle with the five-storey tower which still dominates the town and its modern bridge withstood Turkish assault—and Turkish prisoners were made to dig the castle well, nearly six hundred feet deep—but not the attentions of Čák. After his death the Hungarian king at last dared to venture into this territory and claim it for himself. Later a palace was added, and at various periods the fortifications were extended; but after a fire in 1790 the castle ceased to be lived in.

Trenčianské Teplice is Trenčin's picturesque spa, heaped up in a wooded cleft of the hills. The story goes that a crippled shepherd wandered into this secluded sylvan valley five hundred years ago and, coming to a warm pool which was giving off an odd smell, dangled his aching feet in it. The soothing effect was so noticeable that he repeated his visits, and after a prolonged course of immersion he found that his ailments had been cured and he could throw away his crutch. Spa buildings now enclose the main springs, which produce a hot liquid smelling and tasting so revoltingly like rotten eggs that it must surely do one good. Sulphur baths and hot mud compresses are used to treat rheumatic complaints.

Past three dams on the river, we come to the junction with the main holiday road into Slovakia from Prague and Brno. The number of caravans, trailers, and cars with tents and stoves lashed to their roofs increases. This is a far more spectacular route across the Moravian border than our own unnoticeable slide in near Bratislava. From eastern Moravia this road climbs through more and more imposing hills, the perspectives shifting as light falls on different ridges and is lost in patches of un-reflective forest. There are winding roads, sudden dips, a glimpse of a solitary larch cabin, some strip farming and remains of ancient terraces on precipitous slopes. Huts have logs stacked for the winter, stacked under overhangs, stacked inside open barn doors, rammed into every cranny. It seems that the road will never cease climbing. At three thousand feet we are on the Slovak border, and at last we dip down again. Still there are overlapping folds of mountain ahead, with sawtoothed ridges of firs one after the other, intersecting, some darkened and some the faintest rub of grey crayon against a hazy sky: sugar-loaf shapes, whalebacks, long rollers. So we run into Žilina, where the Váh comes in from scouring its way through the High and Low Fatras. A brisk little industrial town with an outdoor sports stadium and an indoor one for the winter months, this is the real gateway to the Fatras and Tatras. Beyond it, road and rail and river cling protectively together through the gash of rock threatening to press in and squeeze them out of existence, with the weight behind of peaks looming from four and five thousand feet. On one curve of the Váh the road is cramped against a rock face soaring to the pale ruins of Strečno, once a sentinel castle collecting dues from travellers along river and valley, but deserted since its reduction in 1698 by imperial decree. There are times when cloud shadows make it look as if it might shift and collapse murderously on the road below. Round the next loop of the S-bend, and even sketchier ruins crown the opposite bank.

In the heart of this stern landscape lies the idyllic Vrátna vale, dotted with hamlets of wooden houses, some with deeply re-cessed balconies under shingled roofs, their timbers carved and painted with intricate whorls, diamonds and rosettes. These are the homesteads of the *kopaničiari*, smallholders working the narrow terraces of the hillsides. In winter there is ski-ing, but the ski-lift and holiday chalets are just as useful for summer walking; and there are camp sites on the floor of the valley.

One of the villages is Terchová, birthplace of the country's most lauded outlaw. In the seventeenth century many estates were well-nigh deserted because of a decline in population, and foreign noblemen grossly overworked their Slovak serfs to make up for the labour shortage. Protest was useless. The law denied any rights to a serf, who could not seek another employer and might not even marry or allow his children's marriage without his master's permission. There were several organized revolts, all savagely put down. After each futile rebellion many of its survivors would take to the mountains, and recruits fled to join them. Outlaw bands swooped from their eyries to harry their oppressors.

At the beginning of the eighteenth century a major rebellion exploded under the leadership of a noble, Francis Rakoczy, in defiance of Habsburg power. He became ruler of Transylvania for a few brief years and then was ousted. Peasants who had supported him found themselves in worse straits than before, and joined the brigands. Country folk sheltered them and warned of approaching danger. When any were caught and hanged, new tales and ballads were added to the country's store.

Most famous of these Robin Hood figures was Juro Jánošík, much celebrated in song and story and even in Bella's oratorio. He had fought in Rakoczy's army, and later served as a prison guard, finding himself much in sympathy with some of the bandits in his charge. It is believed that his own decision to join the outlaws came after his father's murder by a local lord. Having taken to the mountains he became the most daring adventurer of them all, never ceasing in his vengeful campaign of robbery and destruction. At last he was captured, tried and condemned to death in March 1713. The sentence specified that he should be hanged from a hook thrust through his left ribs and remain on it until he died. 'Now you've got me on the spit', was his last defiant jibe, 'you can devour me!'

Two tributaries of the Váh run below the Martin Peaks of the Fatras, their valleys again sheltering clusters of ornamented wooden houses. On the river Turiec is Turčiansky St Martin, nowadays abbreviated simply to Martin. In 1861, after another and warier approach to Franz Josef on behalf of Slovak cultural and linguistic claims, a society was founded in Martin to encourage Slovak literature and art. This Matica Slovenská set about publishing a dictionary and other books, and raised funds to support educational projects for Slovak students. But as soon as Franz Josef had agreed to the compromise of the Dual Monarchy in 1867, the Magyars set about suppressing the society's activities, and in 1875 abolished it. But the flame did not die. It was here in Martin that the Slovaks in October 1918 proclaimed their alliance with the Czechs in the new republic. Later critics were to say that this was a rushed and impulsive gesture and that Slovakia should have established its own separate representation at the peace conference and after, rather than let the Czechs make all the running. Such views are still held by a number of vociferous expatriates; but perhaps the reorganizations of 1968 and 1971 have gone most of the way towards settling such resentments.

Reopened in 1919, the Matica Slovenská set about promoting lectures and educational courses, not merely for the new generation of free Slovaks but for adults who had been deprived in their own youth of such opportunities. The society's headquarters are now amalgamated with the National Library and the National Museum, with displays recounting the history of the movement. There are other testimonies to Slovak nationalism in the streets of the town, marking the spots where partisans fell during the Slovak National Uprising of 1944. Although this revolt against the Nazis was officially proclaimed from Banská Bystrica on 29 August, Martin was already in the hands of the partisans three days earlier.

Another tributary of the Váh, this time from the north, is the river Orava, making its way down from a dam reservoir covering about twenty-two square miles and edging a short way into Poland. The lake is bordered by holiday hotels, tent sites and chalets, with accommodation for about a thousand visitors.

There are steamboat and motorboat moorings, and during the holiday months the whole expanse is churned up by fast craft and a number of water sports. It is easy to escape the noise, though: paths lead away along forest ridges and up to the peaks, and there are hostels for determined long-distance walkers. Downstream are secluded wooden houses and barns, and an occasional wooden church.

Orava castle stands out superbly above the river in two distinct parts, one a thin grey corridor of stony fortress stuck on the sheer rock, the other a red-roofed clump on a slightly lower, wider ledge. Damaged by fire in 1800—shall we ever come across a castle or township neither burnt nor warped by nineteenth-century restoration?—it has been restored in recent years, and incorporates a museum related largely to the Orava district, and a lookout tower offering a view far out over that district.

A few miles down from the castle is Dolný Kubin, the industrial centre of the valley. It was the birthplace of Janko Matuška, whose poem *Lightning over the Tatras* provided the Slovak part of the National Anthem.

Rejoining the Váh, we keep heading to the east, past cottages and sheep huts of similar shape, like little wooden weatherhouses. There are rows of identical thatched roofs, with boarded gables and stone or daub lower walls. They are made to appear even smaller than they really are by the great bare tops of the High Tatras solidifying out of swirling cloud ranges. The Low Tatras, to the south of the valley, would look impressive enough were it not for this majestic competition. A river chatters icecold over white boulders; forests are distinguishable now on the lower slopes of the mountains, darker than the drifting cloud, thinning away to shrub and then abandoning the climb to the last granite summits; we are entering the Tatran National Park.

The highest peak of the Low Tatras is 6,700 feet, the Gerlach peak in the High Tatras is 8,730 feet. Snow often clings to the heights and lies in crevices until well into the summer months, and the scores of mountain tarns freeze over to provide practice grounds for skaters and ice hockey teams. It is a world created by ice, and still icily remote in certain moods. The convulsions of the Ice Age chopped out these lofty islands and pinnacles and scooped the beds of lakes thousands of feet up. The first human beings to venture into the iegion must have conjured up visions of a dozen lowering gods with heads always wreathed in storms. In comparatively recent centuries, tales of legendary treasure have lured many hopeful explorers to the heights. Ore mining and smelting began in the Middle Ages, despite transport and distribution problems. Sheep farming expanded in the sixteenth and seventeenth centuries, and rich huntsmen found a paradise of wild life. There are still plentiful deer, chamois, bears, lynx and moufflon running wild, and a handful of eagles. The loftiest ski and health resorts are connected by a ridgeway known as the Freedom Road; but the greatest treats are reserved for those who forsake their cars and take to the mountain paths. It is not a terrain recommended to novice climbers. In spite of skilled rescue teams and a corps of knowledgeable guides, many people have met their death here and others continue to do so, as the memorial at Popradské Pleso records.

Poprad, a somewhat undistinguished town on the river of that name, is the main rail junction serving the Tatras, and during summer months operates an airport for holiday traffic. On the way here and on a dozen sites to either side are motocamps, motels, car and caravan parking reservations, and several permutations of same. The tourist industry has become one of North Slovakia's main sources of income. But widespread as its facilities are, the summer visitor is advised to book ahead when possible or, at the very least, find a car or camp site by the middle of the afternoon. Otherwise he will be driving around until long after dark. Yet, having said this, I recall an occasion on which two friends and I had done just what I have warned against, and which worked out most happily. After enquiries at a village inn we were at last directed to a local house above a rippling stream, with a half-finished timbered extension for letting to travellers. The kitchen was not yet complete, but the bunk beds were comfortable and our hosts only too eager to help. They were startled to find an Englishman exploring the region: their guest register had not encountered such a character before, being made up largely of East and West German visitors.

They had just completed a beautiful, bulbous stone chimney and a wide fireplace in my bedroom, and insisted that we should be the first to try it. Arguments that it was a hot night were to no avail. In no time at all we were crouched, perspiring freely, before a log blaze, grilling sausages and agreeing that the fireplace drew wonderfully.

In the valley between the High and Low Tatras is Liptovský Mikuláš, scene of the outlaw Jánošík's execution. There is a literary museum commemorating the remarkable number of Slovak writers born or living at one time and another in the Liptov canton, and other memorials to them appear in the thirteenth-century Gothic church of Sv Mikuláš, or St Nicholas. This church has three Gothic altars, one with a unique moulded monstrance in place of the usual holy figure. Another museum in the town is devoted to the wonders of the Slovak karst and its many caves. In the Demänová vale south of Liptovský Mikuláš are some ten or twelve miles of passages and grottoes clogged with coloured stalactites and stalagmites swelling and twisting into onion domes, crystalline amphorae, science-fiction plants, and a thousand different spikes and sword blades. The Dragon ice cave has been known since the thirteenth century, but others were discovered and opened up only in our own time. The little rivers which originally carved out this subterranean fantasy still weave in and out, disappear into further depths, reappear, and keep the lakes topped up.

An electric railway scales ever-steepening slopes from Poprad to the most beautifully situated holiday resorts in the High Tatras. At Starý Smokovec it emerges between green boulevards and trim gardens. The boldly coloured timber rest homes and hotels, the wooded walks and parks, smart restaurants and smart shops create an atmosphere of leisured prosperity such as the most fashionable Chichester Harbour or Norfolk Broads settlement could hardly hope to match. It is an all-year-round resort: in winter there is a floodlit toboggan run, and all around are ski slopes. A funicular railway to Hrebeniok ends at the focus of tourist paths to and from every promising direction. The main mountain railway turns west from Smokovec to the second largest and most frequently visited of the Tatran lakes,

Štrbské Pleso. It comes as a shock to find this busy, very twentieth-century tourist township at such a breathtaking altitude. The station platforms, crowded with men, women and children in red jerseys and purple trousers, yellow jackets and olive green trousers, knitted hats and leather hats and pork-pie hats, look like those of a seaside terminus in its hey-day. There are souvenir shops, picture postcards, vast quantities of ice cream. It can be alarming to watch one of the red cars start its downward journey, appearing from one angle to teeter on the edge of a precipice and then plunge into oblivion.

The monster of a hotel, Panorama, has stepped balconies giving the most staggering views across mile after jagged mile of the mountain ranges. But there is no need to spend too much time in the crowds around the sweet-shop counter or in the lounge of the luxury hotel: even at its most congested, the long walk around the lake is a joy, and there are plenty of tracks leading away into loneliness for those who prefer it. At one end of the lake is a steep artificial slope with its tip raised high above the water. This, which is a bit of an eyesore against the magnificent wild background, is part of a ski run which races on out of sight. The 1972 world ski championships were held here at Štrbské Pleso.

East of Smokovec the railway ends at Tatranská Lomnica, another centre with smart hotels and a choice of diversions: there are cable cars to the mountain lake above, a chair lift to the ridge known as Lomnica Saddle and mountain walks of varying rigour, and a funicular to Lomnica peak itself, second highest in the Tatras. In the Frozen Valley ski-ing can go on through a fair part of the summer.

The Freedom Road from Lomnica continues to Ždiar, a mountain village which lives on cattle rather than on tourists. As in many a border region, such as that of Northumbria in the days of Scottish raids, the farm buildings here also served as miniature fortresses, set sturdily around a courtyard with only one entrance.

If we go any farther along this road we shall find ourselves in Poland. It is time to turn and begin the descent to the lower lands. Perhaps, within a matter of hours, the whole landscape has changed. Annual rainfall in this range is high, and even when the sun shines on one rock wall there can be sullen shadows on its neighbour. Bright village colours fade and turn sombre. In mid-August one can climb to the peaks in hot, dazzling sunshine, with streams and tarns ablaze with light and verges twinkling with wild flowers; and then begin the descent through November valleys and forest from which all colour seems to have been sucked back into darkness.

Under the wide brows of the mountains lies the region of Spiš, with a number of townships whose names are prefaced by 'Spišský'. These medieval settlements were nearly all developed by German immigrants who worked in the mines and strengthened the sparsely populated area against the Tatars. The confederation of guild towns prospered industrially and in trade with Poland, Hungary, and the German towns from which many of the settlers had come. In the fifteenth century Sigismund pawned thirteen of them to the Polish king, and they remained under Polish jurisdiction for more than three hundred years.

Over a considerable period the administrative centre of the confederation was Levoča, founded in 1245 on an earlier settlement deserted by refugees from the Tatar invaders. The main road from Poprad approaches this walled town through a long avenue of trees, in a valley of gentle water meadows with occasional terraced slopes above. A hill, a turn on the crest, and there spread out below are the spires and pert domes of Levoča. The road descends and runs beside extensive ramparts, then in through a gateway once known as the Polish Gate. Within these substantial relics of the old fortifications, streets are laid out in a grid pattern around the strict quadrangle of the town square. Lining the square are some unspoilt Gothic merchants' houses, with a few Renaissance intruders such as the Thurzo house, which is kept furnished in its original style. Remains of monastic foundations are tucked into the ramparts, and there is an evocatively medieval atmosphere in many of the narrow side lanes. Even the dress of the older women seems in keeping: one would scarcely expect to see folk costume worn every day, but there is still a traditional attire of dark skirts, blouses plain or adventurously brilliant, and patterned head-scarves.

The fourteenth-century church of St James the Greater contains some of the most superb woodwork in Slovakia. The carved and gilded altar-piece of Master Paul of Levoča is sixty feet high and twenty feet wide, with meditative cherubs, the Last Supper in the base, and a number of accompanying relief panels on columns beside the altar and on some nave columns. Pews for town councillors and the legates of the Spiš towns are distinguished by intricate marquetry and painting, each with a personal emblem save for one left austerely blank—said to be the seat of the civic executioner. Where one might expect to see a picture in 'Light of the World' vein is a painting of Christ in the dress of a Slovak shepherd, with broad-brimmed hat set safely forward of his halo. A double cartoon strip of frescoes, discovered only a few years ago, is full of martyrdoms and weird demons, including representations of the Seven Deadly Sins squatting on warped beasts.

A worthy neighbour of the church is the town hall, replacing an original which was gutted by fire in 1550. Its graceful ground-floor arcades are echoed in a first-floor arcaded gallery, and above that rises a fretwork skyline of turrets, gables and weather vanes reminiscent of some Dutch or Danish Renaissance manor. Within is a museum of Spiš history; without, an iron 'cage of disgrace' with a small gate like that of a bird's cage, through which the victim was thrust and then locked in to serve out his sentence of humiliation.

By the late eighteenth century Levoča was declining, and the administrative sessions of the Spiš representatives were transferred some miles south to the mining town of Spišská Nová Ves. The sixteen delegates were accommodated in a set of residences on the river bank, attractively preserved and still known as 'The Sixteen'.

When the townsfolk of old Levoča fled with others of their countrymen before the Tatars they sought refuge in the canyons of the Slovak Ore Mountains, known in rivalry to the Bohemian rock towns as the Slovak Paradise. Deep in this complex of gorges and cliffs, caves and waterfalls, is a height which the refugees gratefully named Salvation Rock. Some of their hastily erected fortifications can be traced, and there are also remnants of a monastery built here but later destroyed by robber barons, giving the place the alternative name which you will find on the map—Kláštorisko.

Most imposing of the Spiš relics is the sprawling ruin of Spišský Hrad, the largest castle in Slovakia, heaped up along an uneven hill, with undulating battlements, walls lurching this way and that, a round tower like a truncated lighthouse, and blank windows staring out over the lands once under their sway. The ruin remains impressive in spite of the inevitable fire—this one in 1780—and substantial losses of its fabric, carted away to make less fearsome mansions.

The best view is that from near Branisko, by the road heading east, which brings us to Prešov. This old royal town has a centre protected as a historic reservation, but the rest of it has grown rapidly into a modern industrial town. Population has doubled since the Second World War, and along with the new factories have come the largest indoor swimming pool in the country, an observatory, and a winter stadium. There is also, significantly, a Ukrainian National Theatre.

Due north of Prešov is Bardejov, with some of the best preserved medieval fortifications one is likely to find. The town square is still cobbled, setting off to advantage the façades of the merchants' houses on every side. In front of the town hall is a cannon rescued from the ruins of Zborov castle, closer to the Polish border, which was badly knocked about by Russian forces in the First World War. Other buildings and villages suffered in 1944 and 1945, though happily a number of strikingly Byzantine wooden churches survived, complete with paintings and icons. Again some of the damage was caused by Russian troops, this time as allies fighting their way in across the Carpathians. To the north-east is Dukla pass, where for many weeks in 1944 Czechoslovak troops sought to break through into Slovakia. A wide area has been signposted and, where necessary, cleared and restored as a battle museum, preserving trenches and gun emplacements and identifying the various stages of the conflict. There is a cemetery holding more than a thousand who fell, with a tall conical memorial at one end.

To the east and south-east we are approaching the border between Slovakia and the U.S.S.R. Down through Humenné, a medieval outpost now with a thriving chemical industry, we can go sailing or fishing on the Morské Oko mountain lake, visit the wildfowl reservation at Senné, or—provided we have had the forethought to apply for a licence—go hunting through the wilds around Remetské Hámre hunting lodge.

There was a time when this end of Czechoslovakia extended a bit further. After the First World War, Carpathian Ruthenia elected to join the new republic, having spent almost six hundred years under Hungarian rule. In 1939 Hungary seized it back as part of its deal with Hitler, but in 1945 it was occupied by the U.S.S.R. and in due course formally ceded to them. The regional capital during its twenty years with Czechoslovakia was Užhorod, now just across the frontier from Vyšné Nemecké.

A different route back towards Moravia will take us through the southern stretches of Slovakia, with Košice lying across our path. This ancient royal town on the river Hornád centres on an inner fortress, whose remains house a museum in the Hangman's Bastion and a torture chamber in the old prison. The Gothic cathedral of St Elizabeth was built between 1382 and 1497 on the site of an earlier church and restored at the end of the nineteenth century. It has a polygonal choir, some fine stone reliefs, and a great carved, painted high altar with four wings. Kosiče gave its name to an agreement negotiated in Moscow in March 1945 by President Beneš for the establishment of a provisional Czechoslovak government now that Soviet troops were well on their way to liberating most of Slovakia. On 3 April Beneš and his colleagues arrived at Košice and began to implement their programme based on a National Front with strong communist representation. On 16 May they were able to move on to Prague.

During the war Košice had been taken back by the Hungarians, who had once had one of their most important universities here. The town is close to the Hungarian border, and the road below the Slovak Ore Mountains to Rožňava takes us even closer. This karst region is fractured by fascinating caves and crevasses, including the nationally protected Zádiel valley where the Blatnica stream and waterfalls have carved out great cliffs and limestone statues. South of Rožňava, the Domica cavern can be visited by boat along the aptly named river Styx, flowing underground into Hungary. North-west, a little way off the road to Banská Bystrica, the Dobšiná grottoes have corridors and caverns coated with ice: the 'great hall', four hundred feet long, has a floor of ice seventy feet deep, wide enough to accommodate a skating championship—the eeriest of all underground ballrooms.

Just outside Rožňava itself, an old iron and gold mining town, is the medieval castle of Krásna Hórka, with pitted and peeling walls and a number of towers whose peaked roofs look remarkably like those of some old maltings. The noble Hungarian family of Andrássy added residential buildings to the original fort, and early in this century the last of them built a marble mausoleum for his wife, a Viennese singer, with a mosaic altarpiece made up of thousands of stones.

Rožňava's cathedral has an altar-piece of a different kind, incorporating scenes from the working life of miners; and the town museum is dedicated to the same theme.

Banská Bystrica, ringed by mountains, has for centuries been the spiritual and administrative centre of Central Slovakia, and a most attractive one. In the thirteenth century German miners settled here and in neighbouring spots such as Banská Štiavnica, whose gold and silver mines were among the earliest to be opened up and exploited in Europe. Banská Bystrica's production and trade in silver and the copper ore extracted from the nearby ranges won it municipal privileges from an early date; and during the sixteenth century it had the monopoly of the European silver and copper market. The influence of the German workers and merchants is clear in much of the town's architecture, especially in the richly ornamented houses around the main square. The castle has an imposing gateway, a Gothic palace, and two Gothic churches, one of them with an altar which is thought to be the work of Master Paul, creator of the Levoča altar.

In the old town hall is a museum devoted to memories of the Slovak National Uprising. After an increase in partisan activity against the collaborationist government's forces, and constant urging that Slovakia should break all ties with the Nazis and openly declare its support for the Allies, a decisive step was taken on 29 August 1944. From Banská Bystrica radio station it was announced that a full-scale Slovak National Uprising had been launched. A National Council established its headquarters in the town, and troops and partisans moved in. German troops entered Slovakia in force to suppress the revolt, but it took several weeks before Banská Bystrica fell, and sporadic fighting went on in the hills until Soviet and Czechoslovak brigades at last came in across the border. Most towns and villages in the region have some monument to the thousands who died: at Nemecká it is a lime kiln in which six hundred defeated rebels were burnt to death.

To the south, on the way to Zvolen, is the little spa of Sliač in quiet parkland, with one spring for bathing and four for drinking. These warm springs have been known since the thirteenth century but for a long time their properties were regarded as harmful rather than curative. Birds and animals were continually being found dead in the vicinity. Nevertheless the women of the village took advantage of the warm water to wash hemp, and gradually some who had been suffering from swollen legs and similar complaints became aware of an improvement in their condition. In the eighteenth century a scientific analysis of the waters explained both the animal deaths and the human cures: the warm carbonated springs were ideal for treatment of heart, circulatory and some muscular ailments; but the release of carbon dioxide could asphyxiate birds and other small creatures.

There is an annual summer music festival in the spa. And there is music all year round in the environs. The Detva district is famous for its invigorating, rhythmically stirring songs and dances, several of whose melodies have been transcribed and arranged by Janáček. The fiery pride in some of them is in keeping with the character of the menfolk, descendants of hardy mountain stock who once formed a special body of fighting men in the royal Hungarian service, known for their courage and ferocity. Although homesteads were scattered thinly across these dry, partially barren uplands, they showed themselves during Turkish invasions the equal of those family fortresses we passed in Ždiar. At the same time there was a tradition of delicate craftsmanship in wood carving. Loving care was expended in the past on making and embellishing musical instruments, and today the old techniques and designs continue to be used in carved gables, gates, wooden crosses, and household utensils.

Like the parsons' castles and peel towers of the Scottish border or the defensive round towers of Norfolk and Suffolk, a number of churches in the Slovak mining towns were once fortified. At Kremnica, with its rich gold mines and its mint, the church was in fact the original main tower of the castle. It is girdled by a double wall enclosing a moat, the outer wall linked to the town fortifications; and an underground passage connects with several houses outside, presumably so that in the event of enemy attack the townsfolk could seek shelter in the castle without having to show themselves in the streets. The mines were at their busiest in the fourteenth and fifteenth centuries, but remained productive well into our own. The royal Hungarian mint was established in a house still standing in Horná ulice. It was later moved to another site and has now been modernized to produce contemporary coinage and a range of badges and medals. In addition to gold and silver, trade in copper from the ore mountains was so profitable that the trade route to Poland came to be known as the Copper Road.

Heading south-west, we ought to turn aside for a visit to Topolčianky, set in a park of about five hundred evergreens from different parts of the world. There is a hunting lodge in the grounds, and beyond are hunting grounds and a game preserve. Deer, wild boar and even bears roam these wild acres, and there is a bison reservation. Within the park is a national stud.

The older wings of the château were built in the seventeenth century by one of the Rakoczy family, three slightly uneven rows of arcades about a courtyard. Later a huge palace was built along the fourth side of the courtyard with a Palladian portico and cupola reminiscent of Chiswick House. It is furnished with antiques from different periods. Between the wars it was President Masaryk's summer residence.

Below these slopes, as we leave for Nitra, is the sweep of the Danubian plain. Flowing down to meet the Danube and the Váh is the river Nitra, and on it stands the town where lived the first truly Slovak ruler whose name has come down to us.

About 830 Prince Pribina reigned over the Slav tribes in this wide river basin and had his castle here. In 833 the first Christian church in these lands was consecrated at Nitra by the archbishop of Salzburg; and in 1006 the town became the first bishopric of the region. Pribina himself was not a Christian when he authorized the building of the church, but he allowed the Christian faith to be preached largely because this enabled him to keep on good terms with his Germanic neighbours. A few years later he was driven out by Mojmír, greedy for territory to add to what was fast becoming the Great Moravian Empire. Pribina was granted asylum by King Louis the German, and in due course accepted Christian baptism. King Louis then entrusted to him the land of Pannonia across the Danube. Now a zealous Christian, Pribina set about bringing the new religion to all his people, and persevered in this until his death in 861. Later Pannonia fell into the hands of the Magyars and became part of what was to be Hungary.

Mojmír tried, after his acquisition of Nitra, to get on with the Germans as Pribina had done, but Louis the German helped to bring him down and put Rostislav in his place—that Rostislav who then turned away from the Roman and German powers and sought enlightenment from Byzantium.

Today the castle and cathedral seem planted eternally and indestructibly on a heavy grey stone platform near the river, attainable by only one gateway in a high, frowning wall. But it has suffered some transformations and some attacks in its time. Earlier churches were truncated or demolished to make way for a more grandiose cathedral and the episcopal palace. In the early eighteenth century the Turks made two major assaults on the town and castle, and destroyed many monuments and other treasures. The weighty ramparts were built in an attempt to hold them permanently at bay. In 1711 work began on repairing the damage, rebuilding the cathedral and converting the bishop's residence to the form we now see.

There is an agricultural university in the town, and an agricultural museum in an old Franciscan monastery. The castle itself has become the home of the archaeological section of the Slovak Academy of Sciences.

And here, once the cradle of Slovak history and then a part of the Great Moravian Empire, we are more or less back where we started in Chapter Two.

The Golden Lane

Some visitors drive home from Czechoslovakia by way of one of its neighbouring countries. For many, the neighbouring country may *be* home: most of the tourist trade in the spas, the Giant Mountains and the Tatras comes from West and East Germany. Few English travellers care for the long journey across Europe, and if driving within Czechoslovakia itself prefer to hire a car from Prague airport. Homeward traffic to London goes largely through that airport. So whatever kind of tour has been undertaken there is usually a day or so at the end for a last stroll round Prague, the best place in which to sum up the experiences of days or weeks. A street here, a church or palace there, take on an added dimension because of some echo from history, the name of some person or place encountered far out in the countryside. The Palacký bridge; the Valdštejn palace; Bilek's sculpture of Komenský saying farewell to his homeland: the names can now be set in a clearer context. Remembering Harrachov in the Giant Mountains, we find a great glass chandelier from its old workshops in the church of St Nicholas in the Old Town Square; and skimming through a 1900 edition of Baedeker I once noticed that Count Harrach had a glass shop in what is now Na příkopě.

And there are lingering contacts with vineyards and villages. The deep vaulted cellar of U Zlatého Jelena—At the Golden Deer—reached by a succession of descending flights and landings is one of those run by a small Moravian-Slovakian agricultural cooperative. U Zlaté Konvice, also deep underground, will now forever be associated with the sun-baked slopes and parkland temples of Valtice. And in quiet corners, unobtrusive entrances lead to the smart little bars where Slovak wine comes straight from the barrel and office workers meet at the end of the afternoon just as English businessmen meet for a quick one before setting off home.

My own last ritual call is always to the Golden Lane; which means a walk through the Old Town again, and on across the Vltava and up through the Little Quarter.

Even in the weeks one has been away in the mountains and fields there may have been planted another coppice of scaffolding, or another great hole in the road may be causing further disruption of the tram services. Work on the Metro has for some years now been blocking off streets with wooden fencing, filling the air with dust, and shaking the foundations and whole structure of irreplaceable buildings. Plans for an underground railway were first put forward in 1926, but forty years elapsed before work started in earnest. The first completed section, just under five miles long, was opened in 1974. The hills and clefts of the city did not make it an easy job. At one stage the line is far below the National Museum station at the top of Wenceslas Square; at another it rides out over a deep gorge in a conduit clamped under the main road bridge, and the passenger emerges through Gottwaldova station on to a wide concourse with a panoramic view of the castle and other distant spires and turrets—one of the most inspired pieces of station planning I have ever seen.

The nine stations are linked with bus and tram stops, but by 1986 it is intended to eliminate buses and trams entirely from the centre of the city, and then to radiate out into the suburbs until by the year 2000 there should be more than a hundred stations along forty miles of line. I confess that, assuming I live that long, I shall miss the trams, though they too have done their unceasing part in shaking old mansions and churches to dust.

About eight million pounds a year are allocated for repair and restoration in Prague alone. Comprehensive listing of graded buildings and the preparation of a long-term conservation programme go hand in hand with urgent protective work. Seismographs and other sensitive equipment monitor weather and traffic vibrations, temperature, atmospheric constituents, and minute changes in plaster and stonework. Sometimes restorers stumble on hidden treasure: beneath a faded fresco, an older and more valuable one; above a nineteenth-century ceiling, a painted one lost and forgotten for generations.

A recently cleaned statue on the Charles Bridge looks a bit raw and self-conscious beside darker and more venerable companions.

The sun shines on a re-gilded weather vane above the Little Quarter.

In the castle, a coach party laden with cameras passes a party of earnest old ladies from the country, being taken round on one of the regular cultural tours organized for both workers and pensioners by local factories and communes.

Here is the flight of steps up to the Golden Lane.

At the far end is the Daliborka, a tower named after the heroic knight Dalibor, who aroused the resentment of his fellow feudal lords by sheltering and employing serfs who had run away from more oppressive masters. He was in continual conflict with the councillors of Litoměřice and a neighbouring burgrave, and after the murder of his best friend he led a peasant rising in which the burgrave was killed. Before the feudal court he was sentenced to a lingering death in this tower, into whose dungeon prisoners were dropped through a hole in the floor above. There is a legend that to while away his captivity he learned to play the violin, and that ghostly music can still sometimes be heard from the dank cell. Smetana used the tale of the violin playing in his opera *Dalibor*, by which he set great store but which achieved little success until after his death; and added some romantic touches of his own. In the end King Vladislav, disturbed by rumours of a probable peasant uprising to free Dalibor, had him executed in 1498.

The buildings along the lane itself are very different from the grim stone tower. In the time of Rudolf II the arches carrying a covered walk behind the parapet of the castle wall were converted to tiny dwellings for the castle gunners. Other castle workers squeezed their way into any little crevice which offered, so that now there is a ragged line of little one-room homes little bigger than garden sheds—but sheds painted in bright, clashing colours and with a motley collection of roofs and gables. Some of the residents tucked an extra room into the cramped space by inserting a half-ceiling of planks, reached by a steep ladder. If you sat up from your pallet in the middle of the night you were likely to crack your head against the roof.

A legend has grown up that these little places were the homes and workshops of alchemists, of whom Rudolf was a great supporter. But in fact the reference to gold in the Golden Lane harks back not to searchers for the philosopher's stone but to goldsmiths who plied their craft here for a time.

Today the cobbled lane might not unfairly be called a tourist trap. Here is where the cameras are at their busiest. Here the tiny rooms, some with windows looking down sheer into the wooded dell which used to be the moat, have become philatelists', glass, booksellers' and souvenir shops. There is not an inch in which to turn round when a conducted tour arrives.

But then, I do not come to this corner for its shops.

Every regular traveller has his own favourite delicacy and his chosen restaurant about which he will on the slightest pretext make himself a bore to friends and passing acquaintances. Some grow rhapsodic over a certain dispenser of cream cakes in Vienna. There is a very special place in a Paris side street which nobody, but nobody, has yet discovered. And in Spain there is one unspoilt corner which the Costa Brava crowds would not even dream of looking for. For myself it must be U Zlatá ulička —At the Golden Lane.

I cannot claim that it remains hidden and undiscovered. Far from it. But in the years I have been visiting it, I have rarely failed to get a table and the most heart-warming welcome. Three stalwarts who have survived the coming and going of younger staff are so much a part of it by now that one gets the impression they built the place with their own hands. Out of the thousands who must pass through these doors each season, they infallibly remember old friends and their tastes, and so far I have never seen them ruffled, even when the hordes cease from photographing the dolls' houses and turn their attention to wine and food. Once installed, there is no question of being chased away to make room for another paying customer. I sometimes daydream of hours I have spent there, especially off season, arriving for a drink and an early lunch, and sitting over another glass of wine and then perhaps coffee, reading, making notes or just thinking. At adjoining tables there will be East Germans and West Germans, Finns and Swedes, Americans and Vietnamese; and the waitress will cheerfully carry on conversations in three or four languages, all relating to their special ham dish, or an omelette just dreamed up, or a very special dish of the day which will be just that—*very* special. Once I heard an animated discussion going on at the other side of the room between Czech, Rumanian and Lebanese wine importers and exporters, wrangling over their trade and delivery problems. The reason I knew this was the subject of their discussion is that in order to communicate across their language barriers they had to speak English. A mixed music of many tongues: improved by the lack of that otherwise prevalent canned music which even the most expensive places in Europe seem to find essential nowadays.

Daydreaming, yes: here, and there . . . above all on that last day, looking back over one's travels. A tapestry of carved Bohemian madonnas seen in museums and cold churches, their demure yet wryly knowledgeable faces tilted slightly, their draperies falling in folds of fading colour; of clouds smoking grey and black through a rift in the Tatras; of corn stooks lashed tightly at the neck, like ranks of prim little men marching up the hill; of rain in a deserted square, and sunshine on the Váh. They can never be precisely sorted out, detached one from the other.

Perhaps, even this late in the day, there may still be one last treat in store. I rounded off one visit with an unexpected concert in the church of St James, contentedly installed near the organ by a friend singing in the choir. As the pews filled up below I felt something in common with Martinů, looking down on the world and its diminutive people from his church tower. More and more arrived, until they had to sit on the steps of side altars and ultimately on the chilly floor. It is a huge church, as big as some cathedrals, with the longest nave in Prague. Rebuilt in the time of John of Luxembourg, on the coronation of whose wife the monks in their monastery next door held a banquet, it has withstood several bruisings. In 1420 the Taborites attempted to burn both church and monastery, but news of their intentions reached the men of the guild whose patron church it was: as this happened to be the guild of butchers, who came to the rescue with a considerable weaponry of cleavers and axes, the assault was not a success.

So many people down there, rustling and settling and waiting, and such an agreeably large proportion of pretty girls!

The concert included a work of suitable frivolity for this languid summer evening. It was a little mass by Hek, a composer whose name is hard to find in any reference book. He had the habit of quite openly appropriating melodies and harmonies from the secular works of other composers, in particular Mozart, and using them to provide cheerful church music. Why, as somebody observed much later, should the devil have all the good tunes? This mass began with a vocal line from *Così fan Tutte*, disconcertingly accompanied by some orchestral thefts from *Figaro*; then *Don Giovanni* made a fleeting appearance before submerging under a few bars from Haydn. It was great fun, and if only there were a gramophone recording of it a great deal more fun could be had with baffled friends and those experts who keep popping up in musical quiz programmes.

But the most significant work was a motet by Černohorský. This was, after all, his church, and the St James' choir, orchestra and organist specialize in his music. Some faces turned palely up from the dark floor towards conductor and soloists, probably seeing only their heads and shoulders from that angle. Others contemplated a Brandl painting or a monument by Fischer von Erlach. A great organ and choral echo shivered along the deserted gallery behind me. Like so many other echoes of Prague it has never quite died away, and I trust it never will.

So it is time to be gone, hoping that the time before the next visit will seem short, and that then it will stretch out to allow more and more exploration of the alluring countryside and the equally alluring townships. Hoping, also, that there will be no world catastrophe or yet more sudden outbursts of conflict across this much-trodden, much-abused terrain.

There is an old Czech saying which Czechs and Slovaks have often had bitter cause to regard as over-optimistic, but which they still deliver with a philosophical smile:

Patience brings roses.

Index

The numerals *in italics* refer to the *page numbers* of the illustrations.